ENTERTAINING LESBIANS

MARTHA GEVER

ENTERTAINING LESBIANS

CELEBRITY, SEXUALITY, AND SELF-INVENTION

ROUTLEDGE
NEW YORK AND LONDON

Published in 2003 by
Routledge
29 West 35th Street
New York, NY 10001
www.routledge-ny.com

Published in Great Britain by
Routledge
11 New Fetter Lane
London EC4P 4EE
www.routledge.co.uk

Routledge is an imprint of the Taylor & Francis Group.
Printed in the United States of America on acid-free paper.

10 9 8 7 6 5 4 3 2 1

Library of Congress Cataloguing-in-Publication Data.

Gever, Martha, 1947–
    Entertaining lesbians : celebrity, sexuality, and self-invention / Martha Gever.
        p. cm.
    ISBN 0–415–94479–1 (cloth : alk. paper) — ISBN 0–415–94480–5 (pbk. : alk. paper)
        1. Gays in popular culture—United States. 2. Lesbianism—United States.
    3. Celebrities—United States. I. Title.

HQ75.6.U5G48 2003
306.76'63'0973—dc21   2003046657

FOR YVONNE

CONTENTS

ACKNOWLEDGMENTS

This book is the result of research conducted over a lengthy period of time, spent in various locations, and there are a number of institutions and individuals I would like to thank for providing myriad resources necessary for its completion and acts of generosity that eased the experience. Everyone who listened to my speculations about lesbian celebrity and offered their own contributed in various degrees to this book, although, needless to say, none are responsible for any of my representations of events or ideas, or any interpretations proposed.

A Constance Jordan Award from the Center for Lesbian and Gay Studies at the City of New York provided funds that allowed me to devote a summer to research and writing. In addition to that grant, which not only defrayed practical expenses but also shored up my confidence in the project, this work was underwritten by employment at Barnard College, the School of the Art Institute of Chicago, the University of Illinois at Chicago, Hampshire College, and Florida Atlantic University. I am grateful to generous and thoughtful members of the faculty and staff at all of these schools. Coworkers at Hampshire, in particular, made my year—divided between teaching in that intense environment and writing substantial portions of the book—a rewarding experience. I recall the many kindnesses, delicious meals, and opportunities for spirited conversation offered by Carol Bergelsdorf, Michelle Bigenho, Joan Braderman, Margaret Cerullo, Chyrell George, Amy Jordan, and Bethany Ogdon. The manuscript was completed after moving to South Florida, where I witnessed the 2000 presidential election debacle at close range and watched from afar the devastation of my former neighborhood in Manhattan the following year. Fellow faculty members at FAU—Stephanie Cunningham, Eric Freedman, Marina Karides, Trudie Coker, Kitty Oliver, Eric Prier, and Naihua Zhang—helped mitigate the effects of these calamities by their genuine collegiality and exemplary commitment to teaching. And Walter Delaney's butterfly garden outside my study window provided many moments of delightful contemplation during otherwise grim times.

Much of the research for each chapter in this book was conducted at a particular library. Most of the work for one was done at the Billy Rose Theater Collection at the Performing Arts division of the New York Public Library. Another draws heavily on materials in the International Gay Information Center Archives housed in the NYPL's Manuscripts and Archives Division. Librarians at both, as well as other branches of that remarkable institution, confirmed my belief that librarians are the unsung guardian angels of our culture. Yet another chapter could not have been written without access to the archives of the Rosenbach Museum and Library in Philadelphia. As she has done for so many researchers investigating the life and loves of Mercedes de Acosta before me (and since, I'm sure), Elizabeth Fuller, as well as her assistants Jason Staloff and Najia Khan, provided a well organized and extremely congenial site for days of reading, note taking, and picture research. The Neilson Library at Smith College also allowed me to obtain a wealth of information that informed yet another chapter.

I am also indebted to those who read early versions of this text and offered suggestions that often enabled me to clarify or refine my analysis or its presentation. First among these is Jack Levinson, whose insights and camaraderie sustained me throughout the entire process, from the formulation of the initial blueprint to composition of the summary comments. Even as I moved around the country to undertake various teaching jobs, Jack encouraged and provoked me to pursue unorthodox ideas and to trust that the pieces of this eclectic assemblage would crystallize into a coherent book. It's fair to say that without our informal study group on the concept of governmentality, which stemmed from our shared interest in how personhood is understood and enacted, the central argument of the book would have remained elusive. And I suspect he will continue to send me clippings of items on Elsie de Wolfe after this book is in print.

I was also able to benefit from the stalwart support and provocative questions of others who read early drafts of the manuscript. Since the days when lesbian and gay critical writing on art and media was scarce, Douglas Crimp has been a constant ally. His scholarship in these areas, as well as his commitment to gay politics, allowed him to critique my work as someone who understands thoroughly its implications. Serafina Bathrick was one of the first people with whom I explored the notion of lesbian celebrity as a fit topic for serious study and who followed up with sound advice about the project as it developed. Stuart Ewen challenged my sometimes convoluted thinking and difficult prose, prompting revisions intended to remedy these problems. Patricia Clough lent her critical intelligence and experience with knotty questions of feminist and queer theory, suggesting intriguing interpretations of several key points. Jill Dolan also offered knowledgeable suggestions, which led to additions that improved the text. Jill Johnston and Ingrid Nyboe graciously allowed me to rummage through Jill's archive, which provided information that might otherwise have never surfaced. Suggestions made by a reader who commented on the manuscript for Routledge also encouraged me to update my ideas to include an appraisal of a newcomer to lesbian celebrity, Rosie O'Donnell, which allowed me to punctuate the last chapter with references to recent events. And I must thank Ruby Rich, who endorsed my tentative idea for this book as we chatted about possible areas of lesbian culture I might subject to critical scrutiny.

Many others offered encouragement and did small but invaluable favors during the time I spent immersed in this project. I was able to count on excellent friends like Rosalyn Deutsche, Dominique Elizabeth, Isaac Julien, Deb LaBelle, Catherine Lord, Nathalie Magnan, Maureen McLane, Mark Nash, Esther Parada, Marianetta Porter, Kim Thomsen, Laura Slatkin, and Bob Ubell to put up with my chatter after days, sometimes months, of lonely work and help me make sense of the disorderly collection of ideas and information I amassed. Gregg Bordowitz, John Erdman and Gary Schneider, Marcia Gallo, Jeff Nunokawa, Marc Stein, and Lynne Tillman gave advice and assistance with crucial problems and questions. Maggie Shader, a Hampshire student I know only through e-mail and long distance calls, provided essential assistance scanning images from an obscure magazine that I was determined to include but unable to locate closer to home. I am also grateful to Candace Gingrich at the Human Rights Campaign Foundation for helping me obtain a copy of another coveted image.

The most important supporter of this work, whose contribution to every phase of its realization cannot be expressed succinctly because that would require at least another book, is Yvonne Rainer. Let me say simply that everyday life with her, whenever we were able to share it, as well as long distance conversations when we were not, enabled me to write this book. And her appetite for bold honesty, rigorous work, creative riskiness, and wacky humor continues to amaze me. My mother, Jean Gever, confirmed her belief in my abilities at every turn. And without Donna Smith, I would never have been able to ride the waves of emotional and intellectual doubt and fatigue that threatened to discourage this project at many points along the way.

CHAPTER ONE

INTRODUCTION

CELEBRITY TALK, LESBIAN STYLE

Ever since I began my research on lesbian celebrity, I have been surprised at the interest the topic provokes among friends and colleagues who do various kinds of intellectual work. I assume that they will find it a subject too frivolous for scholarly study, barely worthy of serious discussion, and I may have not always been successful in convincing them otherwise. Just the same, I routinely find that social occasions become opportunities for intense discussions when I mention the topic. What has intrigued me most, though, is the kind of curiosity I most frequently encounter. The typical question concerns who I am *doing*, as in, "Are you doing Ellen? k.d.? Lily? Are you going to deal with Jodie's refusal to admit she's a dyke? And what about Whitney? Why do you think it took Rosie so long to come out?" After a couple of awkward attempts to answer queries of this sort, I adopted a standard reply: my project isn't intended as a series of biographical sketches, I explain, but rather an inquiry into the social factors that inform lesbian celebrity. By reciting this clarification I hope to earn forgiveness for not dealing with the controversies that swirl around prominent lesbian performers and short-circuit any disappointment they might experience after they find out that I'm not "doing" any of these famous lesbians, even though the names of one or two may appear in the following pages.

The problem I found myself facing in these conversations stemmed from my decision during the early phase of my research that I was not going to deal with the question of closeted stars, at least not in the terms that are generally employed, and I wasn't going to agonize over the debates over outing (funny how "out" has become a verb). And I also decided that I was not going to trace the routes any lesbian celebrity traveled (or did not) to reach the point where she announces that she is a lesbian, gay woman, dyke, or whatever other word she might choose from among the possible self-designations.

None of this stops me from engaging in a good gossip, of course, as well as using such opportunities to test my conjecture that this topic generates a great deal of curiosity and speculation about the presence of lesbians in popular culture. By mentioning these encounters I also hope to caution readers eager to find juicy tidbits about one or another of their favorite stars in this book. There may be a few, but my intent in writing it was not to add to or evaluate the truthfulness of lore about lesbian icons. I do hope, however, that anyone interested in exploring how lesbian celebrities—who before the last decade and a half appeared only as caricatures or as shadowy figures suggesting forbidden desires—have become familiar figures in American popular culture will be more than entertained by this book. Questions about how and why lesbian celebrity came about provoked this study in the first place, and I have found that the possibility of this kind of celebrity involves cultural and political transformations that go beyond more widespread recognition of a constellation of sexual identities and practices defined as lesbian.

Let me return, however, to how this book relates to contemporary studies of celebrity. The existing literature on stars and stardom can be divided roughly into two kinds: biography and social critique. As I have indicated, my project belongs in the second category, although biographical materials often provide points of departure for my analysis. I also devote considerable attention to problems presented by biographical representations, both self-representations in autobiographies and other writers' descriptions and interpretations of the lives of celebrities. There is a further categorical refinement proposed by Richard Dyer in his important survey of the literature on celebrity phenomena, *Stars* (1979), where he sorts academic studies in this field into two additional categories: sociological and semiotic. This work is situated on the sociological side of this divide but employs paradigms and techniques from semiotics from time to time.

I should also alert readers that this book is not an ethnographic study of fans' responses to celebrities, despite what my opening anecdotal paragraph may imply. Nor does it delve into psychological issues or theories meant to unravel the intricacies of fans' fascinations with and fantasies about stars. In other words, I do not undertake a psychoanalytic inquiry into the construction of or engagement with celebrity images. The omission does not result from conceptual sloth but stems from more substantial problems with privileging the psyche as the organizing principle of cultural life. I agree with those who favor psychological paradigms that subjectivity, the problem central to psychoanalytic theory, is a major question for any serious inquiry concerning celebrity culture. However, I find more convincing the proposition that the psychological bedrock of subjectivity is not a primary structure of the human organism but rather a set of effects, historically situated social discourses and practices—as Michel Foucault and others have argued and elaborated (Burchell, Gordon, and Miller 1991; Foucault 1978, 1994; Hacking 1986, 1995; N. Rose 1998, 1999). This decentering of the psyche suggests a radical redirection of the critique of celebrity, away from psychological structures and processes, toward historical studies of the production of particular kinds of persons and concepts of selves, including what is commonly called the inner life.

I have chosen, therefore, to set aside questions of desire and identification—the province of psychoanalytic theory, in particular—in order to concentrate on dimensions of lesbian celebrity related to cultural institutions and practices, discursive configurations, and political debates and developments. I find this approach more suitable for my investigations of lesbian celebrity because the kinds of people involved, both celebrities and lesbians, pose suggestive questions concerning the way personhood has been constituted in contemporary Western societies—how people are made up, as Ian Hacking says, or selves are invented, to adopt Nikolas Rose's idiom. Understanding subjectivity from this perspective involves placing it in the context of cultural reproduction: the processes by which cultural norms and systems of meaning are maintained and undergo change, how social relations regulate individual conduct and, in turn, how conduct is interpreted, and how specific kinds of subjects and subjectivity become legible.

Until recently, however, lesbian personhood was valued negatively in just about every corner of popular culture. Of course, there were a handful of acclaimed lesbians who lived long before the past fifteen years. Think, for example, of Gertrude Stein. Still, because lesbianism was considered a perversion and generally regarded as synonymous with depravity, it was hardly something that someone striving for public recognition would want to aver. During the latter decades of the twentieth century, however, these standards were assaulted by challenges on many fronts. Most importantly for the entity considered here—lesbian *and* celebrity—disciplinary techniques of self-management and practices of self-stylization that became prevalent in the

United States (and other Western nations) in recent years enabled new kinds of selves and descriptions of them.

One such new type of subject is the lesbian, first identified in the mid-nineteenth century, later redefined by those classified (often self-classified) as lesbians in the twentieth. Another is the kind of celebrity who now dominates North American popular culture. Unlike the military conquerors, captains of industry, and religious leaders featured in the halls of fame of previous eras, celebrities nowadays are most often acclaimed on the basis of personal style and individual enterprise. And when celebrities become implicated in public debates over identity—as well-known lesbians inevitably do—the processes and problems involved in shaping contemporary subjectivities are put on display. Thus, both modern stars and lesbians can be described in terms of particular modes of subjectivity achieved through practices of self-fashioning and image management. A detailed exploration of the constitution of such personae is the project of *Entertaining Lesbians*.

Before embarking on a discussion of the specific areas and issues covered in the book, its organization warrants a brief explanation. Its premise as a study of lesbian celebrity can only be conceived within the context of contemporary culture. But this is in many respects, a historical study, although the chapters are not ordered in chronological sequence. Rather, each chapter emphasizes particular historical configurations and developments that resonate in the present, loosely connected by the common themes that occur at the intersection of homosexuality, female gender, and celebrity. As my aberrant chronicle unwinds, skips around, and at times doubles back, one persistent motif emerges, however: self-invention, which is intimately related to opportunities for self-display, as well as the continual monitoring and adjustment of self-image.

Entertaining Lesbians begins, in effect, with an analysis of the claims about the importance of visibility and related concepts of representation that first animated my interest in the topic of celebrity within U.S. lesbian culture and politics, and it seems appropriate that a survey of visibility politics should introduce the discussion.[1] Present-day concerns about lesbian visibility in the United States have been advocated repeatedly as an important political project. The visibility of increased numbers of lesbian stars, it is said, fosters greater freedom for all lesbians. According to this logic, the proliferation of images of lesbians in the media provides evidence of our existence, refutes stereotypes, and provides role models for those who suffer from inadequate self-esteem. The problem that arises with such arguments is that they mistake symbolic representations in the media for political representation and social legitimation. The causal relationship between visibility and power is not only difficult to demonstrate, it is also based on an unexamined faith in the unmediated veracity of documentary evidence, including that produced by photographic media. More pessimistic cultural critics often make the contrary argument that lesbian celebrity serves as testimony to the voracious appetite of media empires, capable of appropriating and manipulating all cultural phenomena and political dissent for profitable exploitation. However, this explanation, too, is seriously undermined by the faulty assumption that lesbian (and other) fans are simple-minded pawns of capitalist machinations. Moreover, these critics may not oppose campaigns for visibility but only protest the recruitment of celebrities for these purposes.

Rather than attempting to decide in favor of one of these positions, *Entertaining Lesbians* treats such contradictions as indications that a different critical approach may provide more satisfactory analyses of how celebrity operates in relation to political identities and social change. Drawing upon paradigms employed by critics of visual and media culture, primarily but not exclusively those developed under the rubric of cultural studies, I outline various tensions and paradoxes found in the enactment of and commentary about lesbian celebrity in the United States. The general outlook I borrow from cultural studies (Stuart Hall's work in particular) theorizes popular culture as a site of struggle over definitions and meanings of key terms in shared cultural vocabularies. But there are additional questions posed by lesbian visibility politics that call for more specific analysis, especially those related to such political issues as the commodification of lesbian styles; connections between sexuality, class, race, and visibility; and the gendered character of cultural expression and social recognition.

These questions recur in chapter 4, although here the problem of visibility is articulated in different terms at a previous historical moment—the late 1960s and early 1970s—when lesbian subjectivity in the United States was radically reconfigured within the crucible of the gay and women's liberation movements. At first, gay and feminist political principles precluded any activist from collaborating with what was believed to be an elitist media system. Celebrity was condemned vociferously as antithetical to the democratic ethos of liberation. Two prominent feminist and lesbian activists—Jill Johnston and Kate Millett—were routinely criticized on these grounds, and their treatment by both mainstream and movement media provides illustrations of the anticelebrity ideology prevalent in radical politics of the sixties.

At the same time, though, the lesbian and gay movement made visibility a centerpiece of its political strategy when it promoted coming out—commonly understood as the realization of self-knowledge, self-possession, and self-esteem—as *the* definitive feature of lesbian or gay personhood. It is no exaggeration to say that coming out became the paramount theoretical and practical weapon in the lesbian and gay political arsenal. But there was an apparent incompatibility between being proudly lesbian but also averse to publicity. Within a few years, though, a rapprochement between the utopian ideals of liberation and visibility was effected when the glorious star became reconciled with the noble lesbian. The truce was brokered on the basis of a shared investment in an ethic of self-fashioning and self-management or, to use the terms introduced by Foucault (1994), the technical practices of governmentality. Lesbian celebrities, I argue, are an effect of this alliance.

Before going any further I should define lesbian celebrity. Stated succinctly, my interpretation of the term is limited to instances where a celebrity is known to be and does not deny being a lesbian. To be more precise, the stardom of these lesbians is achieved and authorized within the institutions of popular culture, endorsed by the mainstream media. As I noted previously, I do not deal with so-called closeted stars and have no interest in debating the pros and cons of outing. Even in its most sophisticated form (e.g., Gross 1993), the discussion of outing presumes that the parameters of lesbian identity have been settled once and for all. Far too much empirical and theoretical work contradicts this assumption for it to remain viable. The political significance of the outing controversy dissipates as soon as social identities are recognized as contingent and often contradictory.

Despite the restrictions I have imposed on lesbian celebrity by ruling out those who would refuse the designation, my definition by no means reduces the scope of my study to a tiny group of exceptional individuals. More importantly, the ideas about lesbian celebrity developed in this book all reject the premise of lesbian celebrity as a result of individual initiative—stars recognizing who they "really are" and incorporating that identity into their public personae—but treat it instead as a social phenomenon. Indeed, this critique of lesbian celebrity attempts to take into account myriad phenomena frequently invoked by commentators on the cultural scene in the late twentieth-century United States. Just naming a few of these—spectacle, mass media, commercialization, sexual politics, socialization—hints at the breadth of the territory visited. Organizing this melange are questions concerning the emergence and expression of lesbian celebrity. Indeed, the pairing of the two

words just a decade ago would have required a lengthy explanation for anyone not privy to lesbian subcultural knowledge. A couple of decades before
that, lesbian celebrity would have been an oxymoron, nonsensical.

As soon as the possibility of lesbian celebrity is proposed, other problems
begin to surface. Can there be lesbian celebrity prior to the conception of a
lesbian person who might qualify? Are changes in the criteria for celebrity
related to the acceptance of lesbians into the charmed circle? These are questions I take up in chapter 3, which presents a historical overview of cultural,
economic, and technological changes in the past 150 or so years that set the
stage for recent lesbian celebrities. My point of departure is a discussion of
the lesbian self-fashioning practiced by Radclyffe Hall, the British novelist,
whose 1928 novel *The Well of Loneliness* produced a scandal when the book
first appeared. Hall's concern for her public image and reputation, as well as her
contribution to conventional ideas about lesbian identity, qualify her as the
first self-conscious lesbian icon. However, Hall's looks and gestures would
have been meaningless without an entire edifice of technological refine-
ments, ranging from the emergence of sexological science (which Hall
endorsed when crafting the archetypal lesbian protagonist of *The Well*,
Stephen Gordon), the incorporation of photography by the mass media, the
related growth in celebrity and gossip journalism, the expansion and democ-
ratization of consumer culture, and mutations in the characteristics of
celebrity. In addition to what could be called celebrity technology, another
significant cultural development took place alongside it: the embrace of
melodrama as the preeminent aesthetic in popular entertainment. The emotionalism and femininity associated with this theatrical form provided a cultural environment where lesbian desires and identities could, and did, proliferate, although normative pressures were sufficient to keep such inclinations
under wraps and underground during long stretches of the twentieth century.

This more or less hidden history has galvanized attention among chron-
iclers of popular culture over the past dozen years or so. Chapter 5 contem-
plates the popular revisionist histories that began to proliferate in the 1990s,
the decade when lesbian celebrity became a feature of the cultural landscape.
These are books that profile celebrities who engaged in lesbian practices but
who never described themselves in those terms—most notably, Alla
Nazimova, Eva Le Gallienne, Greta Garbo, Marlene Dietrich, and the
woman who consorted with all of them, Mercedes de Acosta, as well as the
wider circle of lesbians she knew, befriended, and maybe slept with. Rather
than producing yet another breathless exposé of their love and sex lives, I am

concerned with the rhetorical and social mechanisms that generate knowledge about ancestral lesbian celebrities in the name of historical truth but often reproduce worn out clichés with questionable implications as a result. But I am also interested in another interpretation of the history represented by de Acosta and her friends that emerges when their lives are recast as exemplary studies in image management and theatricality.

Having offered a general outline of the key issues explored in this book a central question remains: who counts as a lesbian celebrity? Perhaps the best example is Martina Navratilova, whose international fame was earned in a cultural domain—sports—where lesbianism has long been, and continues to be, assumed even if not acknowledged or accepted. Others are engaged in more traditional female occupations in entertainment—for example, stage actress Cherry Jones—but depart from convention by refusing to hide or deny their lesbianism, as Jones did when she acknowledged her lover in her acceptance speech when awarded the Tony for best actress in 1995. Television actresses Amanda Bearse (*Married . . . With Children*) and Ellen DeGeneres, of course, whose splashy coming out in 1997 was heralded as a groundbreaking media event, have been equally forthright. Rosie O'Donnell, whose career has run the gamut of theater, movies, and TV, as well as her eponymous glossy magazine, offers yet another example, although she does not fit neatly into any particular professional category. And at a time when fashion models may attain celebrity status and thus have not only their bodies but also their private lives and personalities scrutinized, such lesbian supermodels as Jenny Shimizu and Gia Carangi complicate the traditional notions of idealized femininity that fashion models are said to represent.

Popular music provides plentiful examples of lesbian (sometimes bisexual) celebrity—for example, k.d. lang and Melissa Etheridge, of course, but also Me'Shell NdegéCello, Albita, Sinéad O'Connor, Ani DiFranco, and the Indigo Girls, not to mention the various singers who it is said have taken over the folk music scene in the United States (Hadju 2002). Indeed, lesbian celebrities seem to crop up regularly in this arguably more freewheeling cultural field, and the lesbian histories of such eminent singers from earlier generations as Ma Rainey, Carmen MacRae, Janis Joplin, and Dusty Springfield have not been entirely suppressed. Moreover, this is the only entertainment sector that has consistently produced celebrities who are lesbians of color. I explore some of the historical factors that contribute to the overwhelming—one could say overdetermined—whiteness of lesbian celebrity in the discussion of visibility politics in chapter 2. The absence of a more extensive discussion of this issue could be rectified by a thorough examination of sexual politics in popular music, but that will have to wait for a writer with more knowledge of the field, as well as a more musical sensibility, than I am able to profess.

Out of the increasing number of lesbian celebrities, I selected only Navratilova for an extensive case study of the production of lesbian celebrity in chapter 6, although I devote considerable space to de Acosta's posthumous reputation in chapter 5. The reasons for choosing Navratilova can be summed up in a phrase: image management, one of the recurring themes in this book. Since celebrity is synonymous with celebrity image, lesbian celebrity—or any celebrity, for that matter—becomes in effect an image management project. The self-fashioning practices used to fabricate a celebrity image are well known, epitomized perhaps by the techniques perfected by Hollywood studio publicity departments in the 1920s and 1930s but now performed by a plethora of specialists employed to manage a star's career—personal agents, publicists, stylists, and trainers, to name a few. But until very recently such projects involved primarily cosmetic enhancements.

Although a review of Navratilova's circuitous itinerary on her way to lesbian celebrity provides an account of an elaborate experiment with such methods, the efforts to redesign her image were not confined to looks alone. She also employed ancillary theories and techniques that involved a makeover of her entire physique. The result was a body described by sports reporters in terms of mechanical apparatuses and cyborg metaphors—an ambiguously gendered, perhaps nongendered, clearly human, but also somewhat inhuman or superhuman, lesbian person. And, as many advocates of fitness regimes will attest, this kind of self-enhancement involved mental, as well as physical, discipline. Navratilova and others credited her dominance of women's tennis for close to a decade to the combination of disciplined mind and muscle. Most pertinent for the study of lesbian celebrity, however, Navratilova's image management project also coincided with another kind of self-invention—coming out—which she also enacted in the arena of popular culture. And she was again praised by the press and fans for risking ridicule in her pursuit of self-realization.

But Navratilova's enduring fame, forged by the aggregation of disparate programs for self-mastery, should not be interpreted simply as the just reward for individual initiative confronting and conquering social prejudice. Rather, a thorough examination of her celebrity suggests that Navratilova took advantage of the obligations of self-government that now permeate social and intimate life, as well as the displacement of the moral authority of normative definitions of gender and sexuality by increasingly powerful imperatives to attain physical and psychological well-being. In other words, Navratilova's and others' lesbian celebrity occurs at the point where concepts of the self intersect with relatively new strategies for mobilizing power.

Lesbian celebrities embody such encounters with techniques of social regulation accomplished as willing participants in self-control projects. And these figures demonstrate that individual sexuality and sexual identity, like celebrity image, are articulated through interactions with social norms and systems of representation. Likewise, lesbian culture—including the celebrities who galvanize ideas about and inklings of lesbian personhood—is by definition political. In short, lesbian celebrity is about power and knowledge, and that may be why everyone seems so eager to talk about it.

CHAPTER TWO

VISIBILITY NOW!

THE SEXUAL POLITICS OF SEEING

Chastity Bono, national media director of the Gay and Lesbian Alliance Against Defamation (GLAAD) and daughter of pop singer-actress Cher and the late singer-songwriter turned Republican congressman Sonny Bono, is talking to a *New York Times* reporter in 1997 about her first lesbian love affair in the late 1980s. "No one was out then," she says. "It was before k.d. lang and Melissa Etheridge. I was really afraid" (Witchel 1997). Appearing in the final paragraphs of a breezy profile, the suppositions implied by the historical benchmarks Bono mentions when recalling her personal distress could easily pass unnoticed. At the same time, her version of the past could be a show stopper. *No one?* And this was *when?* For a reader who came out in 1975, and perhaps for countless others whose acceptance or embrace of lesbian identification predates k.d.'s in 1992 or Melissa's the following year, Bono's version of history seems sadly misinformed. But maybe it's not surprising for someone whose knowledge of lesbians seems to rely upon the mainstream media and for whom the possibility of describing herself as a lesbian—accepting the fact that it's all right to say so—was itself constituted as a media event. Bono's first coming out in 1990 was involuntary, insofar as it was engineered by the editors of the *Star*, a supermarket tabloid that capitalized on her parents' fame by emblazoning her name and face, accompanied by eye-catching headlines that screamed "lesbian" and "gay," on its cover and inside pages. Only five years after this exposé did she enact her "official" coming out by granting the gay and lesbian magazine the *Advocate*, an interview (Bono 1995).

No doubt, Bono's faulty historical knowledge can be attributed to the fact that she has lived her entire life within the shelter or, if you prefer, the

Jenny Jones: murder accomplice? • St. Patrick's Day massacre

THE Advocate

THE NATIONAL GAY & LESBIAN NEWSMAGAZINE   SINCE 1967

APRIL 18, 1995

EXCLUSIVE INTERVIEW

Chastity Bono
Out at last

The daughter of Sonny and Cher reveals everything about her traumatic coming-out odyssey

ISSUE 679

$3.95 USA • $4.95 CAN. • £2.95 UK

Chastity Bono comes out officially in 1995, aided by the *Advocate*. Liberation Publications.

fishbowl of celebrity culture, which may be why entertainers serve as the references that authenticated her social identity. But her background also provided her with outstanding qualifications for a post at GLAAD, an organization dedicated to the promotion of "fair, accurate and inclusive representation of individuals and events in the media as a means of combating homophobia and all forms of discrimination based on sexual orientation or identity" (GLAAD 1997a). Bono's easy familiarity with the entertainment business was surely an advantage, as she spells out in a GLAAD fundraising appeal, reproduced in the form of a note written on her personal stationery:

> Some of my friends—even some of my family—wonder what I hoped to achieve by joining the staff of GLAAD. . . .
>
> Here's how I explained it to *USA Today*: "This sweet little blond girl from the *Sonny & Cher* show turned out to be a big dyke. There's something wonderful about that, because that's life."
>
> But getting people's attention to my identity as a lesbian is only the beginning. Converting that attention to real, positive change is the bottom line. . . .
>
> This is an exciting, historic time for gay and lesbian visibility in the media. After decades of being ignored, then defamed, by Hollywood, we're beginning to get meaningful visibility. But we still have a long way to go. (GLAAD 1997b)

The mere fact of Bono's lesbianism coupled with her membership in a pop culture incarnation of the American family circa 1972, when at age two she made her screen debut on her parents' weekly television program, may yield an extremely solipsistic view of what kind of "meaningful visibility" she has in mind. But there is no doubt that the conflation of her own biography with a political program aimed at making lesbianism respectable represents an attempt to engage the media in its own game. She is able to work both sides of the street, appearing as a guest on *Rosie O'Donnell* and then mailing out more fundraising letters citing this kind of attention as an indication of progress.

It is important to point out here that the recurrence of "visibility" in the GLAAD promo piece—elsewhere Bono's note mentions "the struggle for gay and lesbian visibility"—does not result from an editorial oversight or redundant word usage. Instead, it can be read as an emphatic statement that visibility is the primary goal as well as the fundamental rationale for

GLAAD's organizing efforts. (Bono's departure from her GLAAD post in 1998 did nothing to alter this emphasis.[1]) Furthermore, if we interpret the number and quality of representations in the mass media as a measure of social status, as GLAAD literature routinely urges us to do, popular visual culture becomes an important, perhaps *the* most important, focal point for the lesbian and gay political movement.[2] In the bid for greater visibility lesbian celebrity becomes political.

STAR POWER

Unlike Bono, whose career as a rock musician never took off, lesbians whose celebrity is based on reputations acquired as professional performers seem unlikely political organizers, indebted as they are to the power brokers responsible for designating, grooming, and providing platforms for stars in the entertainment business. These obligations apply considerable pressure to avoid controversy, especially the kind that journalists can exploit. More common are cases when the substance of lesbian politics and celebrity manifestly intersect or overlap, for example when women enter the public arena as participants in challenges to homophobic laws, legal judgments, or regulations, becoming public figures as a result. Probably the most high profile instance of this kind of coincidence in recent years is Margarethe Cammermeyer, a decorated colonel in the U.S. Army, whose lawsuit for being summarily discharged following her assertion of lesbianism was memorialized in her autobiography, *Serving in Silence* (1994), then translated into a much publicized made-for-TV movie shown on CBS. What put Cammermeyer on the celebrity map, in addition to the numerous interviews she gave to the press and on the television talk show circuit, was that her story attracted the attention of a bona fide megastar, Barbra Streisand, who produced the broadcast program, and her personification on screen by another prominent actress, Glenn Close. Indeed, it may be that Cammermeyer's star image is indelibly imprinted with Close's likeness.

Other examples of a direct link between lesbian celebrity and politics are provided by lesbians whose renown can be attributed to their familial proximity to political power. Chastity Bono is a charter member of this group, but it is epitomized better by Newt Gingrich's sister Candace. Like Bono, Gingrich explicitly linked her effectiveness as a spokesperson for lesbian issues to her family ties. But while Bono chose to remain close to her show business roots, attempting to convince media moguls and minions alike that

Glenn Close plays Margarethe
Cammermeyer in the made-for-
TV biopic based on her autobi-
ography, *Serving in Silence*.
Photofest.

homophobia is not good public relations, Gingrich acted as a vocal exponent
of lesbian and gay rights in less tony circles, traveling the country on behalf
of the Human Rights Campaign's Coming Out Project and criticizing her
brother whenever he took a public position against gay and lesbian rights. Yet
Gingrich was not above a little glitzy celebrity bonding à la Hollywood, as
when she teamed up with Bono during the 1996 presidential election for a
series of print ads intended to induce lesbians and gay men to vote, which
netted them coverage in the celebrity press. ("Star Tracks" 1996). She also
made a cameo appearance on a 1996 episode of the sitcom *Friends*, playing a
minister who performs a lesbian wedding. By taking this baby step into popular entertainment, she elicited a particularly snide public putdown from
brother Newt and thus produced another opportunity for her to mock him
for his reactionary views.[3] These and other outbreaks of lesbian politics on
the stage of celebrity culture offer ample evidence of an increase in the sort
of visibility Bono, GLAAD, and various others have worked hard to achieve.

Chastity Bono, Sean Sasser, and Candace Gingrich promote the Human Rights Campaign's 1996 voter registration drive. Human Rights Campaign Foundation.

Less obvious, perhaps, are the political dimensions of lesbian celebrity in popular entertainment—theater, movies, television, music, popular magazines, sports—yet this is where the stakes in what can be called visibility politics are raised to the highest levels. The reasons for this are not too mysterious: entertainment in late-twentieth-century Western societies is predominantly visual, and the images produced and broadcast are associated with the power to set cultural agendas. So far, attempts to coax eligible movie stars, arguably the most visible of all celebrities, to come out have failed, but famous lesbians and bisexual women who work in other arenas of the entertainment industries have been less timid: prime examples include Cherry Jones and Lea DeLaria in theater; Ellen DeGeneres and Rosie O'Donnell in television; Martina Navratilova, Diana Nyad, Missy Giove, Muffin Spencer-Devlin, and Amelie Mauresmo in sports; Etheridge, lang, Me'Shell

Ndegéocello, Albita, and Sinéad O'Connor in popular music. In appreciation of their visibility as self-identified lesbians, they are now celebrated by myriad lesbian fans not just for their virtuosity as performers but also for their commitments to increased lesbian visibility. But there is something strangely nebulous about this newfound measure of political achievement. What, we need to ask, is meant by visibility? What, exactly, are the political gains that will follow from it? And are these sufficient to put it high on the list of priorities of politically aware and active lesbians and gay men?

Not only in GLAAD's propaganda but in almost every instance where lesbian visibility is evoked it is presented without elaboration. Indeed, one of the consistent assumptions made is that whatever constitutes visibility is, literally, self-evident: to be seen is to be represented, to be accorded social agency, while to be refused such recognition is to be denied personhood. Visibility confers authority, and it guarantees authenticity. It is transparent, insofar as the thing seen—in this case, a lesbian person—conforms perfectly to an objective category of social identity, while contingent historical and cultural factors that make that identity possible disappear.[4] There are, however, several contradictions contained in the apparent truisms encountered whenever visibility is invoked uncritically. My purpose here is to outline these, examining how visibility has been articulated as a political goal in the ongoing debates over lesbian representation—in both symbolic and political terms.[5]

Lesbian celebrities have come to figure prominently in this discussion as the result of several developments. One of these, the flourishing industry of celebrity journalism in the latter decades of the twentieth century, is not a direct effect of sexual politics. However, as of 1990 the tremendous amount of attention paid to the intimate lives of famous people in the mass media had effectively annulled tacit rules that forbade revelations of homosexual identities and practices of eminent public figures, at least those applied in the "respectable" press (Gross 1993).[6] If stars demonstrate what it means to be an individual in modern societies, as Richard Dyer contends, and crucial to their representative character is our access to knowledge concerning their private lives, then the acknowledgment of lesbian personae among the pantheon of cultural luminaries could signal a change in definitions of the individual and categories of personhood (Dyer 1986).[7]

I begin, then, with the premise that changes in the parameters of lesbian visibility—as well as the prominent attention given to lesbian celebrities that both results from and informs these changes—suggests a broader critique than an empiricist equation of visual perception with knowledge or truth can ever provide. When not only what can be represented but also what can be *seen* is understood as cultural, we are encouraged to refocus our attention away from any fixed notions concerning truthful, objectively accurate representations of lesbians and toward the socially constituted "conditions for visibility," as Teresa de Lauretis has proposed (1988; 1991).

OVEREXPOSURE

The rule of thumb of visibility—visibility is everything; without it your existence is threatened—appears to be confirmed by the desire for recognition among those who are frequently objects, much more rarely subjects, of the visual representations that circulate in contemporary Western cultures. Not surprisingly, the ability of visibility to confer personhood is rarely disputed by those in a position to grant it in the first place, including journalists who cover the culture beat in the mainstream media. Yet, paradoxically, it has become commonplace in these same contexts to treat celebrity, the consummate model of visibility, with extreme disdain, although the popularity of any particular star is generated and maintained by these very scribes and the media that employ them.

It's not just that celebrity occupies an increasing amount of space and time in the cultural environment—exemplified by *People* and *Us* magazines, as well as television programs like *Entertainment Tonight* and *Access Hollywood*, for example, as well as every early morning, midafternoon, and late-night talk show—but complaints abound about how celebrity has infiltrated other areas of social life, politics in particular, but also all branches of cultural activity, from sports to scholarship (Dyson 1993, Nelson 1997, J. Scott 1997, Shumway 1997).[8] Most common are critiques that analyze celebrity—the institution as well as the individuals—as a symptom of social pathology produced by an overemphasis on image consciousness and crafting. A choice example of this analytic bent appeared a few years ago in a *New York Times* piece commenting on the marriage of another second-generation celebrity, John F. Kennedy Jr., to Calvin Klein publicist Carolyn Bessette. Op-ed columnist Maureen Dowd presents the couple as an illustration of a postmodern paradigm à la Baudrillard: "all image and no substance . . . the content is gone." And she sums up her perspective on the takeover of politics by celebrity culture thus: "Jackie Kennedy invented Camelot as public relations packaging after her husband's death. So it follows that its new princess has the perfect lineage for the age. She was a publicist, and spiritual daughter, of the reigning king of fashion public relations. She is our new Obsession" (Dowd 1996). For Dowd, the apparently frivolous interest in celebrity generates serious consequences, since it distorts rational political understanding and judgment.

Consider, too, what another *Times* critic, Michiko Kakutani, has to say about the cultural changes wrought by everyone's favorite icon of celebrity, Andy Warhol. His aesthetic, the author avers, has "become the way we look at the world" (Kakutani 1996, 34). His success in the art market conveys a simple maxim: "The lesson is the same one taught by television: you can sell anything with the right spin—silk-screened prints of race riots, Mao wallpaper, even painting made by urinating on canvases coated with bronze—and with the right spin anything can be art"(36). The "right spin" in this case is the artist's signature. Thus, for Kakutani and innumerable pundits, "Warhol" is employed as shorthand for celebrity worship that encourages anomie and avarice, and therefore corrupts social discourse (cf. Watney 1989). Dowd and Kakutani are hardly alone in their concern. For instance, they are joined by another regular columnist for the *Times*, Frank Rich (1998), whose year-end summary for 1997 invokes the flourishing of celebrity gossip—which he attributes to "peace, prosperity, and falling crime rates"—in order to draw conclusions about the vapidity of fin-de-siècle culture.[9] Indeed, celebrity news, gossip, and imagery is regularly cited as the common denominator of the era's public culture, suffusing everything, from speculations about the culpability of the paparazzi in the death of Princess Diana to debates over O. J. Simpson's trial for murder.

What seems to be most troubling is the tautological nature of the relationship between celebrities and the media: What happens to celebrities is news. Anyone who makes news is a candidate for celebrity. In these and so many other assessments of the Zeitgeist, visibility and its first cousin, celebrity, are presented as evidence of the total surrender to the "society of the spectacle" (Debord 1990) and the "cancerous growth of vision, measuring everything by its ability to show or be shown" (de Certeau 1984, xxi) that cultural theorists have been forecasting for decades, with no respite in sight. Media critics protest the colonization of the public sphere by celebrities, while those engaged in marshaling the flow of information on an everyday basis—magazine publishers and editors, for instance—complain that economic factors compel them to pay great attention to stars. In order to secure the cooperation of publicists and celebrities upon whom sales depend they are therefore forced to sacrifice journalistic standards of objectivity.[10] Critical or complicit, few in the media business dispute the understanding of visibility as cultural capital, and many of those who have little or none are clamoring for more.

PRO-VISIONAL

A skeptical attitude toward celebrity culture, as the critics cited above recommend, is often accompanied by the argument that fascination with fame and the famous is fundamentally undemocratic. Thus, champions of lesbian visibility who regard the acknowledgment of lesbian images in popular culture as a marker of greater social acceptance would seem to be hopelessly naïve, in thrall to the mass media, or, worse, insensitive to social inequities. If the media's exaltation of images represents a hollowing out of cultural meaning, why would we want to endorse this enterprise? In particular, why are gay and lesbian activists pursuing—with encouragement from all sorts of sympathetic allies in the entertainment industries, such as those honored by GLAAD's annual Media Awards[11]—a political strategy aimed at influencing institutions so often associated with superficiality and elitism: the Hollywood star system and all of its latter day offshoots? Is doing so a surrender to the most venal, crass tendencies of late capitalist culture?

To answer these questions, we need to examine how visibility figures in discussions about and strategies employed in lesbian politics. In addition to Bono and her comrades at GLAAD, legions of lesbian spokeswomen have included visibility as a plank in their political platforms. To cite just one example, in 1993 Torie Osborn, former director of the National Lesbian and Gay Task Force, was quoted in the infamous *New York* magazine cover story on "lesbian chic" as saying that visibility constitutes a "big lesbian issue" (Kasindorf 1993, 35). More specifically, this article and a similar piece in *Newsweek* (Salholz 1993) that appeared around the same time outline various phenomena that support the assertion that lesbian visibility has increased: the growing numbers of lesbians who appear at street demonstrations and others who may not be politically active but are open about their sexuality with coworkers, neighbors, and family members, as well as a marked decline in the secrecy and subterfuge associated with such lesbian cultural venues as bars. According to both magazines, visibility is both cause and effect of lesbians' greater political clout in the United States, although how lesbians portrayed in magazines, movies, and television translate into political power is not spelled out in any detail. Rather, these articles indicate that their editors and publishers take the equation of visibility with power for granted, and no further discussion is necessary.

But lesbian and gay advocates of visibility politics are more precise. They foresee three basic advantages that will ensue with enhanced visibility. First, images of lesbians in popular culture proclaim our substantial presence within the population, contrary to the concept that lesbianism is characteristic of a small minority. In addition, images of lesbians whose lives are not scandalous, apart from their lovers' gender, refute notions that homosexual desires and/or identities are caused by psychosexual deficiencies. Such "positive images," it is argued, contradict stereotypes that define lesbianism as a form of psychological and social deviance. Finally, visible lesbians offer role models for young women who are unable or unwilling to conform to heterosexual norms but find no affirmation for their lesbian identities and same-sex desires, suffering from self-destructive emotional disorders as a result.[12]

And these claims are often articulated together. For instance, in her book surveying the history of gay and lesbian politics in the United States, Margaret Cruikshank posits visibility as a key factor in cultivating self-acceptance and a condition for emancipation from social oppression. The representations she favors are not premised on a definition of lesbianism as radical otherness but rather on treating lesbianism as "common and ordinary" (Cruikshank 1992, 164). Instead of news items on lesbian practices of artificial insemination, she writes, "Lesbians would be better understood if the mass media portrayed civic leaders like the two lesbians elected to the San Francisco Board of Supervisors" (163). What Cruikshank would prefer is less sensationalist, less spectacular imagery—an unlikely prospect insofar as the mainstream press is predicated on sensation and spectacle. However, a compromise of sorts has been forged in media coverage during the past decade. Splashy coming out declarations by celebrities attract immediate attention, but the emphasis in the press tends to present their prosaic, "real" lives. In a reciprocal move, vocal, already visible lesbians are just as likely to applaud these normalizing gestures.

UNRULY DISTURBANCES

The view offered by the networks, movie studios, and glossy news magazines can be heady indeed, but this isn't the only perspective available. The interpretation of attention lavished on lesbians in the 1990s as an assimilation into popular culture accounts for only one segment of the pro-visibility contingent. Even *New York* magazine's celebration of lesbian visibility takes notice of activists and cultural producers interested in taking advantage of visual culture to make radical political statements. One example cited is the direct action collective Lesbian Avengers, whose name alone announces its in-your-face challenge to mainstream values. Such groups do not eschew popular media as uniformly compromising but rather attempt to tap into the unruly potential often associated with them.

For much of this century, popular cultural forms—like comic books, music (first rock and roll, later punk, heavy metal, and hip hop), movies, television, and, lately, the Internet and computer games—have been suspected of moral sabotage and inspired appeals for state regulation to curtail their supposedly pernicious effects. From this perspective, popular culture provides an ideal point of departure from which to launch an oppositional critique of sexual and gender norms. And lesbians have been active in this arena: unambiguous examples of this tendency are lesbian producers and readers of lesbian pornography; such comic strips as Diane DiMassa's *Hothead Paisan*, which chronicles the exploits of a fiendish lesbian terrorist; and an abundance of irreverent fanzines and websites.

This dimension of visibility politics is significant, since it underscores the absence of any static configuration of culture itself, especially in those areas often referred to collectively as popular culture, which more and more commands the cultural field as a whole. As Stuart Hall observes, "Popular culture is one of the sites where [the] struggle for and against a culture of the powerful is engaged: it is also a stake to be won or lost *in* that struggle. It is the arena of contest and resistance" (S. Hall 1981, 239). Struggle is the operative term in Hall's discussion of the antagonisms that render popular culture a politically volatile domain. Thus, visibility may disrupt or contradict received ideas and accepted beliefs. It may propose new kinds of social categories or inject new meanings into old ones. On the other hand, such contests often extend the reach of dominant forces, insofar as this arena "is partly where hegemony arises, and where it is secured" (239).

The latter dimension of visibility takes a decidedly sinister form in technologies of surveillance, akin to the Panopticon described by Foucault (1977), transforming newly visible homosexual women and men into ideal targets for social control. From this perspective, it is difficult to disagree with Leo Bersani's acerbic assessment of the emphasis on visibility politics in lesbian and gay circles: "[V]isibility is a precondition of surveillance, discipli-

Diana DiMassa's comic strip *Hothead Paisan: Homicidal Lesbian Terrorist.* © 1999 Diane DiMassa.

nary intervention, and, at the limit, gender-cleansing. . . . Once we agreed to be seen, we also agreed to being policed" (Bersani 1995, 11–12). The Panopticon metaphor is a powerful one, and Bersani's warning should not be deemed irrelevant by lesbians considering a bid for visibility. Yet, given how often contradictions and ambiguities crop up whenever the visibility question arises, Hall's description of cultural friction and mutability seems more applicable than one that understands visibility as a unilateral exercise of power.[13] In fact, the concept of popular culture as a contested field seems closer to Foucault's rejection of the idea of power as property. Power, he proposes, is not something that can be possessed; neither is it a repressive exercise but instead a resource that is affirmative, inventive, and at times even pleasurable (Foucault 1978, 86).

In her study of technologies of gender de Lauretis extends and modifies Foucault's critique of disciplinary power. The technologies to which she refers are practical techniques that "control the field of social meaning and thus produce, promote and 'implant' representations of gender," but not absolutely. For, she writes, "the terms of a different construction of gender [and sexuality] also exist, in the margins of hegemonic discourses . . . outside the heterosexual social contract, and inscribed in micropolitical practices" (de Lauretis 1987, 18).[14] Alongside Hall's assessment of popular culture as sometimes disorderly and always mutable, de Lauretis's comment offers conceptual support for a politics of lesbian visibility—but only if this is conceived as different from the incorporation of lesbians into already existing symbolic configurations, such as that promoted by GLAAD and other standard-bearers who treat visibility as synonymous with validation, social integration, and legitimacy—in sum, immediate reality. What is required, then, is a political understanding of culture as an aggregate of interconnected but not always coordinated institutions and practices that routinely reproduce social identities and relations. These mechanisms (for want of a better word) are inherently conservative and quite resilient but, because these are socially produced, also susceptible to reinterpretation, redefinition, appropriation, and, on rare occasions, sabotage.

BLIND SPOTS

The appearance of lesbians in such prestigious media as broadcast television and large-circulation news magazines is generally interpreted as indication that we have arrived (after all, that is the plot line common to these reports), but it may also generate skepticism or amusement. As a participant in myriad conversations where reference were made to "lesbian chic," I cannot recall any mention of the phrase that was not accompanied by the gestural equivalent of ironic quotation marks—a guffaw or, at least, raised eyebrows. Having become accustomed to the idea that lesbianism is inherently unfashionable and always in bad taste, it is easy to strike a cynical pose when told that we are suddenly in vogue, that someone who shares what has been a stigmatized identity has been anointed a star. Still, if mainstream culture is indeed the arbiter of social reality and status, shouldn't these be read as success stories?

Defenders of lesbian visibility may find the attention gratifying, but there are others who recommend closer scrutiny of the interests involved, as well as the images produced. For instance, in their study of the relationship between the increase in lesbian imagery in popular culture and advertising practices, Amy Gluckman and Betsy Reed (1993) question the market research used by advertisers to rationalize gay- and lesbian-themed ads, which glossy gay publications like *Out* and the *Advocate* rely upon to convince account executives to buy space. Much of this data, the critics maintain, is skewed in its portrayal of lesbians and gay men as relatively affluent compared to their heterosexual peers. Their article cites one set of statistics, published by the gay marketing firm Overlooked Opinions, which presents an average annual gay male household income of $51,624 and $45,755 for lesbian households in the United States, compared to the national average of $36,800.[15] The authors contend that these numbers are inflated because the extent of the lesbian and gay population is unknown; moreover, lesbians and gay men willing to be included in such research projects are only those who can afford to be out. Gluckman and Reed also mention a similar survey, which projected even higher income averages but was just as questionable because the data reflected only responses from the readers of upscale gay magazines.

Gluckman and Reed's point is that attempts to lure advertisers with this kind of faulty information is shortsighted. Presenting inflated income figures as empirically accurate may persuade media professionals that an investment in lesbian and gay imagery is not as risky as they imagine, but these "facts" also provide fodder for right-wing, homophobic political organizations (see also, Badgett 2000). Such groups and sympathetic politicians have used these same marketing statistics as evidence that there is no need for legislation offering protection against homophobic violence or discrimination in employment and housing, since moneyed gay men and lesbians cannot claim to be social pariahs. This strategy has been a cornerstone of arguments against any legal guarantees of what right-wing fundamentalists call "special rights" crafted during the rash of antigay rights initiatives in the early 1990s. Hence, Bersani's dire warnings about the minefields of visibility appear to be well founded. Still, the success of these strategies is not assured. In some cases the corporate sector's embrace of lesbians and gay men as a potentially lucrative pool of buyers, as well as producers, of goods and services, has proved immune to reactionary attempts to authorize homophobia. For example, when the ultraconservative American Family Association and Southern Baptist Convention declared a boycott of Disney Corporation properties and products in 1997—on account of the annual Gay Day gathering at Disney World and their ownership of ABC television, which was responsible for the lesbian-friendly sitcom *Ellen*—Disney refused to respond and seemed to suffer few economic or social repercussions.

No doubt the most important measure of value in capitalist culture is monetary. Recognition within the economic sphere secures and reaffirms social identities, while routinely upsetting traditional social conventions whenever these get in the way of increased earnings. This, as Gluckman and Reed indicate, is why visibility under these conditions is contradictory: we are interpellated as lesbian subjects, as Althusser would say, but also as lesbian *consumers*. However, we should not presume that economic forces will inevitably bring about the collapse of a social identity carved out of political struggles into a consumer identity drained of political content. At the same time, we cannot ignore the possibility that this version of visibility may produce a new form of invisibility. It can be conscripted for a program of normalization whereby women who have been regarded as unnatural perverts will be newly perceived and accepted as ordinary and inoffensive, therefore indistinguishable from heterosexual women.

SEX SYMBOLS

Once we accept that visibility is not an empirical, self-evident fact or inherently progressive, it cannot be understood as a guarantee of admittance to the citadels of power. Indeed, as Peggy Phelan wryly observes, "If representational visibility equals power, then almost-naked young white women should be running Western culture" (Phelan 1993, 11). According to her analysis, political strategies intended to affirm any sort of marginalized identity by means of amplified representations are easily frustrated. This occurs because such schemes fail to take into account the symbiotic relationship between dominant ideology and symbolic constructs that represent certain identities as positively valued—men, whites, heterosexuals, the economically prosperous—and remain the standard against which others are judged. Phelan offers an incisive list of premises that characterize visibility politics, and two of these are especially germane: "The relationship between representation and identity is linear and smoothly mimetic. What one sees is what one is"; and, "If one's mimetic likeness is not represented, one is not addressed" (7).

The problem with these and related precepts common to visibility politics is that they perpetuate the idea that symbolic representations will redress power imbalances. In the process, visibility politics neglects how such social categories as gender, race, sexuality, and class always posit a relationship between two asymmetrical terms—man/woman, white/nonwhite, hetero/homo, upper class/lower class—where the second group is always defined as the opposite and inferior to the first. In other words, the power relations entailed in disparities between terms within each category are reinforced every time they are reproduced. Phelan allows that visibility politics may create feelings of pride among members of underrepresented groups and at times furthers practical political goals but cautions that "the ideology of the visible . . . erases the power of the unmarked, unspoken, and unseen" (7). Invisibility is characteristic of what passes without notice, what qualifies as normal and hence is unremarkable. At the very least, this link between invisibility and power should allow a more nuanced analysis of the effects of lesbian celebrity and interpretations of these as signs of political progress.

There is a further wrinkle encountered when the problem of lesbian and gay representation is posed in terms of an invisibility that will be remedied by inclusion in mainstream culture. As Cindy Patton writes in her introduction to a collection of articles and essays from the early years of the gay and lesbian liberation movement, "[M]ainstream culture has already been queered by us: Liberace, certainly, but also 'voguing'; the adoption by male country and western singers of k.d. lang's butch-pastiche of male country and western singers; Pee Wee Herman's playhouse and its transformation into the pee-pee-peep show; Cindy Crawford and Richard Gere's marriage (not)" (Patton 1994, xxv). These comments appear to contradict sweeping statements about lesbian and gay invisibility that results from consistent, well enforced policies of exclusion. But there is no quarrel here with the basic logic of visibility politics. Indeed, Patton's information provides yet another reason to applaud lesbian celebrities and campaign for an increase in their numbers, since acknowledgment of queer contributions to popular culture will further subvert smug notions of heterosexual cultural hegemony.

Such conclusions may be too hasty, though, if the paucity of lesbians on Patton's list is registered. Indeed, this only confirms the oft-cited handicap suffered by lesbians as compared to gay men where visibility is concerned. Consider, for instance, a newspaper report by Natalie Angier on hostility toward gay men and lesbians during the 1993 gays-in-the-military debate. In one sense, Angier's article is exceptional insofar as she acknowledges the oversight of lesbians. Still, the author then searches for a rational explanation for her acceptance of this apparent truism, citing the parallels between homophobia and sexism to explain hostility toward gay men, as compared to lesbians: "[M]any social critics and gay-rights advocates . . . say that people are much likelier to express animosity toward gay men than toward homosexual women, and that a reason for this is a distaste for anything smacking of effeminate behavior in men" (Angier 1993). Not just homophobia but any aspect of gay culture, it would seem, is largely a male affair, despite frequent efforts to include lesbians nominally. Another writer on gay cultural phenomena does not even bother to question the lack of parity, informing readers of a 1996 issue of *New York* magazine, "By 'gay culture' I mean gay *male* culture. For various historical reasons, lesbian culture has, until just recently, had neither the visibility nor the impact on the larger mainstream culture of its male counterpart" (Mendelsohn 1996, 26).[16] This assessment seems well founded in popular perception, although only if the logic that measures effects in terms of visibility is left unquestioned.

Curiously, media commentators often invoke another, equally clichéd, but apparently contradictory idea about the differential meanings of gay male versus lesbian visibility—that it is less onerous for a female performer to be forthright about homosexuality, more visible as it were, than for her male counterpart. For instance, when rap artist Queen Pen recorded "Girlfriend," a song that brags about stealing a woman away from her boyfriend, cultural critic Michael Eric Dyson was quoted as saying, "This is really going to be a bomb she's dropping. But the *real thing* is going to be when you get some brother coming out" (quoted in Jamison 1998, emphasis added). Similar comments were made during the brouhaha over Ellen DeGeneres in 1997, when critics routinely asserted that a gay male sitcom star and/or principal character remained out of bounds for television programmers, but when that day arrived visibility would be advanced to a new height. But when the breakthrough did occur, lesbians were not in the picture: the NBC comedy show *Will and Grace*, which features a gay male lead character (played by a heterosexual actor) premiered in 1998, the same year *Ellen* was ditched by ABC.

Is visibility more meaningful for gay men simply because they are men? When one group of gay men, African Americans, say, is still not included within the redrawn boundaries of visibility that can accommodate white gay men, do the risks they incur by staking a claim in this domain make their efforts all the more important? These are not minor questions. Rather, in a world where visibility is understood as *the* criterion for reality and gay men represent the "real thing," the *real* homosexual disturbance, the privilege accorded male subjectivity in the field of visual representation comes to the fore. Accordingly, lesbians can be said to occupy an extremely tenuous position: neither "real" women nor "real" homosexuals—that is, visible to the extent that gay men are.

DOUBLE BIND

Whether they believe that gay men are more culturally influential or more likely to be despised, journalists' offhand treatment of the disparity between gay men and lesbians indicates that any discussion of lesbian visibility calls for a more considered analysis of how gender ideology inflects visibility. An important resource for this endeavor is the work of feminist scholars who employ critical methods that deconstruct systems of meaning understood as binary oppositions—not only the structuring of gender as exclusively male or female, but also myriad dichotomies metonymically linked to this, such as active/passive, culture/nature, and the like.[17] Theoretical work dealing with identifications and desires has also adopted these techniques to analyze sexual norms, according to which homosexuality is defined as the inverse or converse of heterosexuality. Thus, femininity appears as the antithesis of and support for normative masculinity, just as the understanding of homosexuality as abnormal or deviant affirms the normalcy of heterosexuality.

Beginning in the mid-1970s, feminists began to outline and then elaborate psychoanalytic theories, which they employed to dismantle the phallocentric logic that informs how women are depicted in practically all dimensions of Western culture. Luce Irigaray (1985) and others feminists working in this vein trace such representations to the unconscious formation of gender identity predicated on phallic superiority within systems of symbolic representation. When the phallus operates as the primary signifier of subjectiv-

ity, masculinity is established as superior to female sexuality, which is castrated, "nothing," marked by an absence, a lack.[18] At the same time, the
"proof" of castration seemingly offered by the sight of female bodies produces
elaborate psychological defenses against the threat of emasculation in the
minds of little boys and is preserved in the unconscious psyches of adult men.
Thus, a masculine/phallic sexual economy generates images of "woman" and
"feminine sexuality" that allay fears of castration, rendering all such images
merely reflections of male fantasies.

A number of features of the representational practices found in Western
cultures can be interpreted in this fashion, including those that constitute
celebrity images. Laura Mulvey does this in her landmark essay "Visual
Pleasure and Narrative Cinema," in which she discusses how Marlene
Dietrich's carefully fabricated image in the films directed by Joseph von
Sternberg in the 1930s "produces the ultimate fetish" (Mulvey 1989, 22).[19]
Von Sternberg's precise orchestration of various cinematic elements—framing, lighting, costume—present isolated parts of Dietrich's body (e.g., legs,
face) or her entire body as perfect objects. On screen, she becomes a phallic
substitute, a "phallic woman," who wards off the association between a female
body and the "fact" of her castration. According to this line of reasoning, the
spectacular quality of feminine display is no more—and no less—than a masculine defense.

Despite the tremendous impact this critique has had within academic
precincts, lesbian commentary on the iconic image of Dietrich has suggested
a form of cinematic pleasure available to women. For instance, in both
Morocco and *Blond Venus* the actress appears wearing a top hat and tuxedo,
and in the former film she flirts outrageously with a woman in the audience
while performing a cabaret act. Such representations have been interpreted as
references to the mannish outfits worn by stylish lesbians around the time the
film was made (1930) and perhaps to Dietrich's own penchant for wearing
tailored, trousered suits and sexual nonconformity—a bit of lesbian visibility,
if you like.[20] But Mulvey declares outright that the visual pleasures of which
she writes are only those that provoke and play to fantasies and desires
defined as masculine *and* heterosexual, because the social identities of all men
and women in Western cultures are unconsciously produced and maintained
on this basis.[21]

Clearly, there's something wrong with this picture, a problem that
Mulvey and others have made efforts to address from within the psychoanalytic paradigm. "[W]hat about the women in the audience?" Mulvey inquires

in her "Afterthoughts on 'Visual Pleasure and Narrative Cinema'" (1989, 29–38). Or, as E. Ann Kaplan asks, "Is the gaze male?" (1983; see also Doane 1981 and de Lauretis 1984). Although these feminists propose various cinematic techniques that might elicit feminine identifications and desires, in most cases these remain well entrenched in heterosexual notions of gender. This is true even when lesbian sexuality is proposed as a conceivable solution for the enigma of female pleasure at the movies.[22] For instance, when Mary Ann Doane describes the "convolutions" of a female spectator's conflicting identifications—with either the female object/image or the subject who has fantasies of possessing the same object/image—she quotes Julia Kristeva's belabored characterization of "what we commonly call female homosexuality": "'I am looking, as a man would, for a woman'; or else, 'I submit myself, as if I were a man who thought he was a woman, to a woman who thinks she is a man'" (quoted in Doane 1987, 157). Similarly, when Mulvey considers the same problem, she discerns an "oscillation between 'passive' femininity and regressive [i.e., narcissistic] 'masculinity'" (Mulvey 1989, 35). This unconscious and irresolute dilemma results in a habitual "trans-sex identification" with the hero, which "does not sit easily and shifts restlessly in its borrowed transvestite clothes" (33). Clearly, it is but a short step from the idea of a woman filmgoer as one occupying "the masculine position" (E. Kaplan 1983, 30)[23] and "who, in buying her ticket, must deny her sex" (Doane 1981, 23) to metaphors of dissonance between female gender and sexual desire. This is hardly breaking new analytic ground. What these feminist critics have reproduced is the all-too-familiar gender inversion model of lesbianism, rendered visible by cross-dressing.[24]

DRESS CODES

Perhaps what confuses feminist film theorists is the irrevocable association in the twentieth-century Euro-American cultural lexicon between lesbian visibility and a certain set of stylistic markers generally associated with masculinity—short hair; austere, tailored clothing; accessories like neckties, men's hats, leather jackets, and sensible shoes; and such gestural traits as a purposeful stride and robust handshake. Certainly, every woman who fits this description is not a lesbian, but it remains difficult to imagine how a lesbian could be visible without at least several of these accoutrements or mannerisms. In fact, the telltale correspondence between "mannish"—butch—fashion and lesbian personality constituted an article of faith among social researchers who attempted to catalogue the distinguishing features of the members of this sexual minority over a century ago. For instance, one of the most prominent, Havelock Ellis, believed that an "actively inverted woman"—a lesbian who courted and seduced other women—exhibits "one fairly essential character: a more or less distinct trace of masculinity," while her typical partner would be always be "womanly," if "plain" in appearance compared to a heterosexual woman (quoted in Newton 1989, 288). Such ideas survive in the present but have been reworked in ways that transform a hegemonic signifier of stigma into a symbolic rallying point for challenges to normative gender and sexuality.

Described as pathology by professionals concerned with classifying deviant sexualities while celebrated by supporters of social legitimation, the butch look is interpreted by both as a self-conscious appropriation of male insignia and therefore different from the quotidian masculinity displayed by men. As such, this particular mode of transvestism might be seen as the antithesis of the masquerade associated with femininity in psychoanalytic discourse. The concept of feminine comportment as a masquerade was first developed by Joan Rivière to explain a distinct type of woman she encountered in her psychoanalytic practice: intellectuals who exhibited the kind of aggression and rationality in their work generally associated with men but who were otherwise paragons of femininity. Rivière's conclusion was that feminine masquerade is adopted as an unconscious defense by "women who wish for masculinity [and] may put on a mask of womanliness to avert anxiety and the retribution feared by men." She did not stop there, but continued, "The reader may now ask how I define womanliness or where I draw the line between genuine womanliness and the 'masquerade.'" Her reply: "My suggestion is not . . . that there is any such difference; whether radical or superficial, they are the same thing" (Rivière [1929] 1986, 38). Rivière conceived her theory of femininity in the late 1920s, when lesbianism and femininity were generally believed to be antithetical. A lesbian participant in a post-1960s political movement who is critical of heterosexual normalcy and the gender stereotypes that go with it might be quite comfortable with her womanliness but want to tear off the mask and flaunt her masculine wishes. Still, when butchness is seen as a political statement the limitations of visibility politics are underscored by what might be described as the femme problem.

In this scenario, where lesbianism is interpreted as a rejection of femininity, there remains the question of lesbians who don't have masculine desires. An article by Lisa Walker, titled suggestively "How to Recognize a Lesbian: The Cultural Politics of Looking Like What You Are," presents this dilemma as pivotal: "The glorification of the butch as authentic lesbian is based on her 'blatant' representation of sexual deviance, and this in turn implies ambiguity and confusion around the femme's sexual identity" (Walker 1993, 882). In other words, when the lesbian in question looks unambiguously like a heterosexual woman, the difference from heterosexual femininity disappears, becomes invisible. Sue-Ellen Case offers a solution to the visibility problems that arise when lesbians do not favor butch style and find femme identity more agreeable by pointing out that "the butch-femme couple inhabit the subject position together. . . . The two roles never appear as . . . discrete" (Case 1993, 295). Since femme and butch are interrelated, both can be incorporated in Case's interpretation of this particular lesbian style as a camp send-up of normative gender.

A butch–femme couple shows up gender for what it is—a mythic edifice that supports the power and authority of men at the expense of women—by highlighting the artifice involved in producing any performance of gender. However, Case maintains that subversive or transgressive meaning is generated by the unsettling butch image, not the femme, which is not a satisfactory resolution if one is not interested in placing the femme in the background. As Biddy Martin remarks, "[W]hen [femininity] is not camped up or disavowed, it constitutes a capitulation, a swamp, something maternal, ensnared and ensnaring" (B. Martin 1994, 105). Thus, the quest for lesbian visibility must come to grips with the devaluation or repudiation of women that produces and reproduces our subordinate position in the gender hierarchy, since (*pace* Monique Wittig) lesbians are also women. When femininity is "played straight," to borrow Martin's excellent pun (1996), femme dress and demeanor become inaccessible as resources for lesbian visibility.

The problem might be solved if hyperbolic femininity is enacted as burlesque, for example, super red and shiny lips, long polished nails, ultrahigh heels, low-cut blouses, and tight skirts that accentuate breasts and buttocks, in other words, the look of a drag queen. Such a performance is said to indicate a critical attitude equal to any butch's. But difficulties also arise with this notion of gender subversion as a visual enterprise, which have been helpfully commented upon by Carol-Anne Tyler. One is that parodic femininity may easily be mistaken for the serious variety. Indeed, she points out, "Sometimes . . . one is ironic without having intended it, and sometimes, despite one's best intentions, no one gets the joke" (Tyler 1991, 54). Additionally, she remarks

that it would be difficult to demonstrate how feminine hyperbole as a political maneuver has challenged men's ability to incorporate these images in
their symbolic repertoire. Think of any "sex symbol"—Monroe or Madonna.

Tyler considers a further paradox produced by this kind of mimicry and
Rivière's concept of masquerade—both playful and straight renditions of
femininity—which bears directly on the class and racial dimensions of lesbian visibility, and of lesbian celebrity as well. She points out that feminine
mimicry is exemplified by female impersonators (her prototype is Dolly
Parton, who she calls a "female female impersonator") whose feminine drag
draws attention to itself through an excessive display of "bad taste"—"too
frilly or flashy" (Tyler 1990, 209)—which is associated with "ethnic" or
lower-class, white women. The critical or subversive meaning that may be
attributed to an "overdressed" feminine outfit is therefore measured by its distance from "real" femininity, symbolized by white, Anglo, middle-class styles
that attract little notice precisely because they signify "good taste." Of course,
the idea of bad versus good taste implies a moral judgment, and there's no
mistaking whose morality is deemed worthy and whose is not, an appraisal of
value that is left unchallenged whenever displays of femininity are deemed in
bad taste, no matter how intentionally "bad" they may be. Thus, ironic femininity may easily miss its target—heterosexual gender ideology—and instead
make fun of women who do not appear to be proper ladies, do not embody
"genuine femininity" (Tyler 1990, 202).

In contrast, butch style is already marked as deviant because it is worn by
an inappropriately gendered person, but its classic forms are also coded
according to class: either upper-class men's wear—finely tailored suits, in
subtle patterns and colors, made from expensive fabrics, and maybe a dia-
mond tie clip and gold cuff links to complete the ensemble—or working-
class fashions like tee shirts, jeans, and motorcycle jackets: in other words,
Fred Astaire or James Dean. And both are indelibly inscribed with cultural
codes of white masculinity. That is not to say that men with cultural identities other than white surrender these when they don such apparel. But it does
seem to be the case that the rare representation of a black lesbian in the mass
media is automatically assigned an aggressive butch persona almost indistinguishable from a stereotypically dangerous black man, who becomes a
deserving target for obliteration. To take an example from popular culture: in
the spate of movies featuring likable lesbian killers released in the past decade
none swaggers and curses as much or incites such extreme violence as the
bank robber played by Queen Latifah in *Set It Off*, who is dispatched by a

Queen Latifah in the
final shootout in *Set
It Off*. Photofest.

barrage of gunfire à la *Bonnie and Clyde* when the police finally catch up with
her. None of the white lesbian murderers in comparable films provoke such
sadistic and bloody punishment, not Gina Gershon in *Bound* (gets the girl
and the money), Sharon Stone in *Basic Instinct* (last seen in bed with the hero
played by Michael Douglas), or Kate Winslet and Melanie Lynskey in
Heavenly Creatures (they receive five-year prison sentences).

True, none of these actors are lesbian celebrities; they just play lesbian
characters. Yet the same treatment applies when it comes to entertainers who
play themselves, so to speak. Jackie Goldsby recalls how the mere hint of lesbianism torpedoed the career of Vanessa Williams and relates this to racial

differences in representations of lesbian sexuality. Around the same time that *Penthouse* published pornographic photographs of Williams in staged lesbian sex scenes during her reign as Miss America in the mid-1980s, Madonna was capitalizing on lesbian innuendo in her scripted and impromptu performances. During an appearance on *Late Night with David Letterman*, Madonna and Sandra Bernhard teased the host and his audience with hints of a lesbian affair, and Madonna's music video for "Justify My Love" included vignettes of the singer engaged in sex play with a woman. "Why is it," Goldsby asks, "that Williams paid such a high price for striking her poses, and that Madonna, appropriating the practices of marginal cultures in her stage act, is rewarded so generously?" (Goldsby 1993, 124). It may be tempting to explain the different meanings of visibility for Williams during her Miss America reign and Madonna during her transgressive period as evidence of the moral categories applied to women—good girl/bad girl. Williams tripped up when her good-girl image was challenged by photographs that indicated this was a sham. Madonna's continued to increase her popularity and her income by exploiting the bad-girl image she had cultivated from day one. However, this implies that race had nothing whatever to do with the difference between the two women and their predicaments, but the more convincing hypothesis is that it had a great deal to do with it.

Williams had to be purer than pure in order to be awarded the supreme prize of ideal femininity, American style, firmly anchored by white bourgeois cultural standards. Indeed, in the moral rhetoric of racial categorization outlined by Richard Dyer (1997, 41–81), "white" connotes purity, innocence, chastity, peace, modesty, honesty, *and* femininity. Although white is not a skin color (no skin tone is actually white), it is symbolically entangled with domination, a system of demarcation between "us" and "them," good and bad. Williams's double provocation—dark complexion and lesbianism—threatened the entire moral edifice. Madonna could capitalize on the same naughtiness that tainted Miss America—remember, both women were playacting lesbianism—precisely because whiteness guaranteed her social superiority, even if she mocked its values. Visibility may be the common denominator in both instances, but the comparison indicates emphatically that this term cannot be applied in any universal sense. Specifically, it cannot be understood without considering how race and sexuality are articulated together in U.S. culture. It is no coincidence that, to date, lesbian visibility and, concomitantly, lesbian celebrity, has been almost exclusively a middle-class, white preserve.

NEW LOOKS

Because celebrity is a representational enterprise constituted through images, the emergence of lesbian celebrities represents the amalgamation of two previously incompatible categories: female celebrity, which involves an ability to project some form of consummate femininity, and identifiable lesbianism, indicated by some kind of display of nonconformity to gender norms by means of stylistic markers associated with masculinity. Thus, lesbian celebrity requires a superimposition of these two images, much like photographic negatives of two faces overlaid to yield a composite portrait. Productive confusion of expectations concerning sexuality and gender may occur in the process, but if more negatives are added the blurry picture becomes unreadable. In other words, the frame can only accommodate one departure from the standard codes of female celebrity—young, white, thin, and preferably blond, and maybe lesbian, too.

An exemplar of this basic configuration is popular musician k.d. lang, who appeared as the cover girl for *New York* magazine's "Lesbian Chic" issue in 1993, was featured in *Vanity Fair* a few months later, and served as a model and spokesperson for MAC cosmetics in 1996.[25] Of all these pictures of lang, the photographs by Herb Ritts illustrating the *Vanity Fair* article seem to rely most upon the old codes of lesbian visibility—or at least use gender inversion as a reference point. The cover and the opening spread of the lang profile show the singer wearing a pin-striped suit, involved in a soft-core shaving fantasy while supermodel Cindy Crawford plays barber dressed in a skimpy leotard and high-heeled boots. Ritts's photos announce themselves immediately as a camp take-off on classic butch–femme iconography, because they are rendered tongue-in-cheek by the exaggerated poses of the two major celebrities.

In contrast, the article suggests that lang's gender ambiguity is an indication of her sexual *nature*, a serious matter and not just an amusing pasttime. Readers are informed that "[s]he is as different from a female icon like Dolly Parton *as if she were another species*" (Bennetts 1993, 98; emphasis added). Ritts's photos, on the other hand, suggest that the only difference between lang and Parton is the gender each chooses to impersonate. This tension between image and text underscores how lesbian visibility may be conscripted for two incompatible ideas: a lesbian proclaims herself by using the vocabulary of normative gender, or a lesbian's mannish guise makes a mockery of normative gender. On the basis of this particular example, I'd say neither

interpretation is definitive, as if the phenomenon of lesbian celebrity provokes confusion and contradiction—which at first may seem a dubious outcome but is surely an improvement on narrow, rigid, immobilizing stereotypes.

It is instructive, then, to compare the treatment of lang in *Vanity Fair* with her portrait on the *New York* cover. Here, lang is presented in an earnest but humorless portrait, where she looks directly at the photographer, and thus at the reader, as if to underline "The Bold, Brave New World of Gay Women" announced in the accompanying headline. Yet another aspect of lang is presented in the MAC ads, which are fairly standard glamour-girl fare, despite an understated but explicit reference to her lesbianism—the lipstick imprint of another woman's kiss on her cheek. Again, the disparate imagery and associations that the ad invokes suggests a departure from earlier countercultural stereotypes. However, the common denominator in all these images—as well as those of numerous other lesbians illustrating the *New York* article (Kasindorf 1993) and the concurrent story in *Newsweek* (Salholz 1993)—is that they are notable for their glamour. Gone are the L.L. Bean outfits, work boots, and makeup-free faces associated with a lesbian-feminist righteousness and high-minded disregard for male approval.

These are members of a new generation characterized as "lifestyle lesbians" by the mainstream press, as well as by more serious commentators. If understated mannish garments and bearing could be said to constitute lesbian visibility in the past, the 1990s witnessed the arrival of a lesbian style that is decidedly more spectacular and, as a result, feminized if not always conventionally feminine—flashy but not necessarily frilly. Lifestyle lesbians revel in shopping and mastering the codes of seduction, although their objects of sexual desire are not men but women; they may assume butch or femme aspects, or a pastiche of both. In her study of this phenomenon, Arlene Stein observes that these younger lesbians may interpret their concern with appearances as a political criticism of cultural norms that equate image and identity, femininity and passivity. According to the protocol adopted by the many members of the older generation of lesbian-feminists, femme style, in particular, signals a retreat from radical political engagement. Challenging this notion, Stein reports that younger, urban lesbians disagree with the reductive notion that apparel reflects political consciousness and justify their miniskirts, high heels, jewelry, makeup, et cetera as an enactment of personal choice, an assertion of freedom in the face of cultural domination. The problem with this formulation for Stein is that "style itself is an insufficient basis for a lesbian politic" that will convincingly challenge the various ways in which lesbians are defined and treated as pariahs (Stein 1989, 41). Without dismissing such practices out of hand, she nevertheless expresses a concern with lesbian politics linked with consumption—shopping and showing off the goods thus acquired—that makes lesbian style a function of the market-place, weakening any claims to radicality.

A more worrisome danger, which Stein hints at and other analysts have dealt with in greater detail, is that lesbian style may readily be appropriated by what Danae Clark calls "commodity lesbianism" (Clark 1993; see also Dittmar 1998). Clark uses this phrase to characterize the growing number of lesbian images in commercial contexts, which she attributes to the slow awakening of advertising account executives to the potential riches to be mined in gay and lesbian niche markets. The most prevalent method developed for these purposes is an advertising technique that employs lesbian-coded imagery—butchy models and poses, for instance—but never makes unambiguous references to lesbianism, as in the k.d. lang M.A.C. ad. This strategy, dubbed "gay window" advertising by those who invented it, "consciously disavows any explicit connection to lesbianism for fear of offending or losing potential customers. At the same time, an appropriation of lesbian styles or appeal to lesbian desires can also assure a lesbian market" (Clark 1993, 196). In other words, fashion-conscious lesbian consumers may easily become handmaidens of capitalist exploitation and alienation. Yet, as Clark points out, resistance to the regimentation of social life that occurs in many self-fashioning practices may also provoke political debates about forms and contents of lesbian identity.

Taking this suggestion a step further, we might question if economic rationality—the mode of social action that characterizes money exchange and the workings of capitalist markets—always trumps cultural meanings and practices. Or, to put this another way, what if, as Arjun Appadurai contends, consumer "demand is the economic expression of a political logic of consumption"? (Appadurai 1986, 31). Implied in this question is an inversion of a central tenet of Marxist political economy, which maintains that modes of production determine forms of cultural reproduction, including consumer practices, at least "in the last instance." Not so, says Chandra Mukerji (1983), who takes issue with both the Marxist explanation of the triumph of materialist culture in the West as an outcome of class struggles over control of productive forces and Weber's theory that Western capitalism flourished as a logical outgrowth of ascetic Protestantism. Indeed, Mukerji's research indicates that the economic expansion that occurred in early modern Europe can be attributed to a growing demand for luxury goods—fashionable clothing most significantly—which motivated technical and entrepreneurial innovations in trade, manufacturing, and communication.

By embarking upon this digression into capitalism's infancy in early modern Europe, with its implications for subsequent global political-economic relations, I may seem to have strayed a great distance from the micropolitics involved in late-twentieth-century U.S. lesbian style, hardly a blip on the radar screens of most social theorists. Even so, these observations may shed light on the contradiction noted by Clark and Stein, as well as pose more precisely a nagging question concerning lesbian celebrity. That is, how can an eminently economic enterprise such as the marketing of style, and the related marketing of celebrity images, possibly provide a foundation for lesbian politics when both rely upon the capitalist traffic in fetishized commodities, whether items of apparel or objects of fascination?

Consider, however, that commodities are objectifications of social statuses—organized in terms of such categories as gender, ethnicity, age, and economic class, but also such social groupings as professions and religions.[26] Consumer practices reaffirm these categories and reproduce their cultural significance, engaging material objects in rituals of everyday life in a manner that invokes their taken-for-granted meanings.[27] Should a commodity's acquisition and use be consciously undertaken, it may assume political significance, whether a bid for upward mobility, as in cases where a particular commodity is associated with higher social status, or in an attempt to redefine prevailing social arrangements. The world of goods is an array of signs that result from but also provide resources for power plays within a cultural matrix. Since the conventional meanings within that matrix must be reproduced *in practice* or become extinct, a cultural system is always vulnerable to threats posed by new or renovated social categories that generate new or renovated objectifications. Is there any difference between popular culture and consumer culture? Not in Western capitalist advanced industrial societies, but that does not mean that economic imperatives automatically prevail, that "commodity lesbianism" or "lifestyle lesbians" will eliminate all radical sexual practices or radical sexual politics. What it does mean is that the previous discussion of popular culture as an uncertain terrain, where adverse ideologies and members of social groups vie for cultural authority, applies to consumer culture as well.

BODIES OF KNOWLEDGE

The struggle continues, or does it? A truce was negotiated in the 1990s in at least one influential sector of lesbian culture—the two mass-circulation gay and lesbian magazines in the United States, the *Advocate* and *Out*. Traditionally, the lesbian and gay press has acted as a cultural watchdog guarding against homophobic disinformation and misrepresentation by the mass media, and these magazines are no different. But this hasn't prevented them from covering entertainment celebrities and the industries that produce and support their careers with great gusto. Indeed, during the 1990s, the attention to Hollywood, commercial television, Broadway theater, and other major show business sites increased to the point that most issues of both magazines contained copious reportage on the doings of various stars, along with an incessant flow of information about new cultural productions and awards, reviews, and, of course, gossip, with a star's face on the cover of just about every issue.

Although the celebratory messages carried by these magazines would seem at odds with their critical function, they hit upon the ideal terms for settling the conflict—visibility politics. Not only do editors and critics writing for these gay and lesbian publications periodically offer visibility as a political justification for indulging in the guilty pleasures offered by mass entertainment, they also seek out examples in mainsteam culture that affirm its progressive potential. For instance, an editor at *Out* magazine reflects,

> By midyear [1995], it was impossible to turn on a TV or go to a local
> cineplex without encountering a plethora of queer-themed characters,
> story lines and music . . . there were more positive, more *real* images of gay
> men and lesbians than ever before.
>
> As with anything in life, change requires a series of slow, successive
> baby steps made by a collective of individuals. If Hollywood sets trends
> and inspires people to take action they normally wouldn't take . . . then
> perhaps we're on to something here. (Koffler 1996)

The reasoning applied here hinges on a belief in the benefits that accrue from *any* representation of "real" lesbians or gay men in the media.

Presumably, celebrities also qualify, since one aspect of their appeal is that they provide a guarantee of reality—these are not only representations but *real* people, who lead *real* lives off camera. It comes as no surprise, really, that profiles and portraits of lesbian and gay celebrities have been given pride of place on the covers of glossy gay/lesbian magazines. As a result, images of *real* lesbian celebrities are accorded the same political influence as documentary representations of noncelebrities. Maybe more influence, as this quote by *Out* author Michael Goff indicates:

> When we look to openly gay public figures, we're looking for a public sug-
> gestion of our lives, which can be so hidden. We may also be looking for
> some help in repairing the damage the closet has done, as well as an
> appropriate target for our fantasies. But most important, openly gay
> people with a high profile give us the power to teach America about us.
> Although the battle for gays in the military was a great motivator, k.d.
> lang and David Geffen, for example, have done as much simply by incor-

porating their personal lives into their public ones. It allows everyone who reads *Time* magazine to "know" someone gay, even if a gay person like you or me is not working in the next cubicle. (Goff 1996)

This interpretation of lang or Geffen as imaginary friends who will accelerate the extension of civil rights to all lesbians or gay men echoes a familiar refrain from coming-out manuals, but the logic of this argument is difficult to sustain. Even though a star's image depends on her being perceived as a real individual, what we actually see is a public persona whose private self is only revealed to us via the ersatz intimacy of talk show interviews and personality profiles that are the bread and butter of the celebrity set. Thanks to such displays, performers become "personalities" elevated to stardom and rewarded for their achievements with fame and fortune.

Contrary to Goff's political rationale for interest in the famous, perhaps what recommends celebrities as exemplars is that they are *not* identical to most of our neighbors, friends, or loved ones. Advocates of visibility may find this a heretical thought, and so they should, but given the significance of popular culture for lesbian politics, a fair assessment of the implications of celebrity seems in order. If the problem that prevents the legitimation of lesbians is our perceived threat to social order, what could be a better corrective than lesbians who are available only as idealized figures and are not likely to muddy the waters of projected fantasies by exhibiting their less-than-fabulous selves? The problem with this outcome is that the visibility of "ordinary" lesbians, which is supposed to increase as the result of growing numbers of "out" stars, becomes even more elusive. Visibility politics centered on the entertainment industry recedes as a viable strategy.

Although what amounts to an ever-deepening disjunction between lesbians celebrities and everyday lesbian lives dislodges a cornerstone of visibility politics, there are advantages that may follow from this schism. If lesbian stars represent the incorporation of lesbians into already existing cultural configurations—including moral schema—then we can learn from them the limits of such integration. In other words, high visibility lesbians like Melissa Etheridge and k.d. lang, Ellen DeGeneres and Chastity Bono provide a measure of the acquiescence to gender and sexual norms required for recognition and inclusion to occur peaceably. But they also remind us that the bulwarks of normative culture are not inviolable, since their visibility as lesbians has resulted from hard-won political battles. Too often, the induction of lesbians into the halls of fame is interpreted as the culmination of these struggles. I am suggesting that it should be seen instead as an accommodation, a negotiated compromise (but not surrender) in the struggle over definitions of personhood.

Meanwhile, lesbian identities and practices will continue to take forms not yet permissible or, perhaps, even imaginable within a culture defined as fundamentally heterosexual. Thus, the group of "invisible" lesbians, always a loose configuration defined according to contingent and local criteria, continues to adopt and adapt the definitions embodied by visible lesbians in selective ways—just as the significance of sexuality, gender, and fame changes over time and across cultures. As does visibility.

CHAPTER THREE

CELESTIAL CONFIGURATIONS
ASPECTS OF LESBIAN STARDOM

In her biography of Radclyffe Hall, her lover of twenty-eight years, Una Troubridge, recalls a momentous conversation:

> John [the name Hall used among friends] came to me one day with unusual gravity and asked for my decision in a serious matter: she had long wanted to write a book on sexual inversion, a novel that would be accessible to the general public who did not have access to technical treatises. At one time she had thought of making it a "period" book, built round an actual personality of the early nineteenth century. But her instinct had told her that in any case she must postpone such a book until her name was made; until her unusual theme would get a hearing as being the work of an established author.
>
> It was her absolute conviction that such a book could only be written by a sexual invert, who alone could be qualified by personal knowledge and experience to speak on behalf of a misunderstood and misjudged minority. It was with this conviction that she came to me, telling me that in her view the time was ripe, and that although the publication of such a book might mean the shipwreck of her whole career, she was fully prepared to make any sacrifice except—the sacrifice of my peace of mind. . . . I am glad to remember that my reply was made without so much as an instant's hesitation. . . . I was sick to death of ambiguities, and only wished to be known for what I was and to dwell with her in the palace of truth. (Troubridge 1961, 81–82)

With Una's permission granted, *The Well of Loneliness* was written and published in 1928. And Hall's career was anything but shipwrecked, although the almost immediate prosecution under Britain's Obscene Publications Act of 1857 of booksellers in possession of copies of the novel, followed by an unsuccessful appeal of the guilty verdict, disappointed and angered her. Nor was the critical reception all she had wished for. Unlike the favorable responses her previous novels had received, reviewers of *The Well* refrained from praising the book's literary qualities while, in a number of cases, affirming its call for greater understanding and tolerance of lesbians.[1] Instead, the book reaped Hall other rewards. It became a colossal best-seller, despite the proscription of its publication in Britain until 1948; 200,000 copies were sold by the end of 1933 and over 500,000 copies prior to publication of the first British paperback edition in 1968. Twenty thousand copies were sold in the United States when Covici-Friede published the book after other, less daring publishers turned it down due to skittishness about the inevitable legal action that would follow (Taylor 2001, 261). Her next novel, published in 1932, sold 9,000 copies in its first two weeks despite bad reviews, and earlier books by Hall reissued in the wake of *The Well*'s success garnered hefty additional sales.[2] Hall did not depend upon the income she received for her writing and could have lived comfortably without it, due to the good-sized fortune she had inherited from her grandfather, but she still enjoyed the financial profits her work generated. This is confirmed by a note she wrote to her agent Audrey Heath: "Do you remember the time when no publisher wanted John Hall, and now they're all at each other's throats—oh, well, as long as we get the dollars!!!" (Baker 1985, 253).

In addition to increasing her private wealth, Hall became a major public figure as the result of the scandal created by those who advocated censoring *The Well*: "Every paper displayed photographs of John and contained descriptions of her 'arresting' appearance and personality. The *Yorkshire Post* showed her in jacket and tie, a cigarette clamped raffishly between the teeth, looking every inch the smooth young man-about-town. The *Manchester Despatch* dubbed her 'the most easily-recognised artistic celebrity in London'" (Baker 1985, 225). This image was something that Hall had long cultivated. From 1920 onward, she and Troubridge appeared regularly at social events in London wearing unconventional, distinctly unfeminine garb—Troubridge with her tortoise shell monocle and Hall in head-to-toe man-tailored outfits (although no trousers until the 1930s), as well as various accoutrements obtained from a London theatrical costume shop. In her negotiations with

Una Troubridge and Radclyffe Hall in 1927, with John Singer Sargent's portrait of Hall's deceased lover Mabel "Ladye" Batten in the background. Hulton/Archive by Getty Images.

publishers of *The Well*, she sidestepped her agent to oversee personally the details of production and promotion, at one point insisting that particular photographs be used to publicize the American edition.

Although she drew upon her own experiences and used her lesbian friends as prototypes for characters in *The Well*, the novel's protagonist Stephen Gordon was not a surrogate for Radclyffe Hall.[3] Stephen was plagued by feelings of inadequacy and injury attributed to what she understood as her aberrant sexuality; the novel concludes with her resignation to the outcast status of a female invert. Hall, in contrast, actively courted the opportunity to make lesbianism a topic of public debate and further her own reputation as a writer. As a result of the considerable publicity she received, "[F]ans mobbed John for her autograph" when she and Una attended an opening night at the theater shortly after the moral crusade against the novel was launched in the conservative press, and "two women admirers stepped forward from the waiting crowd and kissed her hand" as she left the court-room after the London appeal. She also received thousands of letters from supporters during and after the court case (Baker 1985, 232–248). All told, Hall's refusal to dissemble or retreat from the public spotlight recommends her nomination as the first self-styled lesbian celebrity.

DISTINGUISHING FEATURES

Of course, Radclyffe Hall was not the first famous lesbian. That honor belongs without question to Sappho, the Lesbian without whom none of us would be lesbians. Nevertheless, that someone could become celebrated as the author of a popular novel featuring a lesbian hero, or could imagine such a character and narrative in the first place, required a set of cultural conditions that had taken shape only in modern times—that is, since the sixteenth century and acceler-ated during the nineteenth. In addition to the novel form itself, which is arguably *the* expressive form of the modern imagination, the idea of a type of person who could be classified as a lesbian, or some such designation that indi-cated a distinct kind of homosexual woman (Hall preferred the term " invert"), had to be formulated and the qualifications for inclusion specified in order for the protagonist and her story to convey any meaning whatsoever.

It is well known that Hall employed the theories and terminology of late-nineteenth-century sexologists to delineate her main character in *The Well of Loneliness*. Her primary debt in this regard was to Havelock Ellis, who wrote a preface to the novel defending its publication, but she was also famil-iar with the taxonomies of sexual perversions compiled by Richard von Krafft-Ebing and Karl Heinrich Ulrichs. She refers to both in *The Well*, hav-ing Stephen's father read their work in order to comprehend his daughter's odd behavior. By uncritically citing these early commentators on homosexu-ality, she seems to confirm Michel Foucault's (1978) postulate concerning the invention of homosexual *identity* in the late nineteenth century, attributable to a proliferation of scientific attention to sex as a newfound category of knowledge (see also, Weeks 1985, 1991).

Foucault's assertion that this historical moment produced "a new speci-fication of [homosexual] individuals" (Foucault 1978, 42–43) remains a dis-puted question. Other historians have proposed that the theories developed by members of the new professions concerned with sexuality—sexologists, psychologists, psychoanalysts—should not be given credit for inventing what became lesbian and gay identities, since these new categories reflected changes in social-sexual culture that were already underway. On one side of this debate, Lillian Faderman (1991) asserts the priority of professional discourse and takes it a step further. According to Faderman, the invention of a category of lesbian persons determined not only new sexual identities but also enabled women who loved other women to engage in sexual acts that they would have previously abjured: "[T]here was no such thing as a 'lesbian' as the twentieth century recognizes the term; it was only the rare woman who behaved immorally, who was thought to live far outside the pale of decent womanhood" (Faderman 1991, 2). But others, like Emma Donoghue (1993) and Terry Castle, take issue with this version of events. "What the advocates of the 'no lesbians before 1900' theory forget," Castle writes, "is that there are myriad ways of discovering one's desire" (Castle 1993, 9), and she goes on to list plentiful examples from European literature published before 1900 with lesbian themes and characters, beginning with Juvenal's *Satires*.

In his extensive compilation of historical documents dealing with homosexuality in the United States, Jonathan Ned Katz (1976), too, presents abundant evidence of lesbian relationships well before the mid-nineteenth century, including several that refer to lesbianism (though they don't use that word) among white women colonizers and their descendants in the colonial period, as well as lesbian practices observed by missionaries in Native-American cultures during the seventeenth century. Taking this kind of material into account, George Chauncey Jr. cautions us to not place too much emphasis on professional discourses. However, what the nineteenth- and twentieth-century medical literature does indicate, he allows, are "the parameters of the acceptable" (Chauncey 1982–1983, 116). And, in a similar vein, Martha Vicinus (1993) has pointed out that modern lesbian identity has taken a number of different forms, of which the late-nineteenth-century sexologists' influential theory—that lesbianism is as an innate condition of gender inversion, a masculine soul inhabiting a female body—is only one. By the early twentieth century, she observes, several other modes of lesbian desire and identity were widely recognized and practiced, including but not limited to flamboyant hedonists, like the expatriate American heiress Natalie Barney; middle-class, college educated women who forged "romantic friendships," many living together as couples; and peasant or working-class "passing women."

Yet, none of these configurations satisfied Hall's requirements for a hero who would focus attention on the unjust exclusion of lesbians from respectable society—as Vicinus says, they were "either too secretive or too ostentatious" to suit Hall's agenda (Vicinus 1993, 445). Still, there is little doubt that Hall subscribed sincerely to the beliefs about the biological basis for lesbian desires and identity espoused in *The Well*. By aligning herself with the sexologists, Hall joined well-known advocates for removing the social (and in the case of men, legal) stigma of homosexuality, such as Magnus Hirschfeld in Germany, who employed a scientific perspective to argue for sexual reform. Moreover, a crucial dimension of the scientific authority invoked to prove the innate and thus natural basis for homosexuality was its reliance on the empiricist theory of truth prevalent at the time—that is, the belief that reliable knowledge about reality can be obtained only from observable phenomena—which led sexologists to concentrate on identifying lesbians by means of physical traits and behavioral patterns.

For instance, Ellis asserted that among the recognizable characteristics exhibited by lesbians are firm muscles and, in many cases, a "masculine type of larynx," as well as traits that might be understood as cultural but, he believed, derived from an organic basis, such as a fondness for cigars, dislike of needlework, and proficiency in athletics (Ellis [1901] 1936, 250–255). Another example is the research conducted in the 1930s by the Committee for the Study of Sex Variants in New York City, which employed a variety of visual technologies, including photographs and X-rays of the unclothed bodies of their lesbian subjects, as well as drawings of their breasts and genitals, to establish visible criteria that could be used to distinguish lesbians from so-called normal heterosexual women. These researchers also collected additional data they thought would allow them to ascertain and predict homosexual tendencies, such as measures of hormonal levels and psychological tests that were designed to be analyzed using statistical methods (Terry 1990).[4]

Hall paid homage to the professional experts on sexuality in the form of a female character who exhibited congenital physiological and psychological deviance from what was believed to be normal, also inborn, femininity. As Mandy Merck points out, the methods used to delineate the character of Stephen Gordon in *The Well* echo those outlined above: "Hall's lesbian heroine is born a 'narrow-hipped, wide-shouldered' baby . . . [and] throughout the novel she is subjected to the frequent, invariably productive, scrutiny of others as well as herself" (Merck 1993, 87). And in erecting her "palace of truth" on grounds delimited by surveyors of pathological sexualities, Hall may have conferred credibility on one of the most insidious lesbian stereotypes: the miserable pervert, recognizable by her outward demeanor.

At least this is the retrospective judgment frequently leveled at her novel by recent generations of lesbians, beginning with those who made common cause with other groups struggling not for social acceptance but for revolutionary social change in the late 1960s.[5] Hall's literary effort to generate visibility for lesbians, as well as supplying an affirmative argument for lesbian difference, it seems fair to say, received high marks for visibility but failed to effect significant reforms in public opinion. However, another paradigm of modern lesbianism was enacted by Hall herself: artistic, eccentric, *theatrical*.[6] In her study of Hall's friendship with gay composer and writer Noël Coward, Terry Castle remarks, "[W]e need to remember how central a role Hall the public figure played in creating the classic image of the 1920s lesbian. Other women might cut their hair or wear ties—the painter Gluck did, Sylvia Townsend Warner's lover Valentine Ackland did—but it was Hall who became notorious for it, whose picture appeared in popular weeklies, whose personal style became preeminently identified with 'lesbian' style" (Castle 1996, 59–60). Castle also conjectures that photographs and sketches of Hall reproduced in the press in the mid-1920s may have served as the prototype for the *New Yorker*'s Eustace Tilley, the caricature of a sophisticated gentleman in top hat and monocle who appeared on the magazine's cover in 1925 and remained its mascot thereafter (Castle 1993, 198).

Like other mannish lesbians of her day, Hall appropriated the dandy style adopted by urbane men in early nineteenth-century Britain and France. The originator of this fashion, George Bryan (Beau) Brummell, had defined its basic tenets of extreme understatement and perfect tailoring aimed at an impression of unaffected superiority—what Elizabeth Wilson calls "a performance of aristocracy" (Wilson 1985, 182)—bestowed not by heredity but by heroic individualism. The vestments of dandyism subsequently became the trademark of republicans and romantics, Byron and Baudelaire, but eventually evolved into the modern suit, the representative costume of the bourgeois, masculine conformity that Brummell intended to criticize (Hollander 1994, 100–102). Lesbians in the twentieth century, in the United States as well as Europe, harkened back to the original impulses of dandy style by using dress to make an oppositional statement, although one premised on a style associated less with social reform than individual self-possession. The politics of style, though, can be remarkably ambivalent. For some lesbians this fashion was mainly a repudiation of feminine garb that did not in any way renounce the wearer's social class (for example, Hall was an inveterate upper-class snob), but for others it symbolized a more vehement rebellion against bourgeois definitions of gender and sexuality.[7] In either case, the visual effect of self-possession achieved through impeccable grooming without obvious ostentation allowed a dramatic juxtaposition—including elements of confrontation—of ideal bourgeois masculine and feminine traits, of self-control and self-display.

I have devoted so much space to Radclyffe Hall not because of her importance to Anglophone lesbian culture—although that cannot be disputed—but because of her location at a particular historical moment when the parameters and mechanisms of fame had assumed many of the characteristics that apply today. Her fame, then, was double-edged: On one hand, the scandal produced by her publication of what amounted to a public declaration of lesbian existence precipitated a reaction from defenders of the moral status quo. For example, one of the leaders of the campaign against *The Well* wrote, "I would rather give a healthy boy or a healthy girl a phial of prussic acid than this novel. Poison kills the body but moral poison kills the soul" (James Douglas, *Sunday Express*, 19 August, 1928, quoted in Baker 1985, 223). On the other hand, that scandal, coupled with Hall's flair for dramatic self-presentation, was transformed into a publicity coup that ensured her enduring reputation. In this she participated, quite willingly, in the celebrity culture of the time. And why would she not?

FAMOUS PLAYERS

The lives of famous people recorded in the annals of history are most often read as indicators of the moral and political organization of a particular society, and those who achieve renown are regarded as emblems of prevailing cultural values and power relations. Radclyffe Hall's interest in becoming a member of such distinguished company is not too difficult to fathom. Still, it may seem extraordinary that an outspoken lesbian would be allowed entry into the halls of fame at a time when such women were deemed morally enfeebled. An understanding of not only this particular instance of lesbian celebrity, which was idiosyncratic, but also the proliferation of lesbian celebrity some sixty years later requires, at the very least, a sketch of the defining features of fame that had taken shape during the century preceding Hall's appearance on the scene, as well as several subsequent permutations that fostered the boom in celebrity culture so noteworthy today.

Although it is possible to make general statements about celebrity—noting, for instance, that those people who acquire fame embody the qualities and capacities recognized as significant within a particular social matrix—its forms or meanings are never transhistorical. Indeed, celebrities and celebrity itself have emerged as central preoccupations only in modern (or modernizing) societies. Moreover, a particular kind of person came to define celebrity in the early decades of the twentieth century: the entertainment celebrity. Writers and visual artists rarely qualified, although authors of best-selling fiction or popular stage plays might if they were able to produce more than one or two big hits. Painters, sculptors, and photographers rarely achieved fame outside the narrow confines of the art world when alive. There are a few exceptions, and one in particular became the epitome of contemporary celebrity itself: Andy Warhol.

In his historical study of fame in Western European and North American cultures, Leo Braudy (1986) traces this development to changes that began with the eighteenth-century revolutions in France and the United States. In keeping with the republican sentiments that fueled these political upheavals, candidacy for fame was democratized and no longer deemed the prerogative of the aristocracy or those patronized by this class. At first, the most significant change occurred when postrevolutionary political leaders like Washington and Napoleon, who were identified with their nations and not a particular social class, replaced the older types of celebrities (royalty, most frequently). Over the course of the next century, however, a number of interrelated cultural, economic, and technological developments contributed to a complete overhaul of the criteria for fame in the twentieth: the explosion of commodity production enabled by industrial forms of manufacturing and organized by capitalist markets, which increased the amount of goods available to large numbers of people and put money in the pockets of those who wanted to buy them; the spread of literacy combined with the introduction of photography and innovations in printing technologies; the invention of related new media forms like cheap newspapers and illustrated magazines that catered to and capitalized on both the expanding reading public and advertisers for products who hoped to attract their attention; the proliferation of popular, large-scale entertainments like circuses, vaudeville, and amusement parks, and, shortly before the beginning of the new century, cinema.

In very short order, or so it seems in hindsight, movie stars became the paradigmatic celebrities in the United States and Europe. And the various elements that created and sustained stardom according to this model have remained fairly constant ever since. Richard Dyer has described the elements of any particular star's image as

> not just his or her films, but the promotion of those films and of the star
> through pin-ups, public appearances, studio hand-outs and so on, as well
> as interviews, biographies, coverage in the press of the star's doings and

"private" life. Further, a star's image is also what people say or write about him or her, as critics or commentators, the way the image is used in other contexts such as advertisements, novels, pop songs, and finally the way the star can become part of the coinage of everyday speech. (Dyer 1986, 2–3)

Since the promotion of movie stars along these lines began in 1909, some four-teen years after the advent of cinema, historical investigations of its genesis have usually begun with the question about why it took so long for movie pro-ducers to figure out how to capitalize on fans' interest in the actors they saw regularly on their local screens. However, as Janet Staiger (1991) notes, this question may represent yet another instance of the mystification of the process by which movie stars (and other celebrities) are created. In her challenge to this historical interpretation, as well as to the oft-cited explanation that studio exec-utives were reluctant to publicize the names of regular players in order to con-trol salary demands (the argument is that actors would use popularity with the public as the basis for asking for increased pay), Staiger maintains that the prototype for the film industry's star system consisted of methods used by U.S. theatrical producers and managers for almost a century.

Initially devised to publicize prominent foreign performers on tour in the 1820s, the promotion of individual actors cast in leading roles was soon adopted as standard practice. Photographs of featured actors in costume were displayed outside theaters and included in materials circulated by press agents engaged to generate free publicity for performances. Information about the offstage lives of these actors had not yet become a common feature of these promotional packages, but that did not prevent reporters from trying to elicit such data in interviews. Although by 1910 similar methods were integrated into film studios' publicity techniques—lobby display cards and publication of photographs and biographies of contract players in film magazines—Staiger points out that as late as 1912 the named artists promoted by these companies were frequently famous stage actors testing the cinematic waters—Sarah Bernhardt, Réjane, Minnie Madden Fiske—not those whose acting careers began in films. In other words, in the early years of movie mak-ing true stars were those who became famous in already established forms of entertainment (Staiger 1991, 14).[8]

The basic formula for entertainment celebrity in the twentieth-century United States grew out of business decisions made by commercial theater producers in the 1820s, who found it advantageous to identify and promote a few individual leading men and women. Before then, actors were members of stock companies, in which roles were rotated and someone playing a major part in one play might be given a minor role in the next. The stock company was also the organizing principle of the original motion picture companies, but quickly abandoned once the audience appeal of *movie* stars became apparent. But the increasing centrality of celebrity in both theater and film (as well as similar practices in music and dance) was also linked to radical innovations in other media. These changes proceeded along four separate tracks—technological (in the conventional sense), economic, institutional, and ideological—although, as always, these are aspects of the same phenomenon as far as celebrity culture is concerned.

MAGICAL REALISM

Among all the various factors affecting the reconfiguration of fame in the nineteenth century, perhaps the most significant was the public announcement of the invention of photography in 1839. Throughout the twentieth century, the impact of photographic technology on celebrity became undeniable. Not only do photographic media like cinema and television provide a platform for performers in popular entertainment fields, by means of reproducing a performance as an artifact, photography and its spinoffs also allow fans to nullify their awareness of the artifice of stardom. The second effect may be attributed to photography's assumed purchase on reality. "Stars," Dyer notes, "are a particular instance of the supposed relation between a photograph and its referent. A photograph is always a photograph *of* something or somebody who had to have been there in order for the photograph to be taken" (Dyer 1991, 135). Thus, photography provides a key to a particular kind of knowledge celebrities generate: an indication of a real person behind the mask or beneath the surface of a scripted, rehearsed performance. Although this kind of knowledge cannot be conveyed by photographs alone, pictures of the star in question connect other kinds of information about her or him to a corporeal reality, and are therefore indispensable.

At first, photography captured the public's imagination as an ingenious product of science, praised for its marvelous ability to fix an image of a transitory moment. Indeed, Don Slater (1995) has analyzed this as a central paradox of photography: its production of realism as a magic show. Almost as soon as the viability of photography was announced the apparatus was put to use as a method for producing portraits, and the first generation of commercial photographers devoted themselves almost exclusively to portraiture, out-

fitting their studios with ornate furniture and draperies that emulated bourgeois drawing rooms. But even this application, which today seems entirely
pedestrian, was regarded as suspiciously supernatural, even diabolical, insofar
as the materialization of one's likeness in a photograph implied a transfer of
a bit of the soul to the image. For example, the preeminent Parisian portrait
photographer Gaspar Félix Tournachon, better known by his professional
name Nadar, cited none other than Balzac as a subscriber to such notions,
although he also pointed out that this did not prevent the renowned novelist
from posing. "[A]ccording to Balzac," Nadar reported, "every body in its natural state was made up of a series of ghostly images superimposed in layers
to infinity, wrapped in infinitesimal films. . . . Men never having been able to
create, that's to say make something material from an apparition, from something impalpable, or to make from nothing, an object—each Daguerrean
operation was therefore going to lay hold of, detach and use up one of the layers of the body on which it is focused" (Nadar, quoted in Scharf 1975, 107).

Many early photographers understood and capitalized on the illusionist
properties of photography. One of the very first and best known, Louis
Jacques Mandé Daguerre, began his career as a scene painter for the Paris
Opera and graduated to designing and operating panoramas, as well as producing other public, precinematic illusionist spectacles like dioramas. And
Nadar, more than many of his competitors, grasped the importance of the
photographer's ability to manipulate illusion, although he also believed in the
medium's ability to achieve realism. For Nadar, photographic realism was not
automatic, a matter of leaving verisimilitude up to optics and chemistry, but
involved careful manipulation of light, costume, and facial expression. In
order to produce a worthy portrait, he maintained that the photographer
must discern the subject's unique character at the first encounter, "which can
put you in sympathy with your sitter, helps you to sum them up, follow their
normal attitudes, their ideas, according to their personality, that enables you
to make . . . a likeness of the most intimate and happy kind, a speaking likeness" (Nadar, quoted in Scharf 1975, 106).

Before taking up photography, Nadar was a widely published and well-
regarded caricaturist within republican political circles. His previously established reputation among the French artistic and intellectual elite of his day
enabled him to attract many of them to his studio. Between 1855 and the
mid-1860s, he photographed Hugo, Baudelaire, Dumas père, Nerval,
Berlioz, Rossini, Delacroix, Doré, Daumier, Manet, Michelet, and Pasteur,
among others. George Sand was the subject of a series of portraits, including

one in which she appears as a caricature of Louis XIV in a wig and velvet cloak. Bernhardt, then a relatively unknown actress, posed for Nadar in the early 1860s. Nadar printed multiple copies of these celebrity images, each eight-and-a-quarter by eleven inches in size, and sold them to the public for around fifty francs apiece, thus restricting sales to the monied classes. The artisanal methods of production employed in Nadar's studio during this period allowed him to develop a singular style, often described in terms of his skillful orchestration of light and shadow. His pictures also remain exceptional because of the distinctive clothing he encouraged his sitters to wear, as well as what one critic describes as his ability to dramatize "the striking gesture, the bearing, the visible essence of character" (Keller 1995, 79).

Nadar's photography business almost ran aground due to rivalry from another kind of celebrity portrait printed in a format known as the *carte de visite*, two-and-a-half by four inches, and priced at a small fraction of what one of Nadar's larger *édition* portraits cost. In 1854, André Adolphe Eugène Disdéri patented a technique for producing miniature photographs (with a few exceptions, these were portraits) printed on albumen paper and mounted on cardboard backing the size of a conventional calling card, with the subject's name and sometimes her or his signature printed below the image—a forerunner of not just the star photograph but also the photo ID.[9] Because the process involved subdividing one glass photographic plate into ten rectangles that could be printed simultaneously, large quantities of *cartes de visite* could be produced very quickly and with greater economy than any previous process allowed.

A few years later, after Disdéri had begun to mass produce and sell miniature portraits of such celebrities as the French imperial family, the market for *cartes* boomed and, along with related formats like cabinet cards (four-and-a-half by six inches), dominated the commercial photographic trade for the rest of the century (Keller 1995, 80). Nadar's business was threatened by these developments, and he attempted to compete by adopting the format, as well as the rationalized production techniques and newer, less expensive materials used by his rival. He copied photos from his store of celebrity portraits, as well as producing a new batch during the 1860s designed specifically for sales to collectors of *cartes de visite*. As a result, his careful attention to aesthetic refinement was sacrificed to the demands of mass production, while the reduced format made such subtlety irrelevant.[10] In addition to making celebrity portraits easily available to a range of customers, the introduction of *cartes de visite* occasioned a second innovation—the family or personal photograph album, displayed on a parlor table for perusal by guests, which frequently included celebrity photos alongside studio portraits of relatives. In her study of Disdéri's career, Elizabeth Anne McCauley argues that the introduction of celebrity portraits into private homes significantly altered concepts of fame and the famous, "making them more familiar, less heroic" (McCauley 1985, 2).

The peak years of Disdéri's *carte de visite* business were the early 1860s, when he produced a series of portraits of the royal family and other prominent personages, each accompanied by a four-page biography. Two portraits were issued each week, for which his middle-class subscribers paid one franc each, and at least 127 people were represented in Desdéri's *Galerie des contemporains*. Among these notables, McCauley reports, thirty-seven percent were actors and other entertainers, while ten percent were military leaders, and twenty-eight percent were politicians and nobles (55–62). Disdéri also added to his repetoire the collage *carte*, which consisted of multiple portraits (or in one case, merely legs—of ballerinas) printed as composite representations of such professional groups as opera stars or heads of state.

Compared to painted portraits, which were beyond the means of all but the rich and powerful, *cartes* allowed middle-class people representation on the same level as celebrities. Moreover, McCauley points out, the full-length framing favored in *carte de visite* portraiture encouraged popular theories about the meanings that could be gleaned from these pictures: "[V]iewers could interpret character through the details of the figure's pose, with caricaturists and writers in the photographic press outlining the way that the bend of a leg or the drop of a wrist could reveal a profession, personality, class, or temperament" (3). She also draws attention to the influence of fashion plates of the period on *carte de visite* style, noting that both types of imagery were premised on the *flâneur* culture of mid-nineteenth-century Paris, "in which clothes were the man, and character was evaluated on the basis of external appearances" (36).

The *carte de visite* craze quickly spread from Paris to London, then to the United States, where the country's most respected portrait photographer, daguerreotypist Mathew Brady, also found his business endangered by the newer, cheaper method of reproducing images. Like other commercial photographers of his day, and more successfully than most, Brady prominently displayed daguerreotypes of famous citizens, mostly politicians and members of the business and social elite, in his Broadway studio or branches he set up in other cities as advertisements to attract a well-heeled clientele. Not only did Brady's business depend upon income from patrons of his establishment but on

Mathew Brady's photographic gallery on Broadway in New York City, engraving from *Frank Leslie's Illustrated Newspaper*, January 5, 1861. Library of Congress.

sales of copies of his celebrity portraits, for which he charged from between five and twenty-five dollars, compared to one dollar paid by an ordinary sitter for her or his own likeness. By 1860, the photographic market was flooded by inexpensive (as little as twenty-five for a dollar) images of politicians and men of rank, but also famous authors and theater stars (Welling 1978, 143). *Cartes de visite* picturing an obscure lawyer from Illinois were widely circulated during the 1860 presidential campaign, and Abraham Lincoln's election is often credited to the unprecedented publicity he received as a result (Taft 1938, 194–195). As Oliver Wendell Holmes wrote in 1863, *cartes de visite* had become "the social currency, the sentimental 'green-backs' of civilization" (Holmes [1863] 1980, 69). Brady was reluctant to abandon the daguerreotype process and even more disinclined to court lower-class collectors of *cartes de visite*, although he did produce portraits in this format once it became evident that demand for his more expensive photographs had evaporated.[11]

In an article on nineteenth-century celebrity portrait photography in the U.S., Barbara McCandless (1991) presents Brady's career trajectory as the counterpoint to that of a second major figure in this field, the Canadian-born

Sarony's *carte de visite* portrait of
Oscar Wilde, taken during
Wilde's first tour of the U.S. in
1882. Library of Congress.

photographer Napoleon Sarony. In 1866, Sarony set up a portrait studio in
New York City specializing in theatrical portraiture, having learned his craft
in England, where he became familiar with the work of Nadar and the other
prominent French celebrity photographer, Étienne Carjat. Within a few
years, he became the major photographer for the theatrical community in
New York, producing only *cartes de visite* and the slightly larger but similarly
cheap, collectible cabinet cards, which were not sold directly to customers but
through dealers who supplied shops and street vendors. In 1882, there were
six dealers in New York City marketing *cartes de visite* and cabinet cards, and
street merchants alone accounted for one million dollars in sales of these
cards to the public (McCandless 1991, 68).

As one of the most prolific producers of celebrity portraits and a canny
entrepreneur, Sarony prospered. He was known for his ability to coax dramatic
poses and expressions from his subjects, which may have been one of the rea-

sons he was the photographer of choice of the most famous performers. Another reason, however, was that he paid the highest fees, knowing that he could recoup these costs and still make a considerable profit. Prior to 1867, famous people whose portraits were sold by photographers sometimes received free daguerreotypes or paper prints in exchange, but others sat for the commercial photographers' cameras without receiving any compensation because they recognized the value of the publicity such pictures could generate.[12] This changed after Charles Dickens, on tour in the U.S. in 1867, demanded and was paid a fee to have his photograph taken. Word of this arrangement quickly spread, and payment or royalties became the standard practice. For instance, Bernhardt received fifteen hundred dollars from Sarony in 1880, and he paid five thousand dollars to British actress Lillie Langtry in 1882. Around the same time, however, Oscar Wilde posed for free almost as soon as he arrived for his first lecture tour of the United States, because his agent convinced Wilde of the publicity benefits that would accrue from having a Sarony *carte de visite* in circulation (Lewis and Smith 1936, 39).

The antecedents of iconic celebrity photographs, such as those produced by Arnold Genthe, Baron de Meyer, Cecil Beaton, and Edward Steichen in the mid-twentieth century, can be found in Nadar's large format oeuvre. Less memorable photos produced as *cartes de visite* and cabinet cards are precursors of the stock photographs that provide the ongoing outpouring of celebrity images that became a ubiquitous feature of twentieth-century life, although several of Sarony's images—his first portraits of Wilde, for example—can also be counted among the classics.

PUBLIC ADDRESS

Despite the guarantee of reality photographs offer, celebrity portraits only acquire meaning when presented in the context of information about the person pictured. In the case of actors, this additional narrative becomes an extension of their fictional roles, not in the sense of exact correspondence but in terms of what are understood as basic personality traits (sexiness for anyone playing a prostitute or showgirl; no-nonsense toughness for a maverick police detective or Mafia don, for example). Alternately, publicity photos may be conceived to domesticate a star's image, exemplified by pictures of Marlene Dietrich accompanied by her daughter and husband, circulated by Paramount shortly after Joseph von Sternberg's ex-wife sued Dietrich for destroying her marriage.[13]

Marlene Deitrich, husband Rudolf Sieber, and daughter Maria posing for a publicity photo set up by Paramount Studios, on the occasion of Rudi's arrival in the U.S. in 1931, an appearance intended to counteract the scandal resulting from Dietrich's affair with director Josef von Sternberg and von Sternberg's wife's lawsuit against Dietrich. Corbis.

Needless to say, getting the two celebrity personae—the "fictional" and the "real"—in sync has not always been an easy task. However, the Hollywood studios' domination of the entertainment business until the late 1950s made the job somewhat more manageable, since, as Richard deCordova observes, "The narrative which emerged to create the star was entrenched in the same forms of representation as the films in which the stars acted" (deCordova 1991, 28). But systems used to achieve conformity were never airtight, as was proved by revelations of scandalous behavior and several suspicious murders in the Hollywood film colony in the early 1920s (Anger 1975, 1984). Thereafter, deCordova contends, the meanings to be gleaned from information about film stars, the truths they seemed to embody, tended to be primarily sexual knowledge accumulated in a sequential order that replicates the historical stages of the development of the film star system: (1) knowledge about the reality of the star's body, (2) facts about the star's marriage, or, if unmarried, her or his prospects, and (3) the secret of the star's sexual transgressions (deCordova 1990, 142).

Photographs, which fulfill the first aspect of this accretion of knowledge, provide the basic building blocks; official biographical data, regularly updated, supply the mortar; and gossip, innuendo, and fans' own imaginations furnish and embellish the edifice. Obviously, fictionalization can occur at any of the three levels, and it is the resulting precariousness of celebrity knowledge that makes it so productive and intriguing. Once it became feasible to combine the photos and text in a single widely available medium, entertainment celebrity was poised for takeoff.[14] This occurred when, after several decades of experimentation, half-tone reproductions that could be printed using the same presses and page setups as type became economically feasible in the 1890s.[15]

By the turn of the century, people who could not afford to buy photographic prints were able to compile their own celebrity scrapbooks, filled with photos snipped from daily newspapers that cost as little as a penny or popular magazines that sold for only ten cents per issue, and—a bit later—from more specialized movie magazines. Readers were also able to obtain information from printed narratives in the same magazines, which offered a more complete representation and extended the meaning of a particular star's image beyond her or his pleasing face, elegant clothing, or other purely visual characteristics. And these narratives then called for more images—of magnificent houses, posh gardens and swimming pools, sporting events and fancy dress parties, cars and dogs, and so on. The phenomenon, however, should not be attributed to a technological feat alone, nor did it appear without precedents. In many respects, magazines and newspapers that provided coverage of movie stars and other entertainment celebrities in the twentieth century represented an outgrowth of the cheap, popular publications that catered to an expanding reading public made up largely of working people, including a growing number of wage-earning women, that first appeared in the U.S. in the 1830s.

Until penny papers were introduced in New York City in 1833, newspapers cost six cents, were available by subscription only, and addressed upper- and middle-class "establishment" male readers.[16] Two of the four pages of the standard daily, the front and the back, were devoted to advertisements. News in this context was limited to mercantile and political reports, and editorials on political matters were featured prominently. Experiments with lowering newspaper prices were undertaken in Boston and Philadelphia as early as 1830, but the first to revolutionize newspaper contents and methods of distribution was the New York *Sun*, founded by Benjamin Day, followed soon after by the *Evening Transcript* and James Gordon Bennett's *Herald*, also published in New York City. By 1836, other major Eastern metropolises boasted penny papers, and the phenomenon spread westward over the course of the next few decades. All penny papers were conceived as vehicles for daily news items geared toward working-class, mainly immigrant readers and concentrated on "human interest" stories, like crime reports, presented in lively, colloquial language.[17] Furthermore, they were sold by newsboys on the street, which meant that they were widely available and the price of a single issue was easily affordable for wage laborers. These journalistic upstarts proved enormously popular: from 1830 to 1840 newspaper circulation in the U.S. increased almost fourfold, from approximately 78,000 to 300,000, largely attributable to the introduction of penny newspapers. In comparison, the urban population increased from .9 million to 1.5 million during the same decade, a sixty percent increase. The average circulation of a metropolitan daily in the 1820s was between one and two thousand subscribers; the *Sun* sold around 15,000 copies a day in 1835.

Another important cornerstone of mass circulation media was put in place when Joseph Pulitzer bought the failing New York *World* in 1883. He lowered the price to one cent (by this time, the *Herald* cost three cents and the *Sun* was two) and refashioned the paper into a provocative daily, akin to current and former penny papers, that combined muckraking political reporting with attention to other sorts of scandal. The *World*'s circulation rose rapidly as a result, from 15,000 when Pulitzer bought the paper to over 125,000 three years later (Schudson 1978, 92). But the innovation that gave the *World* an edge over its competitors, according to Michael Schudson, was its liberal use of illustrations and Pulitzer's willingness to publish large-format advertisements, some of which used pictures—something other newspapers, from the plebeian *Sun* to the upper-crust *New York Times*, eschewed. Pulitzer's personal dislike for illustrations in newspapers at first motivated him to reduce the number in the *World*, but he soon reversed his position when he discovered "the circulation of the paper went with the cuts" (Schudson 1978, 95; see also Lee 1937, 129–130). An additional achievement in engraving techniques—half-tone reproductions of photographs used on a regular basis in newspapers beginning with the New York *Tribune* in 1897—gave advertisers one of their most effective methods for attracting readers' attention. And in due time, 1915 to be precise, ads using entertainment celebrities to endorse products began to appear (deCordova 1990, 110).

The penny papers and their descendants then begot the tabloids, a term that at first referred solely to a newspaper format, half the size of the conventional broadsheet. Although the earliest penny papers were also printed on smaller pages as a purely economic measure, Frank Munsey is credited with establishing the first, but short-lived, sensationalist U.S. tabloid, the *Daily Continent*, in 1891. (An earlier predecessor was the New York *Daily Graphic*; published between 1873 and 1889, although this did not fit the profile of punchy prose and sex-and-crime reportage that distinguishes the genre.) Munsey's paper soon succumbed to competition from the *World* and William Randolph Hearst's *Journal* (bought by Hearst in 1895 and the *World*'s primary competition for years). Only in 1919 did the tabloid press in the generic sense take root in the United States, modeled on the London *Daily Mirror* founded by Lord Northcliffe (Alfred Harmsworth). The first sustained venture in this field was the New York (*Illustrated*) *Daily News*, published by the company that owned the Chicago *Tribune*; in five years it became the largest-selling daily in the city.[18] When Hearst brought out a revamped New York *Daily Mirror* as a tabloid in 1924, he promised readers "90 percent entertainment, 10 percent information—and the information without boring you" (Bird 1992, 19). Not surprisingly, news about and profiles of celebrities, along with plentiful pictures, were important elements of the enticements Hearst and other tabloid publishers proffered. Another tabloid that first appeared in 1924 was Bernarr MacFadden's *New York Evening Graphic*. With absolutely no pretense about providing news for informational (as opposed to entertainment) purposes, the *Evening Graphic* created the template for the papers we today often call supermarket tabloids.[19]

PRYING EYES

Perhaps the most pertinent feature of this genealogy is not the material form of the medium but the style of gossip reporting that these early tabloids devised. Most significantly, Walter Winchell's "Your Broadway and Mine" column first appeared in the *Evening Graphic*, introducing readers to what became the standard for modern celebrity gossip. One of Winchell's colleagues remembered the impact of his new style of gossip reporting: "The effect of his Monday column [in the *Evening Graphic*] woke up Broadway to startled self-consciousness. People could hardly believe what they saw in print.

All the old secrets of personal sex relations—who was sleeping with whom—were exposed to the public gaze" (Sobel 1953, 301). In his account of Winchell's career, Neal Gabler observes that before Winchell began publishing his items, collected during nightly rounds of Times Square speakeasies, editors and writers subscribed to the maxim that "certain things weren't done by decent people, including decent journalists. Certain proprieties had to be maintained" (Gabler 1994, 137). But Winchell didn't respect these principles. His racy columns proved enormously popular and greatly enhanced the circulation of the *Evening Graphic* and then the New York *Daily Mirror*, the Hearst tabloid that served as his home base from 1929 to 1962.

The *Mirror* also provided Winchell with an outlet for national syndication. In 1930, Winchell began to air his gossip on network radio, and his audience expanded exponentially as a result.[20] In a mere six years, his influence spread from a local community, albeit a large urban center, to the entire nation, able to tune into his witty, sometimes caustic commentary. According to Gabler,

> It all seemed mildly illicit—this world that Winchell hurled each Sunday night [in his early radio broadcasts] into the teeth of Depression America. It was a glamorous world governed by none of the ordinary rules of behavior or responsibility. It was a world where romance was a euphemism for sex and where each listener was a voyeur, vicariously enjoying the suggestion of perpetual sexual availability of these stars, celebrities and socialites who changed lovers, husbands and wives like clothes. And it was Walter's presentation that made it seem so. By piling one item on another and by wrenching them all from any context, he created a new context: a dizzying and disorienting bacchanalia, almost prurient in its appeal. (Gabler 1994, 162)

By all accounts, Winchell established the gossip columnist as the arbiter of fame. Boasting about his own influence, he remarked, "Social position is now more a matter of press than prestige." To which Gabler adds, "A mention in his column or in his broadcast meant that one was among the exalted. It meant that one's name was part of the general fund of knowledge" (185). The gossip columns written by Winchell and his rivals at the other major dailies covered all sorts of show business and artistic celebrities, along with members of the upper class—social register members as well as the *nouveaux riches*, and European aristocrats who kept company with fashionable folk from the United States—as well as recent additions to celebrity ranks like award-winning athletes and record-setting aviators. He also wrote about sensational crimes and those accused of committing them. The kinds of topics he introduced as acceptable, even essential, items of public information concerning prominent people—couched in euphemistic language, of course— were tolerated, if not encouraged, by editors.

Gossip writing was also given a boost by the expansion of journalism into coverage of the motion picture industry, first in trade magazines like *Moving Picture World* (1907) and within a few years in those geared to fans like *Motion Picture News* (1910), *Motion Picture Story* (1910), and *Photoplay* (1911). We tend to think of these magazines as the prototypes for more recent forums for celebrity gossip like *People*, and by the end of World War I they had settled on the parameters that still govern this branch of publishing. However, issues from the formative years of the fan magazines, until 1917 or thereabouts, exhibit a less coherent idea of what the format should be and what information people would pay money to read. For example, in its first few years *Photoplay* included numerous articles on the technical aspects of filmmaking—for instance, explanations of how elevated platforms are used to position a camera above the action—whereas the private lives of actors received very little attention. What little gossip they carried tended to be concerned with upcoming productions and casting decisions. In keeping with the widely held belief that gossip is a feminine preoccupation, its relative absence in prewar issues indicated that publishers imagined that the ideal reader was male, a supposition born out by the kinds of products they advertised: correspondence courses in law (almost exclusively a male profession), barbershops and Turkish baths, subscriptions to *Popular Electricity* magazine. There were ads pitched to women as well—millinery courses, custom-made skirts, bust enlargement therapy, for example—but these figured less prominently. The magazines' ads also solicited "photoplays" and offered courses in professional screenwriting, an occupation open to women as well as men. The most profitable group of consumers anticipated by these magazines in their first years, however, were film exhibitors, wooed by promotions for lobby display stands, film titling services, theater decorations, and popcorn-making machines.

Around 1914, the balance between ads directed at men and those clearly intended for women shifted decidedly toward the latter, and by late 1917 the classification of these magazines as feminine reading material had solidified. By then, the overwhelming number of products advertised were for distinctly feminine commodities—sanitary napkins, laundry and face soap, hairpins, perfume, diet pills, and fat-reduction creams. Additionally, by the early 1920s

THE FINEST INTIMATE PICTURES OF YOUR HOLLYWOOD FAVORITES

MODERN SCREEN

10¢

MARCH

HOLLYWOOD HEARTBREAK by VICKI BAUM

Janet Gaynor on the cover of the
March 1932 *Modern Screen*.

the faces these magazines presented to the public on their covers and
employed to appeal to readers' curiosity were uniformly female.[21] Yet this gender segregation did not necessarily reflect their readership, insofar as published
letters from readers included many from men, who, like women, inquired
about their favorite stars. Still, a feminine slant prevailed, and men who participated in the activities of fandom had to do so within this framework.

Over time, the gossip pages in *Photoplay* and *Modern Screen* moved from
the back to the middle, and eventually to the front, middle, *and* back of each
issue, organized as separate columns presented under different headlines. The
space assigned to gossip expanded as well, from two pages in 1915 issues of
Photoplay, to three in 1916, five in 1917, and up to nine by 1930. In keeping
with the redirection of the agenda, away from the mechanisms of film production towards news about "personalities," the constitution of gossip, too,
changed markedly during this period. Gossip in the early years often concentrated on finances, lawsuits, and other business matters; stars' off-screen
lives were discussed in relation to careers and salaries, and romances or families were rarely mentioned. A photo spread entitled "Who's Married to
Who" in a 1917 edition of *Photoplay* represented the magazine's timid entry
into the territory of intimate relations in Hollywood.

By the mid-1920s, these monthlies offered a steady diet of detailed information about who's not only married to whom but also who's dating and maybe sleeping with whom.[22] The fan magazines provided a visual catalog of couplings in numerous photos of those attending parties, resorts, and sporting events (often polo matches), as well as news of marriages, divorces, and childbirths. Other features offered makeup and hair-styling tips, information about the fashions favored by particular performers, and their favorite recipes. In the thirties, articles on how celebrities dealt with personal difficulties were added to the mix. An especially intriguing subgenre of this consisted of cautionary tales about starstruck young women so obsessed with fantasies of becoming movie actresses themselves that they left home and ended up lonely and miserable or, worse, victims of predatory men.[23] What is most interesting about these pieces is that they acknowledged and reinforced popular conceptions about the carnality rampant in Hollywood.

HEROIC MEASURES

From this review of the rapid expansion of popular print media and proliferation of celebrity images in the nineteenth century, which then converged in the early twentieth century to create an array of magazines and newspapers illustrated with photographs, it is not difficult to recognize the outlines of today's prodigious celebrity culture. No doubt, the effect of electronic media—radio and television, and now the Internet—on the exponential growth of celebrity culture from the 1930s to the present is indisputable, but the synthetic quality of entertainment celebrities has been a consistent feature of their constitution and their cultural significance since early in the century. What remains more obscure, however, is how changing concepts and practices of gender and sexuality affected and were affected by the increased attention to entertainment celebrities. Indeed, many of the commentators who see contemporary forms of celebrity as symptoms of social malaise have paid little attention to these factors and taken heterosexuality for granted as intrinsic to celebrity.

Social critic Daniel Boorstin (1961), for example, who is responsible for the oft-quoted definition of a twentieth-century celebrity as "a person who is known for his [sic] well-knownness," has argued that the growth of entertainment celebrity in the U.S. exemplifies the cultural decadence, artifice, and posturing that has eclipsed traditional notions of heroes and heroism. Boorstin adopts a highly moralistic tone and uses metaphors that speak of deceit—his synonym for celebrity is a "human pseudo-event"—to explain the

modern fascination with celebrity, which he links to the narcissistic personality typical of industrialized Western societies. But there is no recognition of
the masculine attributes of the kind of fame he finds most laudable, apparently oblivious to the implication that he finds the newer kind of celebrity
reprehensible *because* it is feminine.

A similar argument appears in the work of Richard Schickel (1973, 1985),
a prominent film critic and author of two books on twentieth-century celebrity,
who bemoans the false sense of intimacy fostered by attention to celebrities in
the media. Celebrity culture, according to Schickel, undermines traditional
modes of respect and "may substitute for a sense of organization, purpose, and
stability in our society" (Schickel 1985, 22). Like Boorstin, he sees the stakes as
nothing less than the collapse of political, psychological, and moral order:

> [Celebrities] are turned into representations for much more inchoate
> longings; they are used to simplify complex matters of the mind and spirit;
> they are used to subvert rationalism in politics, in every realm of public
> life; and, most important, they are both deliberately and accidentally
> employed to enhance in the individual audience member a confusion of
> the realms (between public life and private life, between those matters of
> the mind that are best approached objectively and those that are best
> approached subjectively), matters that are already confused enough by the
> inherent tendencies of modern communications technology. (viii–ix)

The tendentiousness of Boorstin's and Schickel's analyses may raise hackles,
but in many respects they only magnify a theme found in one of the first scientific studies of celebrity phenomena, social psychologist Leo Lowenthal's
1944 (1968) analysis of the increase in biographical profiles in popular magazines (the *Saturday Evening Post* and *Collier's*) during the first four decades
of the twentieth century. In addition to finding a general trend toward individual success stories, Lowenthal detected a shift from features on men of
industry and state to entertainers and athletes—in other words, decreased
interest in production and increased concern with consumption.

Although Boorstin's writings and those by other cultural conservatives
evince a nostalgia for past cultural values—what Mike Featherstone (1992)
has identified as a Weberian narrative of disenchantment common to paeans
to the heroic ethic—Lowenthal and other leftist media scholars interpret
entertainment celebrities as figments of ideology, understood in the Marxist
sense of "false consciousness." It's not surprising to find this attitude in

Lowenthal's work, since he was a member of the Frankfurt School and shared the views of his colleagues Theodor Adorno, Max Horkheimer, and Herbert Marcuse regarding the consciousness-numbing effects of popular culture. From the perspective of many Marxist scholars, it is not the homogenous mediocrity and sheepishness of "the masses" that is deplored, as it is in Boorstin's treatise, but capitalist commodification and greed. Thus, reports about the accoutrements of entertainment celebrities' sumptuous lives can be interpreted as invocations of the bourgeois imagination and the capitalist property relations this world view expresses—"Bovaryism" is the felicitous term employed by Edgar Morin (1960). Morin and others have also elaborated the various ways in which celebrities function in tandem with capitalist forms of media production: stars can be seen as capital itself, employed to produce profits for themselves and for their employers; they can be understood as commodities, manufactured by publicity apparatuses; or they can operate as fetishes used to promote purchases of other commodities via product tie-ins with movies or other entertainment vehicles, as well as endorsements for unrelated merchandise.[24]

No matter what political orientation is involved, though, all these discussions of celebrity depend upon a causal logic, whereby negative values—for example, crass desires, gullibility, unrealistic fantasies—are instilled in audiences by the star system. Paradoxically, another group of social researchers have found the same skeptical sentiments among star-gazing fans, the very "masses" assumed to be deceived by mass culture who, in fact, reveal themselves to be quite astute critics of the apparatus of celebrity production and suspicious of its motives (Barthes 1993; Gamson 1994; Stacey 1994). For some, however, familiarity with the mechanics of celebrity culture is but proof of its insidious nature. Consider the position taken by Todd Gitlin, a veteran of the New Left and prominent media sociologist: "What is peculiar . . . is American culture's relentless hunger for celebrities, along with a fascination with the process by which celebrity is manufactured. The culture of mythmaking is a culture in which the genuinely heroic has been downgraded. When everything is 'theatricalized' . . . then what is noble? what is valuable? what matters?" (Gitlin 1993, 352).

Surveys of theories of celebrity tend to divide the field into those that emphasize the production of celebrity and those that concentrate on consumption, but the two approaches are united in a common concern with the detrimental effects of spectacle, theatricality, superficiality, and illusion, as Gitlin's brief statement so eloquently shows. According to this logic, a fascination with celebrity is spawned by the circulation of celebrity images and texts, which become commodities susceptible to the sort of fetishism Marx described in *Capital*: "nothing but the definite social relations among men [*sic*] themselves which assumes here, for them, the fantastic form of a relation between things" (Marx 1977, 165). Individual stars can be likened to brand names of products manufactured according to industrial specifications and consumed as items of monetary exchange, while the actual labor necessary for their production remains concealed.

All these established theories of celebrity's significance in a media-saturated world neglect, however, the longstanding affiliation between entertainment and consumer culture. This history indicates that entertainment's link with markets and consumer activity is not necessarily determined by economic forces alone and is more extensive and more complicated than disparaging critics of celebrity recognize. From its formative period onward, public spectacle—exotic and sumptuous wares, colorful entertainers, and the crowd itself—was a key component of modern consumer culture. Even in pre-modern Europe, at late medieval merchant fairs theatrical entertainments played next to vendors' stalls and shops. The birthplace of modern banking and financial speculation, as well as a center for buying and selling goods, these markets also served as a gathering place for people from all social strata: the concept of "society," became tangible in such places where people intermingled at "the center of networks of display, communications, spectacle" (Slater 1993, 195). In short, consumer activity is intricately bound up with sensual and emotional pleasure as much as with participation in abstract economic exchange.

Still, class identities and relations are central to such activities, especially in a world where economic exchange is the privileged medium of social interaction and consumer activity the most effective enactment of social status. In fact, class identity and consumer culture are inseparable, for, as Don Slater (1997) notes, the reason consumer culture became so ingrained as a taken-for-granted defining feature of social life was that it provided the answers to questions raised by the breakdown of the rigid feudal system. Once power could be exercised in the realm of commercial relations, which was one of the crucial achievements of the eighteenth-century bourgeois revolutions, goods and acts of consumption that signaled identity and status became highly negotiable, but within limits that maintained the modern moral order predicated on the model of the ideal citizen—industrious, white, male, heterosexual, married. Thus, by the mid-nineteenth century, when the middle class had secured its hegemony, consumer culture largely catered to bourgeois interests, and the most awe-inspiring spectacles of the time—shopping arcades and departments stores, museums, international exhibitions (e.g., London in 1851, Paris in 1855 and 1887, Chicago in 1893)—and illusionistic displays like dioramas, panoramas, wax museums, and early cinema—were similarly designed to appeal to this group.

The basic activity of consumer culture—shopping—is the practical expression of the modern idea of the social subject as a self-defining individual. And consumerism, Slater remarks, represents the "pre-eminent social training ground" for the production of liberal individualist ethics (Slater 1997, 61). Acts of consumption signify autonomy, privacy, and freedom. But, because modernity is contingent upon impersonal, rationalized production, consumption under these conditions also implies manipulation. This contradiction results in what Slater has called the "dialectic of shopping," with corresponding concepts of two types of consumers: the rational hero and the irrational patsy. What's more, the gender disparities associated with this dichotomy—the trite but no less authoritative opposition of active masculinity to passive femininity—are glaring: "Mass consumption and the mass cultural audience . . . attract gendered imagery. They are described as whimsical and inconstant, flighty and narcissistic; they can be seduced, or their resistance overcome, by stimuli or persuasion in order to achieve market penetration" (Slater 1997, 57). Slater also notes the difficulties encountered when examining how gender operates in critiques of consumer culture: "[I]n writing a book that surveys [theories of consumption], I have symptomatically found it difficult to raise these issues consistently: they get structured out of the field" (ibid.). Tania Modleski observes a similar but more specific effect when the critics are women: "Not the least of the problems involved in equating the masses and mass culture with the feminine is that it becomes much more difficult for women to interrogate their role within that culture" (Modleski 1991, 34). These problems also occur in the discourse on celebrity. There is the same dichotomy, although the opposition in this case takes the form of heroic, rational (masculine) cultural critics providing the analytic frameworks that render irrational (feminine) consuming fans passive. Entertainment celebrities become agents of capitalist deception or the decay of moral values, likewise feminized by their symbiotic relationship with mass audiences.

Of course, these masses, or the even more menacing mob, as nineteenth-century social critics liked to describe communities of working-class, often foreign-born, women and men, were condemned as vulgar and unruly by some middle-class women reformers, as well as many of their male colleagues, who advocated an ethic of "social purity." Nonetheless, current detractors of popular entertainments and associated celebrities—predominantly but not exclusively men—frequently express condescension, if not outright antipathy, to mass culture by means of analogies with women and passive or seductive femininity.[25] In this arena, class and gender are rarely addressed explicitly but continually alluded to. In the process, the separate but overlapping histories of two groups—workers and women—become intertwined. This is not merely a rhetorical trick but can be traced to the conflation of women's and worker's political movements by the guardians of the established social order both faced. As Andreas Huyssen points out,

> [W]hen the 19th and early 20th centuries conjured up the threat of the masses "rattling at the gate," to quote [Stuart] Hall, and lamented the concomitant decline of culture and civilization (which mass culture was invariably accused of causing), there was yet another hidden subject. In the age of nascent socialism *and* the first major women's movement in Europe, the masses knocking at the gate were also women, knocking at the gate of a male-dominated culture. (Huyssen 1986, 39)[26]

When an interest in consumption is deemed inherently feminine, as it is in modern bourgeois culture, the irrational, vulnerable consumer manipulated by merchants' hype becomes analogous to the emotionally impressionable consumer of sentimental drama. Not surprisingly, by the end of the nineteenth century the most popular theatrical form in Europe and North America, melodrama, was disdained by critics who regarded it as inferior to serious dramatic art—realism or tragedy—and dismissed as yet another type of trifling mass culture. This was part of a more sweeping separation between high and low art that occurred in nineteenth-century Europe and, by proxy, North America, which Christine Gledhill correlates with "a re-masculinisation of cultural value . . . recentering the hero and claiming tragic value for the failure of heroic potential" (Gledhill 1987, 32). The result was a sexual partition that rendered emotional expression on stage and by audiences feminine. As Gledhill says succinctly, "Men no longer wept in public" (ibid.). When movies became the most popular form of entertainment in the early twentieth century, possibilities for melodramatic plots and performances were extended further.[27] And by the 1930s paternalistic warnings issued by social scientists about the dangers of mass culture increasingly concentrated on the beguiling effects of motion pictures on naïve, passive spectators (Blumer 1933; Hauser 1935).[28]

There are additional connections between the defining characteristics of melodrama, the emergence of entertainment celebrities, and femininity. First of all, melodramatic characters and stage or film stars (as well as other celebrities) are cut from the same cloth: each relies on an ability to evoke affective predicaments and embody social identities; each takes on meaning through expressive gestures, including speech, using techniques that put emotions on display and make them legible.[29] Once again, the emphasis on states of feeling, rather than reason, and on self-display imprints entertainment celebrities with particularly feminine features and has the same effect on fandom as well. At the same time, acting has been one of the few occupations in which ambitious women could prosper financially and professionally, because, as Huyssen argues, this particular kind of artistry "was seen as imitative and reproductive, rather than original and productive" (Huyssen 1986, 51). A curious addendum to the feminization of celebrity culture is that even male stars become suspect. A classic example is Rudolph Valentino, whose exotic costumes and elaborate makeup in films like *The Sheik*, as well as his marriages to two women suspected of being lesbians, provoked sarcastic comments about his masculinity in the press (Hansen 1991, 245–268; see also, Neale 1983). It is not difficult to fathom, then, why an interest in entertainment stars is taken as a sign of emotional immaturity or intellectual inferiority. It is, in a word, unmanly.

DRAMATIS PERSONAE

For all the power exerted by the idea of lesbians as would-be men—women who are unfeminine or "mannish"—and therefore presumably averse to the excessive emotional display of melodrama, the concept of how lesbian subjectivity is expressed and lived that became predominant in the twentieth century is remarkably melodramatic. Consider how Peter Brooks describes the characteristics of melodrama, keeping lesbians in mind:

> [M]elodramatic rhetoric, and the whole expressive enterprise of the genre, represents a victory over repression. We could conceive this repression as simultaneously social, psychological, historical, and conventional: what could not be said at an earlier stage, not still on a "nobler" stage, nor within the codes of society. The melodramatic utterance breaks through everything that constitutes the "reality principle," and all its censorships, accommodations, tonings-down. Desire cries aloud its language in identification with full states of being. (Brooks 1984, 41)

If lesbian personhood itself can be said to be infused with melodrama, it seems reasonable to ask why the melodramatic disposition of the star system and enduring popularity of melodrama itself didn't make the sphere of popular entertainment more hospitable to lesbians? The scant lesbian material produced before the 1970s—and I would include novels like *The Well*, along with more spectacular forms like plays and movies—was often censored. The cast members of the 1927 Broadway play *The Captive* were arrested and subsequent performances banned, although the lesbian who threatened the marriage of the play's two main characters never appeared on stage. Crucial scenes in the 1931 German film *Mädchen in Uniform*, which deals with lesbian desire in a girls' boarding school, were cut from the version shown in U.S. movie houses. When the Nazis came to power in 1933, the film was withdrawn immediately from circulation in Germany, and those responsible for its production fled the country. Once the Production Code was adopted by Hollywood studios in 1934, the possibility of the slightest, saddest lesbian character was eradicated until after the Code was gradually set aside in the 1950s.

Within a cultural climate that banished lesbians from stage and screen, it's no wonder that until the late 1980s the idea that any woman working in show business would willingly proclaim herself lesbian was practically unthinkable (the phrase most often used was "professional suicide"). Indeed, hints aplenty could be dropped (and were—see chapter 5) but the tacit agreement to not make outright statements (or accusations) regarding lesbian performers was sufficient to police the boundary separating lesbianism and celebrity.

And yet the conditions for lesbian personhood in the twentieth century and those for entertainment celebrity seem to be particularly well matched. This is not solely an effect of temporal coincidence but of a firmly established structural relationship, albeit one where the presence of lesbians and lesbianism is paradoxically evinced by erasure or disavowal. In every sector of modern consumer culture and all the key areas where contemporary celebrity is constituted—popular entertainment, mass media, and related publicity techniques—normative definitions of sexuality, gender, and class are routinely mobilized and reinforced. At the same time, the devices used to arouse and satisfy audiences' desires establish an imaginary, but also material, foundation for lesbian passion: activities coded as feminine, where the pleasures of women's company may be taken for granted; opportunities for voyeuristic delight in the display of female bodies;[30] enactments of fiery relationships among women, even if overtly asexual; and depictions of forceful, not always typically, feminine women. All such common features of popular culture can be plausibly described as potential lesbian occasions.

That may be the reason why backstage and offscreen show business communities have always been suspected of fostering lesbian tendencies, as well as licentiousness of every variety. There is certainly a voyeuristic component to this notion, as the tenor of the following passage in Havelock Ellis's 1901 text on lesbianism indicates:

> Passionate friendships among girls, from the most innocent to the most elaborate excursions in the direction of Lesbos, are extremely common in theaters, both among actresses and, even more, among chorus- and ballet-girls. Here the pell-mell of the dressing rooms, the wait of perhaps two hours between the performances, during which all the girls are cooped up, in a state of inaction and excitement, in a few crowded dressing-rooms, afford every opportunity for the growth of this particular kind of sentiment. (Ellis [1901] 1936, 215)

These words appear as a quotation, which Ellis attributes to "a friend," although it's not at all clear what relationship this friend has to the setting she or he describes. However, a line further on in the text offers a hint: "It is ... *among the upper ranks*, alike of society and of prostitution, that Lesbianism is most definitely to be met with, for here we have much greater liberty of action, and much greater freedom from prejudices" (Ellis [1901] 1936, 216, emphasis added). Few social commentators were concerned about threats to the decency of lower-class performers—who were presumed morally deficient in any case—while bourgeois women, who were expected to embody the principles of feminine virtue, were perceived as "fallen" if they pursued an acting career. Tracy Davis's work on the gender ideology that circumscribed the lives of actresses in Victorian England, but also in the U.S. during the same period, elaborates this point:

> [L]ike the *demi-mondaine*, [an actress] is marked as a social adventuress, flaunting her beauty to accrue influence and wealth; and like the prostitute, she must perpetually stoke the fires of admiration, or perish. The incompatibility of *naïveté*, modesty, and theatrical ambition was interpreted as unfeminine, anti-family, and anti-male tendencies in women who chose to contravene their properly gendered upbringing. . . . She was criticized for doing exactly what men did: turning outside the home for

social intercourse, intellectual stimulation, and occupational fulfillment.
(Davis 1991, 85–86)

The correspondence between disdain for proper female behavior, attributed to
women who opted for careers on stage, and masculine tendencies associated with
lesbianism, which was the defining characteristic of an "invert," becomes clearer.

Despite the prevailing suspicions about the sexual debauchery of actresses
and other female performers, unambiguous references to homosexuality were
rare when actresses played theatrical or cinematic roles. Allusions, however,
were not. Sanitized representations of offstage life can be found in the *Stage
Door*–type movies, which feature lots of intense, but never overtly sexual, relationships between women. A pre-Code film like the 1929 *Pandora's Box* went
even further by alluding to the lesbian *demi-mondaines* in pre–World War II
Berlin music halls. But since the logic of the celebrity system presumes that
the "real hero behaves just like the reel hero" (deCordova 1991, 27) and until
very recently unmistakable lesbian *heroes* in the repetoire of popular entertainments were unthinkable, any particular star's heterosexuality was taken for
granted. Therein lies the basis for the aura of secrecy that hovers around lesbian celebrities and results in what Terry Castle describes as the "apparitional
lesbian," who "remains a kind of 'ghost effect' in the cinema world of modern
life: elusive, vaporous, difficult to spot—even when she is there in plain view,
mortal and magnificent at the center of the screen" (Castle 1993, 2).

One strategy frequently used by advocates for historical recuperation
intended to give the lesbian ghosts in popular culture substantial form has
been biographical research, resulting in the compilation of annotated lists of
illustrious lesbians. Another, which I find more agreeable, is inquiry into the
haunting of modern (and postmodern) popular culture in the United States
by the specter of lesbianism. In particular, those concerned about the oversight of lesbians by popular media might consider how the tremendous
growth of consumer and visual culture, which is so often cited as the culprit
for the proliferation of celebrity, has produced at the same time a sexualized
field where the lesbians and lesbian themes flourish, unacknowledged and
therefore as the sort of open secret Eve Kosofsky Sedgwick writes about
(1991). For some, secrets about sexuality may suggest danger, the terror of
being discovered, the threat of being exposed. For others, however, this kind
of secrecy can be thrilling, information shared only by insiders, members of a
private club. But it is important to remember that not all keepers of sexual
secrets occupy equivalent positions in relation to power. As Foucault states,

> Silence itself—the things one declines to say, or is forbidden to name, the
> discretion that is required between different speakers—is less the absolute
> limit of discourse, the other side from which it is separated by a strict
> boundary, than an element that functions alongside the things said. . . .
> [W]e must try to determine the different ways of not saying such things
> [about sex], how those who can and those who cannot speak of them are
> distributed, which type of discourse is authorized, or which form of dis-
> cretion is required. (Foucault 1978, 27)

As a result, the impetus for disclosing the unspoken, or unspeakable, may easily precipitate a disturbance in orderly public discourse, with dire consequences for whomever gives the show away.

The reputation of a lesbian celebrity like Radclyffe Hall may be interpreted in this context. Some thirty-five years after *The Well of Loneliness*
appeared and became a centerpiece of lesbian culture, as well as broader cultural precepts concerning lesbianism, its protagonist and its author remained
commanding iconic figures for members of a growing number of politically
ambitious lesbians. And it is telling that the two were frequently conflated.
When Una Troubridge's biography of Hall was published in 1962, the only
North American lesbian journal in existence at the time, the *Ladder*, reviewed
it as a "biography of 'The Well'" and recommended it as a companion to "that
monumental lesbian love story" (Damon 1962, 10). A subsequent article in
the *Ladder* devoted to Troubridge's paean to Hall, written by leading gay
author Donald Webster Cory, also insisted on the correspondence between
Hall and Stephen Gordon. Cory, however, did note the discrepancy between
the imagined character and her author: Hall "required no false front of con-
cealment" and suffered no terrible social censure, while Stephen and her lesbian friends were lonely, "miserable and outcast and driven to suicide" (Cory
1963, 8–9). Nevertheless, he avers that social stigma, the lot of many homosexuals that led inevitably to feelings of alienation and an internalized sense of
inferiority, must have been as true of Hall as it was of her fictional lesbians.

The antidote, as Cory understood this social-psychological dynamic, was
twofold. First, heroic individuals needed to furnish public representations of
homosexual women and men. This, he believed, had been Hall's major contribution: "It was one thing for the world in its silence and its gossip to know
about John, as they knew about many of her contemporaries, men and
women. It was quite another thing to make an official fact out of something
that everyone just knew to be." Second, these representations also needed to

The Ladder

We are
coming
And our name
is legion
You dare not
disown us

Radclyffe Hall

Courtesy of Barbara Grier

be heroic: "They would be portrayed, not as human beings, but as superhuman beings. . . . [M]illions of people felt that this was the portrait that the world required, to lessen the antipathy, to accept the invert into the family of humanity" (Cory 1963, 7–8). On these terms, a lesbian celebrity automatically attained the stature of an idol, even if this meant that she was also fated to be a martyr. In Cory's words, "[W]hether she rejects the society or accepts its judgement and looks upon herself as an aberration, no matter what course she chooses, she is a lonely human being" (9).[31]

As recently as 1970, Hall was still invoked as the standard bearer for lesbian personhood. In that year, a cover of the *Ladder* featured words from the final passages of *The Well* inscribed in Gothic lettering with Hall's name printed underneath: "We are coming/And our name is legion/You dare not disown us" (*Ladder* 1969–1970). By then, however, the women's and gay liberation movements were gathering steam, and the quotation took on a different tone in this context. In the novel, these phrases are uttered as a petition for deliverance, addressed to God by the ghosts of lesbians who had died over the course of the novel, with Stephen acting as the medium. Printed in large letters, without illustration, in 1970 these words read as a militant declaration, a vaguely menacing statement issued by impatient amazons as a secular call to arms against a homophobic world. Martyrdom was no longer an appropriate stance for lesbian celebrities.

CHAPTER FOUR

GOING PUBLIC

STAR WARS IN THE LIBERATION MOVEMENTS

From the outset, the gay and women's liberation movements that burst forth on the public stage in the late 1960s looked forward to a world transformed by political and cultural revolutions, but members of these movements also forged historical arguments to counter the idea that homosexuality was unhealthy and socially pernicious. Where lesbians were concerned, famous women—from Sappho to Gertrude Stein—whose homosexuality had been practically erased, were posthumously recruited as distinguished forebears. The justification for the attention given to eminent lesbians of past eras was similar to that most frequently encountered today: role models. This was not a novel argument, insofar as the homosexuality of distinguished individuals has been a consistent feature of organized efforts to obtain social approbation and decriminalization of homosexuality. Magnus Hirschfeld, who founded the Scientific Humanitarian Committee in Berlin in 1898 and later established the Institute for Sexual Science to promote sexual reform and tolerance of homosexuality in particular, compiled lists of famous homosexuals to promote his cause. However, the difference between the rationale for these earlier efforts and those made since the 1960s is that Hirschfeld and his contemporaries believed that this information would change social mores in a population they considered largely heterosexual, while members of liberation groups were more concerned with problems of self-regard among gay men and lesbians.

In 1969, Dick Leitsch, executive director of the New York City chapter of the Mattachine Society, called for research into and publication of information about notable lesbian and gay men by members of the nascent gay liberation movement:

> Homosexuals, like everyone else, need people to identify with. We need
> heroes, homosexuals who have "made it", to show what we can do if we
> try. . . . Increased interest in homosexual heroes and homosexual histories
> would help solve the identity crisis so many homosexuals feel by bringing
> home the realization that we are not "freaks", but part of a group that has
> always existed and contributed its bit toward civilization and culture.
> (Leitsch 1969)

For Leitsch and like-minded comrades, a parade of accomplished cultural
and political figures who could be identified as lesbian or gay offered psychological benefits for shame-ridden gay men and lesbians who were potential members of the movement. Awareness of these dead heroes would instill
pride, which quickly became the watchword of the gay liberation program.

Living lesbian and gay heroes were another matter, all famously occupying more or less transparent but securely guarded closets. And, although it
might seem inconsistent with efforts to identify noteworthy representatives,
any lesbian who became renowned due to her involvement in the women's or
gay movement was suspected of using politics for self-aggrandizement.[1] In
other words, the concern with celebrity in lesbian cultural milieus was treated
as a political problem as often as it was interpreted as an achievement.
Documents from the extremely volatile and often contentious late 1960s and
early 1970s confirm the difficulties presented by lesbian celebrity, which could
be summarized as one general question: how to deal with the media. At that
time and from the perspective of the young radicals who constituted the first
gay and women's liberation groups, television and the mainstream press were
not looked upon as neutral publicity vehicles. Instead, these media were
assumed to be ideological instruments of repressive patriarchy and capitalism,
an assessment amply supported by much of the coverage they offered—or
neglected to give—about these movements. Women's liberation fared slightly
better in this regard, although its more radical contingents were routinely
treated as extremists. Gay liberation activists and actions, on the other hand,
were either ignored completely or rendered as eccentric curiosities. The uprising in New York City sparked by a police raid of the Stonewall Inn in June
1969, for example, either was given little mention in the local news media or
treated as an amusing escapade with little political import (Alwood 1996).

The gay and women's liberation movements, like other radical political
and countercultural groups active in the 1960s and early seventies, regarded
media that did not emanate from friendly quarters—alternative, non-

commercial media—with deep suspicion. In addition to general skepticism about the ideological slant given to reports on events and issues by dominant media, members of radical organizations resented its power to authorize spokespeople and leaders. The ideals of democratic decision making often upheld by these groups, combined with an effort to incorporate Maoist principles of self-government in North American oppositional politics, created an atmosphere of mistrust concerning leaders or any structures that reproduced and institutionalized power differentials among individuals. The Gay Liberation Front (GLF), the name chosen by the first militant gay liberation organization formed in New York City in the wake of the Stonewall Rebellion, is indicative of its political principles, which consciously aligned this group with the popular national liberation struggles in Asia, Africa, and Latin America that emerged in the post–World War II period.

SHOOTING STARS

Another source of gay and lesbian activists' ire regarding the press was the common journalistic practice of seeking conventionally attractive members of these groups as de facto representatives. The chosen spokespeople were almost uniformly white and middle-class, often conservatively attired and well mannered by bourgeois standards. The gay press of the era, which consisted primarily of locally distributed, inexpensive newsprint periodicals, routinely registered antagonism to what was viewed as the commercial media's imposition of an individualistic ethic on fundamentally collective efforts. Anyone quoted as a spokesperson was likely to be castigated for her or his cooperation. For example, a feminist gay man, writing in the pages of the New York GLF newspaper *Come Out*, disparaged an article on gay liberation in the *New York Times* in a typical fashion: "[W]e can tell who are those among us who had the lowest consciousness—the straight identified homosexuals who compete with each other for access to the pig media." More optimistically, he added, "All the media in the world cannot erase the products of a gay consciousness" (Gavin 1972).[2]

The same theme was taken up most vigorously by lesbians involved in both the feminist and gay movements, so it is not surprising that lesbians were among the most vociferous media critics. A regular contributor in both contexts, Martha Shelley, was particularly contemptuous of a new phenomenon she designated the "Women's Liberation Media Star," who she profiled for *Come Out* readers:

Generally a college-educated, white, well-heeled woman who knows a
great deal about publicity and publishing but who never has the time for
consciousness raising, she is prone to make apologetic statements to the
male press, prone to waste her time arguing with Hugh Heffner or Dick
Cavett when she could be organizing women. "I have a wonderful relationship with my husband," says one denying her lesbian relationships in
Life magazine—when only a week before she brought tears to the eyes of
gay women with the stories of her ill-fated lesbian affairs. (Shelley
1970–71, n.p.)

Shelley goes on to explain the political repercussions that will ensue from
efforts to use mainstream media to publicize feminist and gay arguments for
liberation: "These media stars, carefully coifed and lathered with foundation
makeup, claim to represent all women. In actuality they are ripping off all
women. . . . These women will betray us when the *cock* crows. . . . If large
numbers of women are going to passively depend on a few stars to liberate
them, instead of getting themselves together to do it, the movement will
surely fail" (ibid.). According to Shelley's logic, efforts to secure media coverage were distracting, at best, if not utterly antithetical to the principles and
purposes of liberation.

Shelley's decision to omit the name of the offending woman featured in
Life is curious and deserves further reflection. On one hand, it could be interpreted as a refusal to acknowledge someone the media chose to shine a spotlight on as worthy of additional publicity. Or it might be construed as recognition of that woman's claim to membership in the movement, despite her
willingness to be singled out for attention. Therefore, not indicating her
proper name may have been an effort to spare her embarrassment. (Shelley
was less circumspect when she dealt with Betty Friedan in this article, perhaps because condemnation in this instance was directed at a feminist who
had publicly distanced herself from radical feminists and lesbian activists, and
attempted to do so in the name of the entire women's movement.) But there
was little mystery concerning the reference for anyone involved in radical
feminist or gay politics, at least in New York City.

She was clearly identifiable as Kate Millett, whose 1970 best-selling
Sexual Politics gave feminists conceptual ammunition for a full-fledged attack
on patriarchal, sexist culture as represented by Sigmund Freud, D. H.
Lawrence, and Norman Mailer, among others. However, Millett didn't count
on—nor could she have predicted—her elevation to media stardom as the

Kate Millett (second from right), with lesbian and women's liberation supporters.
Photograph by Diana Davies, New York Public Library, Manuscripts and Archives
Division.

result of her book's popular success. Her portrait was displayed on the cover of
the August 31, 1970, issue of *Time*, which devoted eight of its pages to a feature on "the politics of sex," including a sidebar profile of Millett, "Who's
Come a Long Way, Baby?" She was, as Shelley noted sarcastically, interviewed
at length by a reporter from *Life* for its September 4, 1970, feature on women's
liberation (Wrenn 1970). She appeared on radio and television talk shows. All
of this attention might have been lapped up greedily by someone trying to
make a career as an actress or politician, but Millett was a literary scholar and
artist, and her much-touted book was her Ph.D. thesis. She was also an avid
participant in a political movement that distrusted all such fanfare.

Not that mainstream media univocally praised Millett. She was lam-
pooned viciously in an *Esquire* illustration; her work was also dismissed as
unnecessarily strident and poorly documented by a reviewer in the same issue
of *Esquire*, as well as in *Harper's*, the *New Republic*, and *Commentary* (Decter
1970; Howe 1970; Lawrenson 1971; Malcolm 1970). Indeed, she became the
symbol of everything that opponents of feminism despised. On top of that, a

subsequent *Time* article cited a statement concerning her bisexuality that Millett had made to a gathering at Columbia University in November 1970, using this as evidence of her writing's dubious value. "The disclosure is bound to discredit her as a spokeswoman for her cause, cast further doubt on her theories, and reinforce the views of those skeptics who routinely dismiss all liberationists as lesbians," the article stated matter-of-factly ("Women's Lib" 1970). The New York City chapter of the National Organization of Women (NOW) immediately set out to dispute the underlying argument that a lesbian is automatically disreputable at a demonstration for child care and abortion rights held several days after the *Time* article appeared. Demonstrators wore lavender armbands and distributed leaflets declaring support for Millett and condemning *Time* for trying to undermine their movement. When the press failed to cover this aspect of the event, a group of feminists called a press conference to state plainly once again the solidarity between women's and gay liberation, with Millett prominent among the speakers. This time, the media took note. According to Sidney Abbott and Barbara Love's account of this affair, "Media coverage was excellent. . . . It virtually halted dyke-baiting" (Abbott and Love [1972] 1985, 125).[3]

For Millett, however, this display of sisterhood could not offset entirely the effects of the treatment she received from within movement ranks. The attacks began as soon as *Sexual Politics* was published and an unsigned leaflet denouncing Millett for grandstanding was distributed at a meeting of Radicalesbians, a group formed in response to homophobic statements by prominent members of the women's movement like Friedan and Susan Brownmiller. Friedan had become infamous within U.S. lesbian circles as the author of the remark that lesbianism was a "lavender menace" as far as women's liberation was concerned. Nor did she stop there, but later engineered a purge of lesbian officers in NOW. Brownmiller echoed Friedan when she dismissed lesbians' presence within women's liberation as a "lavender herring" in a piece she wrote for the *New York Times Magazine* (Brownmiller 1970). Taken together, these condescending comments by leading feminists inspired the militant Lavender Menace action by Radicalesbians at the Second Congress to Unite Women in 1970 in New York City (Abbott and Love [1972] 1985, 108–116). And it was a member of Radicalesbians who challenged Millett to admit her lesbian affairs at the Columbia event (Jay 1999, 232–233).

In *Flying*, Millett's autobiographical account of the year following her publishing success and her anointment as a women's liberation luminary, she writes about several grueling months on the college lecture circuit, after which "you come home to find everybody in New York invents scandalous legends while you're gone, and three purists have just put forth an edict on your treason" (Millett 1974, 93). Shelley could be counted as one of these purists, but so too could any of a number of radical feminists, such as the authors of "What Can We Do about the Media," a set of resolutions proposed by a feminist collective called the Class Workshop at the 1970 Congress to Unite Women. Among the tenets the group advocated were the following:

> Women's Liberation is getting popular enough that the media needs
> us as much as we need them. We can and must dictate our terms to them:
> present prepared statements and refuse to give personal information. . . .
> From now on anyone who refuses to follow this policy must be assumed
> to be doing so for her own personal aggrandizement. . . . No member of a
> group can appear as an independent feminist—whether for fame or for
> money. . . . No individual or group can earn a living by writing or speaking
> about women's liberation. . . . Anyone who wants to write should write for
> the movement, not for the publishing industry. . . . Any individual who
> refuses collective discipline will be ostracized from the movement. (Class
> Workshop 1970)

Millett was guilty on all counts. But the resolutions were not endorsed by those attending the conference. These were extreme and ultimately impractical guidelines for a political movement with a constituency as broad as women's liberation. The publishing industry was eager to cater to a growing audience for writings by feminists and about feminism, and the movement counted a goodly number of members with literary ambitions among its active members. However, such sentiments were very much in line with the antiestablishment stance characteristic of the more radical segments of both gay and women's liberation.

In many respects, disdain for the media and the fear that it would dilute radical messages by transforming movement spokespeople into celebrities had been a feature of American radical politics since the mid-1960s. The civil rights, Black Power, and anti–Vietnam War movements had all grappled with the problem but were never able to resolve it. As Todd Gitlin explains in his classic study of the relationship between the New Left and the media, *The Whole World Is Watching*, movement leaders like Mark Rudd of Columbia

Students for a Democratic Society, Abbie Hoffman and Jerry Rubin of the Yippies, and Stokely Carmichael of the Student Nonviolent Coordinating Committee became so newsworthy that they often ignored the principles of egalitarian decision making officially endorsed by the groups they represented. As the result of the media attention, Gitlin says, "Narcissistic motives, once negligible or contained, inevitably flourished, fattened by rewards, while more cooperative impulses withered" (Gitlin 1980, 161). In his analysis, the feminists who built the women's liberation movement in the late 1960s reacted against such preening ambitions and macho posturing with efforts to guard against this phenomenon, although they, too, could not control journalists' compulsive focus on individual personalities. Kate Millett captures well the impossible situation that faced any feminist who was singled out as a public figure: "[T]he movement is sending out double signals: you absolutely must preach at our panel, star at our conference . . . at the same time laying down a wonderfully uptight line about elitism. Why can't we stick by what we knew was right to start with—no bloody leaders?" (Millett 1974, 92–93).

OUTER SPACE

Unlike feminists, gay liberation groups rarely faced the need to deal with the possibility of their leaders becoming media stars, because at this time outspoken members of this political constituency were automatically deemed objects of scorn and derision. The mainstream press never seemed eager to identify gay or lesbian leaders, or even to acknowledge that homosexuality could be a political identity, as opposed to a shameful condition. Even a sympathetic article, such as a profile of the recently radicalized Daughters of Bilitis (DOB) that appeared in a 1971 issue of the *New York Times Magazine*, devoted considerable space and little criticism to theories concerning the psychopathology of lesbianism (Klemesrud 1971). No one who believed that the mass media pursued a repressive social agenda would be surprised by the repeated insinuations of perversion among lesbian activists in so much of the reporting on feminist and gay politics. But for revolutionaries like Rita Mae Brown, a leading radical lesbian feminist polemicist in the early 1970s, this kind of treatment could be interpreted as a political advantage. "For those who build toward a new world, women's liberation is a dead movement twitching its limbs in the vulgar throes of establishment recognition," she wrote. "Women-identified women will not sell out" (Brown [1972] 1992,

195). Like many others at that time, Brown believed that radical lesbians possessed the political analysis and revolutionary resolve necessary to bring about the liberation of all women.

However, there was at least one American lesbian, beside the ambiguous Kate Millett, who attracted abundant notice from the press due to her outspoken advocacy of lesbian issues and her unrepentant sexual identity. This was Jill Johnston, known mainly as regular contributor to the *Village Voice* and author of one of the first books to champion the new radical lesbian politics, *Lesbian Nation* (1973). Many lesbians expressed their admiration for Johnston's work, for the courage exhibited by an established, albeit avant-garde, art and dance critic publicly proclaiming her lesbianism and writing about her lesbian life. But she also encountered extreme animosity from lesbian feminist militants, which she also chronicled in her weekly column, reprinted in *Lesbian Nation*, and recalled in a 1998 republication of much of this material. Looking back on the hostile reception she often received from members of both women's and gay liberation, Johnston credits the media for producing her "new giantess misshapen profile rigged up in the glare of national publicity" and the "'false self' of stardumb" (Johnston 1998, n.p.) that resulted. Still, she remained mindful of how she abetted the production of her own notoriety and therefore put herself directly in the line of fire.

The kind of high jinks that landed Johnston in this predicament were often designed to garner attention from journalists who couldn't resist a juicy tidbit, although precedents can be found in the dadaesque prose she had been producing for the *Voice* for years. Starting out as a fairly conventional critic of avant-garde art and dance in the late 1950s, she developed a quirky, rambling, sometimes whimsical, often intimate writing style by the mid-1960s. Her columns could be described as the literary equivalent of the happenings, Fluxus performances, and similar aesthetic attacks on the pretensions of high art that she championed as a critic—"an art of high amusement and contempt for authority," as she put it (ibid.). Predictably, in the early days of women's liberation, Johnston ran afoul of more respectable feminists like Friedan, who was interested in press coverage of the movement but not the kind generated by outrageous behavior. In summer 1970, Women Strike for Equality, a coalition made up of various women's liberation groups and headed by Friedan, held a fundraising cocktail party at the East Hampton home of avant-garde art collectors Ethel and Robert Scull. But Johnston upstaged representatives of the feminist group by taking a topless swim in the hosts' pool while society reporters from the *New York Times*, *Newsweek*, UPI, and others took notes and snapped photos. "Have gun, will travel. See pool, will swim," she wrote in her gleeful account of the episode, "Bash in the Sculls" (Johnston 1998, 10). Later she explained that she had not planned the action to "protest the discrimination of lesbians by feminists" because, in her words, "I wasn't nearly so organized" (Johnston 1973, 16).

Then, in the spring of 1971, Johnston published a piece in the *Voice* entitled "Lois Lane Is a Lesbian," no more impassioned than her previous writings but unusual in that she no longer mentioned lesbianism in passing but explicitly aligned herself with gay liberation and offered a theory of lesbian feminist politics. One would assume that such an unvarnished statement of affiliation in a widely read newspaper would be welcomed by gay and lesbian activists. But Johnston was too eccentric for many involved in either women's or gay liberation. As she noted in the same article, "I'm persona non grata with every 'group' in the country. . . . The women's lib people don't like the way I swim. The Gay Liberation Front says I wouldn't get any support from *them*. . . . Gay newspaper says I'm an exhibitionist" (Johnston 1998, 31). The last count of the indictment, at least, seems justified, although *Gay*'s coverage of Johnston could also be attributed to their overall tendency to dismiss or belittle women's liberation and anyone associated with it.[4] *Gay*'s sexism aside, Johnston's performance at Town Hall in New York City in May 1971, a media circus staged as a confrontation between Norman Mailer and his feminist critics, could easily be put down as exhibitionist. Indeed, Johnston did not shy away from this characterization but saw her public buffoonery as classic *épater-le-bourgeois* theatrics meant to upset well-heeled supporters of fashionable radical causes. As far as she was concerned, her antics were also intended as a critical commentary on the event's premise—that "women's liberation is a debatable issue" (Johnston 1973, 17). She refused the terms of the debate and also its format when she rose from the conference table to join a couple of friends in sexual horseplay on stage.

But she did not repeat her performance or otherwise disrupt a local television talk show on which she and DOB president Ruth Simpson were scheduled to appear along with two conservative psychiatrists. Simpson and other members of her organization left in protest after attempting to oust the male guests and host, while Johnston stayed behind and attempted to contradict the doctors' ideas about sexual perversion (Johnston 1971a; "Lesbians Zap Bandy" 1971). And when she teamed up with author Germaine Greer, feminist media star of the moment and copanelist at Town Hall, on another TV talk show, Johnston was outspoken but not particularly raucous

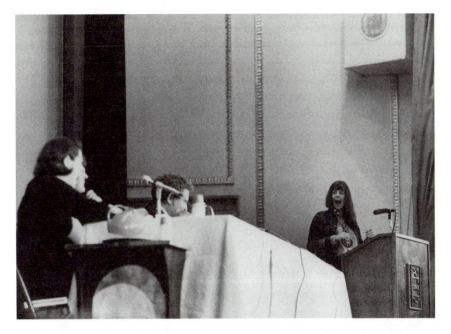

Jill Johnston speaking at the 1971 panel on women's liberation at Town Hall, with Norman Mailer and Germaine Greer in the foreground, from the documentary film *Town Bloody Hall*. Pennebaker-Hegedus.

(Johnston 1971b). In a way, though, it didn't matter whether she played the game or not, whether she answered the interviewers questions or turned the tables on them. She was invited to participate in these discussions because of her notoriety for being colorful, which included being unbashful about her lesbianism, and if she lived up to her reputation the producers got what they were after. For Johnston, as well as other lesbians, a coherent, effective strategy for being taken seriously by the dominant media at this time was structurally impossible. As a result of these and similar skirmishes with the media, Johnston adopted an analysis similar to Shelley's and other movement critics of the time, even though she was vulnerable to the charge that her high visibility made her a collaborator with the enemy.[5]

Jill Johnston's clown persona may have allowed her to overcome the strictures that prevented the mass media from creating gay and lesbian liberation icons (n.b. there were no lesbians on covers of major national news magazines until 1993),[6] although it permitted them to dismiss this newly open and prideful lesbian as a kook. On occasion, a relatively conservative, not at all amusing gay spokesman like Dick Leitsch was quoted as a representative of the old-guard homophile activists in the Mattachine Society, and serious DOB officials like Ruth Simpson in New York or the group's founders Del Martin and Phyllis Lyon in San Francisco would be called upon for authoritative lesbian viewpoints. But none of these political leaders became as widely identified with the movement as did Johnston. Nowadays her or Millett's notoriety would be celebrated as a milestone in the contest for visibility. Then it was a millstone that each had to drag around from speaking engagement to speaking engagement on the lecture and talk show circuit that constituted movement stardom.

TALKING TRASH

Johnston and Millett may have been media stars, emblems of the women's and gay liberation movements that provoked major press coverage at the end of the sixties, but they were also objects of what became known as trashing by feminist and lesbian activists critical of celebrity. Johnston even engaged in a bit of this activity, accusing Millett of "posing as 'straight' for the media" prior to *Time*'s outing of the *Sexual Politics* author, although that didn't spare Johnston the same treatment when the media nominated her as the representative for lesbian liberation and she didn't decline.[7] In her case, the charge was that she was male-identified, because she boasted of her sexual exploits in print (Johnston 1973, 132–133), and elitist because, as she put it, "the entire dyke community from coast to coast was not invited" to a meeting she tried to organize on the intersecting interests of lesbians and feminists (Johnston 1974, 189). Similarly, Jo Freeman, a women's liberation activist based in Chicago, was shunned and surreptitiously denounced by supposed "sisters" in Chicago in the early seventies. Some years later she published an article in *Ms.*, using her movement *nom de guerre* Joreen, that analyzed trashing as an unacknowledged enforcement of traditional concepts of proper feminine behavior (Joreen 1976). In another article on the subject Freeman examined how the charge of elitism was used as a wrong-headed attempt to adhere to democratic ideals but led inevitably to covert power plays (Joreen [1972] 1973). When these bitter struggles over media representation were taking place, however, few were prepared to speak up or write publicly about this form of callous behavior because the tactic left them estranged from the movement they were accused of betraying.

Rita Mae Brown, who was willing to antagonize anyone, undertook a critique similar to Freeman's in an essay entitled "Leadership vs Stardom" (1972), written while she was a member of the Furies lesbian collective in Washington, D.C. But this didn't prevent her doing a bit of trashing of celebrity spokeswomen herself. In Brown's analysis, "The rule of thumb for stars is this: she gets money from the white, rich, male world. . . . [T]hese tokens will in no way change the structure of government nor of the economy" (Brown 1972, 20). Having taken swipes at sellouts, she did assert that attacks on stars from within the movement, although motivated by justifiable animosity, "play into the hands of the male supremacists who then use these attacks to illustrate the 'fact' that 'women hate each other and can't work together'" (ibid.). The more important point for Brown was that a star should not be mistaken for a leader, "a woman who comes from the ranks of the movement. . . . She is not receiving rewards from male supremacists to divert our movement" (ibid.). What worried her is that the trashing of stars had spread to the trashing of leaders, which threatened to destroy the movement by driving away the most dedicated and talented organizers and thinkers.

The implicit assumption of this argument is that leaders never become stars and vice versa. The two categories—which could be distinguished as (deserved) political reputation opposed to (arbitrary) entertainment celebrity—were deemed utterly incommensurate, although, as Brown herself demonstrated in her own career, the wall between the two could be and was breached within a decade and crumbled altogether within two. Perhaps because she proceeded from cultural notoriety to political activism, and not the other way round like Brown, Johnston remarked in her contribution to this debate—an essay irreverently titled "Delitism, Stardumb, and Leadershit"—that "a star is not necessarily *not* a leader and vice versa" (Johnston 1974, 193, emphasis added). Johnston wasn't putting herself forward as a candidate for leadership in the movement (although it's possible to read Brown's comments in this light) but seemed less willing to rebuke those who abjured all contact with the mainstream media.

Distrust of stars, and the media in general, may have been a hallmark of radical gay politics in the late 1960s and early 1970s, but that did not preclude dreams of recruiting closeted celebrities whose support would speed liberation—of all gay people, including the stars in question. The president of one of the first gay liberation groups in the country, Homosexuals Intransigent! (HI), a student organization founded at the City College of New York in April 1969, advocated just such a project in an issue of *Gay*

Power, another alternative, "underground" paper. "Celebrities who are homosexual could do a lot to change public attitudes towards homosexuality," he wrote. "Any *one* celebrity publicly declaring himself [*sic*] homosexual would risk retaliation, but if dozens or hundreds of thousands of gay public figures declared themselves at the same time, their declaration would *force* the public to change its attitude toward homosexuality more than toward themselves" ("HI!" 1971). The plan was to draw up a list of famous gay people and write letters asking them to allow their names to be used in ads or, if they were uneasy about this option, to donate money that would be used to recruit others who might be bolder.

Needless to say, the proposal never got off the ground. What it does indicate, however, is that from the beginning coming out was the central tenet and strategy of gay and lesbian liberation politics. Given their apparent faith in the persuasive power of celebrity, it is curious that representatives of HI described the group as "leaderless," and the article cited above has no byline. The contradiction between engaging in fantasies about gaining support from rich, famous homosexuals and disavowing any differences in status among individual members indicates how the logic of visibility politics created blind spots in the radical gay movements as they grew and attracted supporters. But the main contradiction this produced emerged almost immediately, when gay and lesbian activists recognized and set out to exploit the political implications of coming out. Although the effects did not become manifest for some time, it is at precisely this juncture that lesbian celebrity and politics intersect.

THE PERSONALITY IS POLITICAL

Although much has changed in the decades since the concepts entailed in lesbian/gay liberation first took shape, the axiom that coming out is an essential requirement for viable lesbian or gay politics has not. Indeed, coming out quickly became the cornerstone around which the movement was built—its most important feature—and the closet its most influential metaphor, to the point that both terms have been applied in all types of contexts that have nothing to do with homosexuality.[8] Coming out also drew celebrities into the liberation project because of their emblematic significance within mainstream culture. The political valence of such notables shifted from their position as questionable agents of social conformity—since their silence served as a reminder that homosexuality was reprehensible—to potential role models if (but only if) they were willing to assert their homosexuality publicly. Coming out became the defining feature of the new politics of homosexuality, which logically generated and accelerated interest in lesbian and gay celebrities, both in the ranks of the liberation movement and in the culture at large.

A typical argument for coming out as a political strategy was made in the early days of gay liberation by New York GLF member Martha Shelley: "The worst part of being a homosexual is having to keep it *secret* . . . the daily knowledge that what you are is something so awful that it cannot be revealed. . . . [T]he internal violence of being made to carry or choosing to carry the load of straight society's unconscious guilt—this is what tears us apart, what makes us want to stand up in the offices, the factories and the schools and shout our true identities" (Shelley 1970). Significantly, *Come Out* was the name of New York GLF's newspaper, first published in November 1969. Although the political implications of coming out seem to have been first publicized by local media produced in New York City, these ideas quickly proliferated around the country. For instance, Shelley's remarks on coming out appeared first in the East Village radical newspaper *Rat* and then in the *Detroit Gay Liberator*. The *Chicago Gay Liberation Newsletter* reproduced excerpts of a speech given by GLF founding member Michael Brown at the first New York City Gay Pride rally in June 1970: "[W]e'll never have the freedom and civil rights we deserve as human beings until we stop hiding in closets and in the shelter of anonymity. We have to come out into the open and stop being ashamed or else people will go on treating us as freaks" (Chicago Gay Liberation 1970, 1).

The implication of the rapid diffusion of these ideas is not that New York City was the source of all lesbian/gay liberation theory and propaganda during this era. In many respects the movement's dynamism as a national phenomenon can be attributed to conditions that were not specific to any particular locale. On the other hand, local formations were not uniform nor were there any national organizations that could claim to represent lesbians and gay men on a national level. For example, issues of the *Detroit Gay Liberator* offer evidence that the socialist contingent in GLF in that city was even stronger than in New York, which could be attributed to the history of working-class militancy in Detroit's auto industry. Likewise, the *Chicago Gay Liberation Newsletter* carried more and longer articles about racism within the movement than any of the New York gay liberation papers. However, a loose communications network existed among the various gay/lesbian groups and their constituents, who stayed in touch largely through the publications that circulated among them. Thus, reprinted remarks made by New York GLF

Jill Johnston (right) at a GLF meeting in New York City. Photograph by Diana Davies, New York Public Library, Manuscripts and Archives Division.

members signaled that affiliated groups understood themselves as part of a national movement and generally endorsed the sentiment that coming out should be placed high on the gay liberation agenda.

The provocation to come out quickly enlisted supporters outside the active membership of gay liberation organizations as well. Inspired by the radicals in GLF and other lesbian/gay liberation groups, Johnston amplified previous references to herself as a lesbian she had made in print and alerted *Village Voice* readers that such deeds were political acts: "Gay people are now expecting and demanding the same sanctified regard for their sexual interests and unions as they have rendered for so long as they can remember to the weird forces that endowed them with life in the first place. Now there is *only one way* for this social change to take place. And that is for all gay people, those who know it and accept it, to stand up and speak for themselves" (Johnston 1998, 29; emphasis added). In her own coming out statement, Johnston encapsulated what became the prevailing wisdom among champions of gay and lesbian liberation: coming out will precipitate social recognition and respect, thus liberation.

As mentioned previously, GLF groups were modeled on the national liberation movements that sought freedom from colonial domination in the post–World War II period, armed conflicts that were still raging in areas of Asia and Africa at the end of the 1960s.[9] In this context, coming out was advocated as a means of declaring an oppositional identity as a member of the oppressed group, thereby taking the first step toward building a militant gay political movement. Although making a public declaration of one's homosexuality was less frequently mentioned as a method for achieving a sense of personal self-worth, this, too, was sometimes described as a side effect of collective organizing. Like the radical factions of the women's liberation movement of that period, GLF and affiliated groups advocated consciousness raising, which they believed linked self-awareness and self-respect to solidarity with others who shared one's social marginality. According to GLF's philosophy, the primary goal of the process was to understand how the oppression of lesbians and gay men was related to that directed at others on the left and to forge alliances with them on the basis of a common interest in overthrowing all systems of discrimination and exploitation.

From the start, though, gay liberation groups included activists who weren't interested in GLF's socialist and feminist theories but wanted to "obtain political power . . . by working within the present system rather than trying to destroy it" (Owles 1970). This was the rationale behind the formation of the reform-minded Gay Activist Alliance (GAA), created by disgruntled GLF members in late 1969. GAA and its supporters at *Gay* had no argument with capitalism and were not interested in making connections between social injustices like racism or sexism and the political-economic system. Nor did they want to participate in unstructured, leaderless groups, since they deemed these ineffective for planning and carrying out political lobbying, legal challenges, or fund-raising activities. For adherents of this position coming out was the *primary* organizing principle of their political program, because, as the group's first president stated, they believed, "Before a gay is willing to fight for anything he [*sic*] has to be aware of his own repression" (ibid.). However, this dispute was not confined to differences in political ideology between the rival organizations, since a number of GLF members endorsed the idea that a vibrant, open homosexual counterculture, not political revolution, should be the movement's top priority. Coming out figured prominently in strategies for realizing such a community. And the same split between political and cultural activists could be found in the ranks of GAA (Jay 1999, 89; Marotta 1981).

For a fleeting moment, the political/cultural split within the movement placed differing emphases on the interpretation of coming out. In early 1970, *Gay* published a letter in its advice column that epitomized the disagreement:

> Q. I am a lesbian belonging to the *Gay Liberation Front*. We have had some internal dissension over a question of priorities. Which is more important, do you think, political liberation or mental liberation?

> A. Liberation of the head, of course. . . . If we do not *feel* free inside, where we *really live* most intensely, we are not free anywhere. (Kaiso 1970)

The schism between gay liberals and revolutionaries, as well as between political versus cultural interests, in New York City was replicated in cities around the country. Around the same time many lesbians deserted both camps to form separate, often separatist, lesbian-feminist groups. Within three years, champions of a unified, revolutionary gay and lesbian politics with ties to other liberation movements had retreated and their organizations had all but disbanded, while the ascendant liberals transformed the gay movement into a campaign for civil rights, in contrast to the sweeping social transformations the radicals had envisioned.[10]

In the process of this political displacement, an emphasis on *individual* self-knowledge and well-being became the predominant rationale for coming out, compared to the *collective* goal of organizing a substantial oppositional movement informed by revolutionary consciousness. This is often interpreted as fallout from the implosion of left radicalism in the United States, due to disillusionment with the ultramilitant rhetoric and violent methods championed (and actualized in rare instances) by frustrated revolutionaries, coupled with important political victories for the right in the national political arena (Nixon's election as president in 1968, for starters). This is the commonsense explanation of the disintegration of many radical left political organizations that occurred in the mid-1970s. Yet, gay politics and culture indicate that there is a more compelling argument that accounts for the success of what were considered reformist strategies for achieving liberation. The connecting link is the practical production of new kinds of gay and lesbian identities after 1968, which rendered coming out the most potent weapon in the liberation arsenal.[11]

Although the conflicts that erupted in GLF were real and often bitterly fought, in several important respects the cultural/political, liberal/radical factions did not differ significantly. Indeed, many defining elements of the branches of the reform movement that succeeded that contentious period were informed by theoretical and strategic approaches advocated by the revolutionary faction. And these, in turn, were linked to broader developments in social practices and technologies having to do with permutations in definitions of personhood, what Nikolas Rose describes as "identity projects" (N. Rose 1998, 157).[12] The term "technology" is also borrowed from Rose, who elaborates concepts introduced by Michel Foucault in order to analyze the historically contingent production of particular kinds of persons and notions of selves. Technologies in this sense are not physical instruments or institutional systems but practical and technical methods for administrating populations and individual subjects. Rose explains, "Technologies of the self take the form of elaboration of certain techniques for the conduct of one's relation with oneself, for example requiring one to relate to oneself epistemologically (know yourself), despotically (master yourself), or in other ways (care for yourself)" (N. Rose 1998, 29). Coming out is such a technology.

UNLIKELY BEDFELLOWS

Advocates of gay and lesbian liberation or, later, gay/lesbian civil rights conceived coming out as a means to counteract social conformity and complacency in matters related to sexuality and gender. Where the public was concerned, coming out was intended to precipitate two effects: (1) exposure of homosexuality as a trait of seemingly "normal" individuals, which would unsettle assumptions about definitions of normalcy, and (2) demonstration of prideful gay and lesbian identities. Having been pigeonholed for the better part of a century throughout the West as both unfortunate and dangerous aberrant creatures, anyone who thought of her- or himself as a homosexual person (not everyone who engaged in homosexual practices did, or does) was encouraged to take part in overthrowing the various mechanisms that guaranteed the odium meted out to homosexuality and homosexuals. Thus, rationales for coming out frequently invoked socialization and social roles, usually gender roles, to explain how homosexuality has been defined as deviance and how it might be reformulated as a positive identity.

Consider, for instance, how GLFers Allan Warshawsky and Ellen Bedoz introduced the problem in *Come Out*: "We are all the products of an oppressive society. . . . The institution of the nuclear family socializes us to meet the inhuman needs of the system. It defines our roles and pressures its members into fulfilling them. These roles no longer serve the needs of the individual" (Warshawsky and Bedoz 1970). "The Woman Identified Woman" manifesto issued by Radicalesbians, a New York group made up of dissident members of both women's and gay liberation organizations (including Martha Shelley and Rita Mae Brown), struck a similar note and described how socialization and roles affect lesbians in particular:

> [A lesbian] may not be fully conscious of the political implications of
> what for her began as personal necessity, but on some level she has not
> been able to accept the limitations and oppression laid on her by the most
> basic role in her society—the female role. . . . To the extent that she can-
> not expel the heavy socialization that goes with being female, she can
> never truly find peace with herself. For she is caught somewhere between
> accepting society's view of her—in which case she cannot accept herself—
> and coming to understand what this sexist society has done to her and
> why it is functional and necessary for it to do so. (Radicalesbians [1970]
> 1973, 240–241)

In the latter call to arms, attention shifts from statements about how social forces conspire to impose normative heterosexuality to explanations of why individual opposition to these processes promises social and political liberation.

Yet, despite their interest in revolutionizing family structures and sexual-gender norms, advocates of gay and lesbian liberation frequently employed the terminology and concepts used by adherents of the dominant social theory at the time, structural-functionalism, which proceeds from the premise that societies are integrated systems that tend inherently toward equilibrium, with internal mechanisms that contain any disruptive elements. The primary architect of this influential branch of American sociology was Talcott Parsons. His book *Family, Socialization, and the Interaction Process* (1955), co-authored with Robert Bales, is the classic structural-functionalist treatise on the relationship between family structures and socialization, defined as the process of internalization of norms and values that produces individuals who perform given social roles. According to Parsons, the family in modern societies serves the function of ensuring the differentiation of gender roles. Although not inborn, these roles are nonetheless natural, because they are products of the public-private dichotomy in social life, which Parsons sees as evidence of objective increases in social differentiation and complexity. In Parsons's words, this is a "positive 'progressive' development" (Parsons and

Bales 1955, 51). Thus, sexual and gender norms are socially necessary. For instance, Parsons avers that "the prohibition of homosexuality has the function of reinforcing the differentiation of sex roles" (103), which is precisely the dynamic lesbian and gay critics aimed to dismantle.

Although they clearly did not endorse Parsons's belief that the taboo against homosexuality was socially "progressive" or similar structural-functionalist justifications for bigotry, the arguments made by Warshawsky, Bedoz, Radicalesbians, and various like-minded analysts of homosexuality were informed by functionalist reasoning. In other words, they accepted the basic tenets of functionalist theory, which treats social phenomena in terms of each one's contribution to overall social stability (e.g., definitions of crime function as demarcations that limit collectively approved behavior). Rather than challenging the basic premise of functionalist theory, that social structures require and ensure consensus, these lesbian and gay theorists advocated establishing a different consensus. They hoped that exposing the operations of this system would spur proliberation forces to counteract its effects and pave the road to a new set of cultural norms.

Take, for example, socialization, perhaps the most significant concept appropriated by gay liberation from this strain of social theory (although this term has come to dominate the vocabulary used to talk about the relationship between individuals and social structures to such an extent that its theoretical lineage has become obscure). Socialization is at heart a theory of social reproduction. It explains how individual participants in the social world—that is, everyone—are integrated into it and therefore guarantee its continuity. The theory of socialization depends on the bedrock assumption that most humans will adapt to the world as given to them because they will be rewarded for doing so; social norms are learned by means of an overlapping system of frustrations and gratifications (Parsons and Olds 1955, 193). Briefly stated, this integration is achieved through the internalization of norms, which begins at birth for every individual within the family circle. The theory of socialization is antithetical to disorder or antagonism, other than as instances of pathology, and neglects questions of power. In theory, socialization produces individual selves that mesh neatly with the requirements of an orderly society.

Closely related to socialization is the concept of social roles, the positions individuals occupy within the social order. Structural-functionalism employs the concept of roles to explain the allocation and performance of the diverse individual undertakings that constitute the social system, and sex roles provide an all-purpose shorthand for how gender identity is taken up and lived. Similarly, the concept of sex roles provided the theoretical framework used within both the women's and gay liberation movements to explain conventional gender and sexual behavior and attitudes. However, sex role theory, like socialization, supports an integration-oriented functionalism that promulgates normative ideals about social relations and structures. Moreover, the most influential theoretical support for sex roles is that provided by Parsons's writings on the nuclear family. In this context, roles divide responsibilities and personalities found within that institution into two categories: "instrumental" and "expressive." Each of these complementary attributes conforms to a gender role, with the husband-father characterized by the former and the wife-mother by the latter (Parsons and Bales 1955, 22). Once again, a normative imperative is engraved indelibly on the theoretical model.

Curiously, the role paradigm, which emerged in the 1930s and flourished in the 1950s and 1960s, had been roundly criticized and largely rejected by social theorists as early as the mid-sixties. But, as R. W. Connell notes, the concept of sex (or gender) roles survives in sociology and social psychology textbooks, and continues to inform applications of those discourses in myriad practical settings: education, corporate and industrial management, and social work, as well as popular social commentaries produced by news and entertainment media. Connell's explanation for why role theory was widely embraced in the first place and has remained prevalent is that it "attempted to show the functional necessity (for social survival) of role performance." It was, he writes, "the classic illustration of social determinism" that offered a scientific rationale for social hierarchies (Connell 1979, 11), "a theoretical ideology developed to cope with the stresses in the cultural order *created* by movements of resistance," including political activism in favor of sexual liberation (14). To quote Connell again, "Role theory plainly appeals to those who like to think that the social order works by mutual agreement; that people ought to do what they are told; and there is something wrong with those who don't. . . . This association of role theory with concepts of 'deviance' and programmes of therapy is thus not accidental at all" (15).[13]

Conflict presents a dilemma for role theory, as it does for socialization, since the model presumes an efficient, integrated, self-regulating social system. In other words, a functionalist approach assumes that conformity and consensus are essential, intrinsic features of social life. Roles are not freely chosen nor subject to idiosyncratic manipulation. They merely define the various interrelated positions that individuals occupy within the social system.

Proponents of role theory believe that its scientific basis can be substantiated further by the statistical methods used to ascertain role definitions, so that what most people do and believe becomes synonymous with objective imperatives of the social system. Harnessed to the apparently scientific truth provided by statistical evidence, roles take on an objective, coercive quality, even when contradictory roles and role performances are acknowledged. This entire theoretical edifice consists of a grand tautological argument for adaptation to social norms.

Again, I don't want to imply that lesbian and gay liberation activist-authors, along with other members of the gay liberation movement, endorsed the conservative positions held by structural-functionalists like Parsons. Quite obviously, they did not. They hoped to create new models of sexuality and gender, doing away with oppressive concepts of normalcy. They adamantly opposed the roles and processes of socialization that were said to inculcate these, as well as the structures of domination that rely upon the inferior status of femininity and homosexuality. Some advocated destroying the entire system, doing away with all roles, all authority. The antidote to oppression they recommended was the demolition of the structures that secure social domination and control. For example, the Radicalesbians imagined eliminating categories of sexuality (but not gender), entirely: "In a society where men do not oppress women, and sexual expression is allowed to follow feelings, the categories of homosexuality and heterosexuality would disappear" (Radicalesbians [1970] 1973, 241).

I doubt that very many, if any, of the movements' polemicists had studied Parsons's or others' structural-functionalist texts firsthand. If they had, they might have been less inclined to reiterate the key words used in this discourse: socialization, sex roles, et cetera. It is more likely that they picked up the basic structural-functionalist idiom and ways of thinking about social processes by virtue of the theory's translation into nonacademic descriptions of social life (think, for instance, of the everyday use of the word dysfunctional, another borrowing from the structural-functionalist lexicon). Moreover, the normative dimension of structural-functionalism gave its descriptions of social phenomena the authority of realism, so that sex roles, say, were understood as empirical forms of acting and thinking imposed by an impersonal, objective culture.

It's important to recall, one more time, that constructing a critique of gender and sexuality without these dominant concepts would have been quite difficult, since popular as well as academic discourse concerned with sexuality and gender was so thoroughly saturated with structural-functionalist assumptions about how social life is organized and how people operate within it. That doesn't mean, however, that the effects of hewing to this theoretical legacy are inconsequential. By reiterating the interpretation of Parsons's theory of social organization and operation, the gay and women's liberation movements endorsed unwittingly a conceptual framework that posits norms and consensus as essential features of social order. If this order is not thoroughly obliterated, if the revolution doesn't occur, the social system established and supported by functional imperatives will remain firmly in place. The ideal of liberation around which resistance was to be rallied demanded a romantic belief in the elementary antagonism between individual fulfillment and social constraint, or a variation on Freud's thesis about civilization's discontents. But those who took up such arguments—reformers along with revolutionaries—also borrowed from the despised discourse of social control—allying themselves with theories that assumed the calculability of all human actions, which if adequately analyzed and rationally criticized can be reengineered.

The gay and women's liberation projects preserved vestiges of structural-functionalism at the core of their critique and retained these in various practices intended to develop it further. Two widely embraced attempts to rationalize structural solutions to sexism and heterosexism were: consciousness-raising groups, which consisted of rule-governed and highly controlled discussions about shared personal experiences intended to reveal the larger political hierarchies and constraints underlying them; and separatist collectives founded by lesbians in order to devise mechanisms that would foster new forms of subjectivity, as well provide incubators for vanguard revolutionary activities. Not even the dissolution of many of these groups and disillusionment of many of their participants would undermine the powerful currents of functionalist thinking, which survive in various concepts bandied about in lesbian political analysis to this day.

One is the idea of role models, which is so frequently invoked that the roles to be modeled seem to be objectively determined. Another is the belief in and reliance on quantitative data, usually the results of opinion surveys, used by lesbian and gay journalists and policy analysts to plot political progress (or regress), and by lesbian and gay political organizations to set agendas and formulate strategies. This is the distinctively twentieth-century form of objective knowledge about social phenomena, which, as Rose observes, "takes a very material form—diagrams, graphs, tables, charts, num-

bers—[and] which materializes human qualities in forms amenable to normalization and calculation" (N. Rose 1998, 120).[14] A related development is
the technical interpretation of and justification for coming out: an increase in
the number of self-declared lesbian and gay men will strengthen advocates'
claims for greater recognition and less discrimination, based on irrefutable
measures of scientific fact. But perhaps what this almost casual citation of a
dubious theoretical paradigm bespeaks most of all is social science's authority in shaping commonsense beliefs concerning social reality.

Proponents of gay and women's liberation may have taken what Parsons
and others had to say about socialization and sex roles at face value, but that
didn't mean that they were willing to become compliant social subjects. It
isn't surprising, then, to find the authority of social scientists responsible for
promoting functionalist explanations of social behavior endorsed implicitly
by Warshawsky and Bedoz in one paragraph of their *Come Out* article—"The
institution of the nuclear family socializes us to meet the inhuman needs of
the system. It defines our roles and pressures its members into fulfilling
them"—and vigorously challenged in the next:

> Divergence is labelled "sick", "deviate", "unhealthy", "abnormal" by the
> establishment's social scientists who function as the system's official agents
> of guilt and shame. They establish arbitrary norms so that those who dif-
> fer can be made to feel "abnormal". . . .
>
> Thus the pressure for "deviates" to camoflage [*sic*] their differences to
> avoid scorn: the Black passing as white, the clean shaven Jew . . . , the
> homosexual who leads a double life. These people have sacrificed their
> selfhood for the safety of acceptance. They have victimized themselves.
> (Warshawsky and Bedoz 1970)

This is where the activists outline their oppositional stance regarding
prevailing approaches to "social problems," one critical of the structural-
functional maxim that defines deviance as evidence of defective socialization,
which the social system will necessarily correct, or as role conflict that may
trouble an individual but not affect the social order. Either account provides
support for the diagnosis of homosexuality as a psychological disorder—
embodied by a dysfunctional kind of person. Of course, it was this psychiatric
definition of homosexuality that gay liberation was most intent on disman-
tling, and which coming out was intended to vanquish. However, by hewing
to structural-functionalist paradigms, activists and theorists of the gay and

women's liberation movements lay the groundwork for the ambivalence about celebrity that can be found in lesbian and gay contexts to this day—proud embrace of those the mainstream media treats as movement representatives on one hand and disdain for or ridicule of media stars on the other.

EXPERT TESTIMONY

Numerous historians contend, with ample archival support, that medicalization superseded morality as the primary mode of the social regulation of sexuality over the course of the twentieth century (Davidson 1987; Foucault 1978). By the 1960s, the understanding of homosexuality as a matter best handled by medical professionals had become ubiquitous, and various psychological therapies were applied in attempts to control, if not "cure," those who were diagnosed as homosexual. One remedy regarded as promising in the sixties was a type of behavior modification called aversion therapy. A patient would be given an injection of apomorophine, which produced nausea while he (less frequently she) was shown images of individuals of the same sex. Or the patient received a jolt of electricity after reading a series of descriptions of homosexual behavior, followed by reading passages describing heterosexual behavior without any shock (Nathaniel McConaghy, quoted in Alinder [1970] 1992, 143). In effect, the doctors who practiced this therapy hoped to reconfigure what they understood to be a neurological stimulus-response mechanism.

More conservative—and more common—treatments were various talking cures, which may have been more insidious than the overt cruelty of electroshock or injections of noxious chemicals because the patient was expected to assume responsibility for failure if homosexual desires could not be eradicated. In all but a very few instances they could not. Feelings of guilt and shame were oft-cited consequences of such ordeals. While it is quite likely that many gay men and lesbians may not have believed that they suffered from mental illness, the heterosexual imperative was so rigorously enforced through a variety of cultural and legal mechanisms that self-perceptions became moot. Personal narratives from the preliberation era in twentieth-century North America and Europe are riddled with accounts of gay men and lesbians seeking professional help to rid themselves of homosexual desires and of minors whose parents imposed psychiatric treatment upon them.[15]

Homosexuality, it can be said, was (and in some places, still is) a disqualified identity, at the same time that it was an illicit practice. This was addressed cryptically in the founding principles and purposes of GLF, which asserted, "We are going to be who we are" (*Come Out* 1970, 2). While indicating the importance of self-definition to the movement, strategists never questioned accepted concepts of what a *self* is, assuming that it is (we are) unified, governed by self-awareness, author of its (our) own desires and actions. Instead of encouraging debate about such fundamental notions of the self, they concentrated on redefining homosexuality as a *valid* category of personhood. To accomplish this, the enemy was identified—psychologists, psychiatrists, and the media that popularized their ideas—and scientific expertise on homosexuality was forcefully challenged.

One of the most dramatic actions taken by gay liberation activists was an invasion of the annual meeting of the American Psychiatric Association (APA) in 1970 (Alinder [1970] 1992). The intruders declared solidarity with the antipsychiatry movement spearheaded by former patients in mental hospitals and inspired by the writings of radical psychiatrists like the Marxist–humanist David Cooper (1967; 1968) and R. D. Laing (1967), whose approach was based on phenomenology. Jill Johnston, for one, applauded this development, which she predicted would result in a "comprehensive political-psychological theory and counter consciousness that will be a more effective subversive deviation from the patriarchal authoritative hierarchical law enforcement reality oriented materialistic sexually repressive fucked up culture in which we live" (Johnston 1974, 256). In the short term, this promise was actualized, since challenges to the psychiatric profession provided gay liberation with one of its first victories: in 1973 the APA agreed to remove homosexuality from its list of approved diagnoses in the *Diagnostic and Statistical Manual*. And in 1980, gay activists and sympathetic professionals defeated an attempt to reintroduce a comparable diagnostic category.

Therapists began to advertise their acceptance of homosexuality almost as soon as the movement was launched, and a number of lesbians and gay men established professional practices geared specifically to helping others regard their homosexuality in a positive light. The gay press ran columns dealing with psychological issues. For example, *Gay* regularly published commentary and advice by psychologist Dr. Stephen Kaiso under the heading "The Well of Possibility," signaling the movement's rejection of Radclyffe Hall's conclusion that loneliness is the inevitable consequence of homosexuality. In addition, many of the activities sponsored by the newly constituted lesbian and gay organizations—the recitation of individual coming out stories in writings by members of the movement, and in less formal settings, as well as cultural events intended to instill pride in lesbian/gay identity and camaraderie—can be understood as therapeutic. Talk shows and magazine articles offered opportunities for lesbian and gay liberationists to confront their psychiatric foes in public forums, since mental health was the preferred frame for media coverage of homosexuality, even after gay liberation proclaimed the rejection of medical expertise.[16]

Retrospective accounts of gay liberation have described the first organizations as riddled by divisions. Histories of the movement recall how lines were drawn and positions staked out that pitted politics against culture, street demonstrations and militant confrontations against social companionship and pleasure—dancing and psychedelic drugs being two of the favorite diversions offered, in addition to opportunities for sex, at GLF social events—and political revolution against tolerance of gay and lesbian lifestyles (Jay 1999; Marotta 1981).[17] But, from the start, the political rationale for coming out entailed cultural justifications, and both promised to promote personal well-being, conceived as self-awareness and self-expression. The Radicalesbians summed up the goal as "real-ness, feel[ing] at last that we are coinciding with ourselves," leading to "a revolution to end the imposition of all coercive identifications, and to achieve maximum autonomy in human expression" (Radicalesbians [1970] 1973, 245). The slogan "gay is good," echoed the Black Pride movement's "black is beautiful." And Warshawsky and Bedoz underlined the political effects that would follow: "We will no longer mutilate our true self-potential in an attempt to measure up to false 'norms'. In liberating ourselves from our shame we make our first attack upon the system" (Warshawsky and Bedoz 1970). It doesn't seem an exaggeration to say that the new gay politics and the cultural counterpart made self-esteem a first principle.

Paradoxically, this kind of rhetoric connects the objectives of gay liberation with what Foucault designated "governmentality" or "mentalities of government," which characterize liberal modernity (Burchell, Gordon, and Miller 1991; Foucault 1994). In his elaboration of this concept, Rose points out that governmentality does not refer to state power alone but can be applied to any ethical system that seeks to "act upon the lives of each and all in order to avert evils and achieve such desirable states as health, happiness, wealth, and tranquillity" (N. Rose 1998, 152). Although we may be inclined to interpret any notion of liberation as inherently opposed to the coercive practices of government, Foucault and Rose argue that the kind of subjectivity characteristic of modern Western democracies—the autonomous self—is

Martha Shelley at the Oscar Wilde Bookstore in New York City. Photograph by Diana Davies, New York Public Library, Manuscripts and Archives Division.

itself an exercise of disciplinary authority that places ever more responsibility on individuals to monitor and regulate their own deeds and beliefs, to know and improve themselves, to become self-governing. How is this achieved? Major resources for governmentality are what Rose refers to as the "psy" disciplines and technologies—psychology, psychiatry, psychotherapy, psychoanalysis, "through which self-governing capabilities can be installed in free individuals in order to bring their own ways of conducting and evaluating themselves into alignment with political objectives" (155).

The gay liberation movement attracted notice for its scandalous impulses and intentions, with provocateurs like Shelley throwing down the gauntlet to straight folks with such statements as "We want to reach the homosexual entombed in you, to liberate our brothers and sisters, locked in the prisons of your skulls" (Shelley [1970] 1992). In settling on strategies that emphasized psychological factors, though, movement strategists were mainly concerned with shifting the realm of expertise from accredited professionals to individuals. In Rose's analysis this is characteristic of modern subjectivity in general: "[E]ach of us has *become* a psychologist, incorporating its vocabulary into our

way of speaking, its gaze into our ways of looking, its judgments into our calculations and decisions" (N. Rose 1998, 123). Likewise, the significance of
coming out, routinely explained as an individually accomplished antidote for
internalized guilt, fear, shame, and the lack of integrated sense of self, situates
this practice as a "therapeutic technology of the self," which involves techniques
for cultivating self-respect and developing a suitable identity narrative (195).

Self-image assumes an central position in such projects. The very first
issue of *Come Out* featured a piece entitled "A Positive Image for the
Homosexual." Written by psychologist Leo Louis Martello, who became a
regular contributor to the paper, the article offers a vision of gay liberation
that reflects concerns about its symbolic representation: "Homosexuality is
not a problem in itself. The problem is society's attitude toward it. Since the
majority condemns homosexuality, the homosexual minority has passively
accepted this contemptuous view of itself. . . . The greatest battle of the
homosexual in an oppressive society is with himself [*sic*], more precisely the
image of himself as forced upon him by non-homosexuals" (Martello 1969).

Thus, the demand that media institutions replace negative stereotypes
with positive images emerged as a central feature of lesbian and gay liberation politics early on. The importance accorded positive images stems from
their presumed truthfulness, as opposed to the pathological depictions of lesbians and gay men the liberation (later, civil rights) movement deemed mali-
cious falsehoods. The first candidates for exemplary standard-bearers might
include such bohemian, countercultural icons as Johnston, but once the heyday of confrontational liberation politics had passed—by the mid-1970s—
the ideal positive image took on a more respectable cast. And the argument
for such images became more specific: wide publication and broadcasting of
positive images would render homosexuality socially legitimate.

Underlying both approaches, though, a more important kind of realism
was at stake: all famous lesbians and gay men were called upon to endorse the
truth of self-knowledge attained through coming out and crafting a self-
image that reflects pride and self-possession. These positive images were
defined as realistic representations of self-affirming lesbians and gay men,
who then provide role models worthy of emulation by the next generation.
Once again, however, the influence of functionalist paradigms of socialization
and roles can be detected in the efficacy accorded positive images, as well as
the related idea of role models. What, exactly, is modeled as the result of
exposure to an image (visual or linguistic) of a self-proclaimed lesbian? Is it
simply that the role model is not closeted, and therefore not ashamed of her

lesbianism? Is that a role? What possible function could such a role serve? An obvious place to look for an answer might be Mary MacIntosh's article "The Homosexual Role" (1968), which explains how this deviant role enforces hetero-masculine norms and is not a social position accepted by all, or even most men who actually engage in homosexual practices. MacIntosh criticizes the normative function of the disreputable and marginal role she describes, confirming the connection between role theory and functionalist ways of thinking. In contrast, subsequent discussions about role models and positive images have overlooked the linkage between these concepts and their conservative sources, and are thus limited to attempts to pour new homosexual wine into old structural-functionalist bottles.

Another, more productive way to think about this question is to consider the pressures brought to bear on social norms, for instance by women who do not conform to feminine standards. Add to that the emergence in the nineteenth century of what Ian Hacking calls "a particular medico-forensic-political language of individual and social control," which employed the newly developed scientific technique of statistical analysis to define forms of deviance and rendered norms meaningful (Hacking 1986, 226). In this environment, a new kind of person, a new social identity was minted, the lesbian. Now, the process of making up people that Hacking describes is dynamic, neither wholly the contrivance of forces of social control nor an innovation by nonconformists. Instead, both interact and react in the process of producing the definition of a lesbian person. This approach allows for improvisations for which the static and determinist logic of role theory cannot account.

Commenting on how the generation of new kinds of people affects individuals, Hacking remarks, "Who we are is not only what we did, do, and will do but also what we might have done and may do. Making up people changes the space of possibilities for personhood" (229). For instance, at the beginning of the twenty-first century we can define ourselves as transgendered, transsexual, lesbian, female homosexual, bisexual, heterosexual, or any combination of these. And we do not require a medical expert to verify the definitions. A self-determined categorization carries sufficient authority. But, in spite of these proliferating options, Hacking reminds us, "our possibilities, although inexhaustible, are also bounded" (ibid.), bounded, first of all, by prevailing concepts of how subjectivity can be achieved and lived, how personhood is constituted.

By the end of the 1960s, lesbians, along with gay men, created a political movement that promised to remove all barriers that cordoned them off from participation in social institutions. Talk of liberation was not just a rhetorical gesture; activists of this period were committed to the ideal of freedom and their ability to realize it. But one of the most formidable boundaries they didn't take into account was precisely that imposed by notions of personal freedom, which were then and remain central to the concept and practice of coming out. Intended as a technique for achieving personal liberation through collective identification, coming out became contingent upon and supported by a paradigm of subjectivity—self-knowledgeable and self-assured—that emphasizes "mental health" above all. The privileging of coming out suggested that political solidarity with other lesbians can only be attained by ridding oneself of any trace of self-loathing, which is assumed to be characteristic of the condition of being a lesbian in the first place.

The type of lesbian person who would be produced through a combination of self-examination and self-approbation was seen as the antidote to the despised and therefore depressed, self-hating lesbian described by definitions of homosexual pathology. The vocabulary and techniques of psychological diagnoses and treatment could be used to convince the leery that release from self-contempt is worth the risk of being regarded as deviant. Moreover, coming out has been undertaken not only as a project of self-validation but also self-fashioning. Rose describes this process as becoming an entrepreneur of the self, "seeking to maximize its own powers, its own happiness, its own quality of life, though enhancing its autonomy and then instrumentalizing its autonomous choices in the service of its life-style" (N. Rose 1998, 158). It wasn't that lesbians were supposed to become "normal," co-opted by the culture that had disparaged them, but the gay and women's movements crafted an approach to lesbian identity that can be interpreted as the fullest, most ambitious realization of this entrepreneurial character.

However, the idea of lesbian identity itself has produced a welter of theoretical challenges from feminist and gay thinkers, who point out the problems that accompany any fixed notion of this kind of person. As Judith Butler, one of the most thoughtful and provocative among such theorists, asks, "If to be a lesbian is an act, a leave-taking of heterosexuality, a self-naming that contests the compulsory meanings of heterosexuality's women and men, what is to keep the name of lesbian from becoming an equally compulsory category? What qualifies as a lesbian? Does anyone know?" (Butler 1990, 127). The category may not be clear-cut, and attempts to give it definitive meaning have produced as much political rancor as unity. Yet, the dilemmas created by the notion of lesbian identity have been taken beyond the

Rita Mae Brown (right) and other participants in the Radicalesbians' Lavender Menace action at the Second Congress to United Women in 1970. Photograph by Diana Davies, New York Public Library, Manuscripts and Archives Division.

subcultural level, to the pages of large circulation print and broadcast media, occasioned by the trickle-up effect of coming out. The logic of coming out, which rests on the belief that sexuality is a basic—perhaps *the* basic—dimension of subjectivity, combined with an entrepreneurial concept of individual existence, made lesbian celebrity feasible.

INDIVIDUAL INITIATIVE

What lesbian celebrity would become, or that such personages were possible in the first place, was anticipated in the career of one veteran of the militant lesbian liberation movement I have mentioned several times—a prime mover in the Lavender Menace action and coauthor of the clarion call for radical lesbian revolution, "The Woman-Identified Woman"—as well as one of the vociferous critics of celebrity in its ranks: Rita Mae Brown. By the end of the 1970s, Brown had moved from the underground success of her first novel, *Rubyfruit Jungle* ([1973] 1977), issued by the small feminist press Daughters Inc., into the world of major publishing houses, mainstream publicity, and widespread notoriety. Never shy, Brown encouraged her racy reputation by identifying herself as the model for *Rubyfruit* bad-girl, hot-lesbian protagonist Molly Bolt. Although it seems accurate to say that her subcultural reputation acted as a springboard to the larger public stage, this move was not generally duplicated by many of her contemporaries from the lesbian liberation days.[18] Nor could Brown's celebrity have been predicted by her political history or the writings she produced as a movement firebrand: essays that castigated respectable, middle-class feminists (1976) and a collection of poems with the incendiary title *The Hand That Cradles the Rock* (1971). In 1972, she had proclaimed in print that "star rip-offs must be stopped." By 1978, she and her supporters were knocking on the doors of Hollywood studios with hopes of bringing *Rubyfruit* to the big screen, presumably with a star or starlet playing the leading character based on Brown herself (Rubyfruit Jungle Productions n.d.).[19] And by 1980, her status as a famous lesbian, in the United States anyway, focused the attention of the tabloid press and their paparazzi stringers on the lesbian sexuality of a rising star in another cultural arena: tennis player Martina Navratilova.

Despite the fact that the affair between Brown and Navratilova was made public when they were spotted together at the Wimbledon tournament and photographed by reporters from British tabloids, then made the object of much broader publicity that reached readers around the world, this liaison did not manage to render Navratilova a lesbian celebrity—yet. Eventually, she became the most famous lesbian in the world, a prototype of lesbian celebrity. A closer look at the twists and turns in the path leading to her stardom is the topic of chapter 6. As a conclusion to this one, suffice it to say that radical lesbians may have railed against stars, but eventually celebrity culture caught up with the movement. Or, it could be said, the movement's politics of coming out converged with cultural definitions of celebrity. None of this occurred overnight but over several decades, nor has it proceeded without dispute— legal, political, cultural. But the seeds of this development were sown in the initial formulations of what liberation would mean.

CHAPTER FIVE

IN RETROSPECT

LEGENDS OF MERCEDES DE ACOSTA AND COMPANY

Even though lesbian celebrity is a recent phenomenon, it is quite easy to assert that there have been celebrities in the past who were lesbian, or perhaps bisexual, without encountering too much opposition. Since the early years of the lesbian and gay liberation movement, the lesbian/gay press has made repeated efforts to establish the enduring presence of lesbians in Western culture. To this end, publications devoted considerable space to profiles of such famous lesbians as Radclyffe Hall, Gertrude Stein, and Djuna Barnes, who achieved wide recognition earlier in the century. Of course, members of the movement researched even more remote epochs in the quest for ancestral lesbians. In this spirit, the first issue of the *Furies* included a lengthy article on Queen Christina, the seventeenth-century Swedish monarch, an odd choice given the antielitist stance of the radical lesbian publishing collective (H. Harris 1972). More interesting yet is their choice to illustrate the article with photographs of Greta Garbo playing Christina in the 1933 Hollywood biopic but without mentioning Garbo's underground reputation as a lesbian. Either the author and editors were unaware of this, or they decided not to contradict denials of homosexuality by the famously reclusive movie star, who was still alive. In 1972, when the article appeared, her disavowal was enough to make any attribution suspect. Today the kind of ambiguity Garbo engaged in would be chalked up to prevarication, however forgiving of this we may be. Celebrities from earlier eras are not evaluated according to our present-day standards, since we are aware that they lived and worked at a time when coming out was either not an option or "lesbian" accepted as a valid social identity.

In many respects, famous dead or retired actresses and other entertainers constitute a distinct category within the pantheon of lesbian celebrity. Because they climbed the ladder to stardom without submitting to social dictates—what Adrienne Rich (1980) and others have called compulsory heterosexuality, in particular—they are hailed as courageous. More importantly, the discovery of lesbian histories involving standard icons of glamour and charisma promises to give contemporary lesbians an impressive ancestry, which was previously hidden or censored but can now be made public. Once we can say, without being dismissed as deluded, that Greta Garbo, say, was a lesbian, the presupposition of a cultural idol's heterosexuality will be undermined and homophobia counteracted. Additionally, the disclosure of the secrets of dead lesbian celebrities appears to support the understanding of lesbian history as a linear narrative of progress—from oppression to emancipation, from self-loathing to pride.

I intend to challenge that model of history and the overstatement of invisibility in earlier times that it requires. For these purposes, I offer the example of Mercedes de Acosta: born in 1893, died in 1968, poet, novelist, playwright, Hollywood screenwriter, journalist, and amateur spiritualist. What makes de Acosta a compelling figure for a study of lesbian celebrity is the breadth of her social—and amorous—connections, which she chronicled in her memoir *Here Lies the Heart* (1960), which has become a much-cited source of information, anecdote, and innuendo concerning the lesbian lives of a number of very visible women in twentieth-century American culture. And she never lived what we would call a closeted life, although in committing her life's story to print she attempted to fabricate one retrospectively.

MAKING A NAME

Like lesbian celebrities in general, de Acosta presents something of an enigma, provoking more interest from historical researchers in the past dozen years than she ever did during her lifetime. Undoubtedly, her enhanced renown stems from the combination of her verifiable lesbianism and her familiarity with just about every accomplished actress on Broadway and in Hollywood, as well as ballet dancers, opera divas, cabaret singers, music hall and vaudeville performers, from about 1915 to the late 1940s. Her friends and acquaintances also included Amy Lowell, Marie Laurencin, Noël Coward, Igor Stravinsky, Alice B. Toklas, Jean Cocteau, Cole Porter, and Cecil Beaton. I doubt, however, that anyone would regard de Acosta as role model material, either before her death in 1968, at age seventy-five, or now. True, many might envy her affairs with Isadora Duncan, Alla Nazimova, Eva Le Gallienne, Greta Garbo, and Marlene Dietrich, just to name a few of her more eminent lovers. But being a lesbian Lothario is not the stuff of which role models are made, which suggests that exemplary status can only be attained by a sanitized kind of lesbian whose sexual desires remain incidental, at best. In other words, de Acosta demonstrates an unspoken assumption: the role model is expected to inspire productive endeavor, not evoke scenes of sybaritic pleasure.

So, Mercedes may not be a model lesbian, if setting an example for social acceptability is the standard, but her legend offers a particularly intriguing perspective on the affiliations between twentieth-century celebrity and lesbian culture, one that role models—and the positive images they are said to generate—cannot accommodate. But she has acquired her posthumous fame precisely because her very visible lesbian persona acts as a divining rod pointing toward a number of lesbians occupying neither marginal nor subcultural positions but residing at the center of U.S. popular culture. That does not mean that de Acosta ever publicly proclaimed her lesbianism, although how and why she demurred on this point is not consistent with a narrative of shameful subterfuge or outright denial. No, de Acosta, like twentieth-century celebrities in general, lived according to the precepts of spectacle, and the mustering of appearances, fantasies, and seductions needed to produce it.

Indeed, theater was de Acosta's vocation, although not always her profession. And her background may have predisposed her for a dramatic life. Her mother came from an aristocratic Spanish family and in the mid-nineteenth century inherited a large fortune, although she underwent considerable hardship before she was able to retrieve the estate from a wicked uncle who had stolen it. Her father, also born into the Spanish upper class, narrowly escaped execution by a firing squad by diving off a cliff into the sea that borders on Havana's notorious Moro prison, following his capture as part of a student rebellion against the Cuban government; later he became a successful businessman. They were introduced and married in New York City, where they raised eight children in high style—Mercedes was the youngest—but were extremely careless with money. Her father committed suicide; her mother died almost penniless. As an adult, de Acosta lived for many years in Hollywood, although she was not an actress but worked as a screenwriter whose scripts were never produced. Prior to her career in the movie industry, she was a familiar figure in New York art and intellectual circles, a playwright as well as a poet and novelist, but only two of her plays were ever produced in the United States. One, *Sandro Botticelli* (1923), was an unqualified failure. The other, *Jacob Slovak* (1927), had a very short Broadway run due to a series of production miscalculations and mishaps, and, despite positive reviews, an indifferent public.[1] She published several volumes of poetry (de Acosta 1919, 1921, 1922) and two novels (de Acosta 1920, 1928), but her literary career never took off.

Thus, a quibbler could say, de Acosta wasn't *really* a celebrity, not even in her prime. She may have been granted occasional notice by prominent syndicated society gossips like Cholly Knickerbocker (1935) and Elsa Maxwell (1943).[2] But she was most frequently mentioned as an adjunct to her glamorous older sister, Rita de Acosta Lydig, who was considered to be one of the most beautiful, stylish, and artistically cultivated women of her day.[3] Although, like Rita, Mercedes's appearance attracted attention, she was more likely to be called striking or exotic than beautiful. Still, she shared with her sister a lack of interest in keeping up with fashion; they both expected others to catch up with them instead. In order to express her particular sensibility, Mercedes created a signature costume, for many years wearing only black or white clothing, a topcoat with a tight waist and circular skirt custom made for her by the Paris couturier Paul Poiret, shoes with oversized buckles, and a tricorn hat or beret. She also wore trousers long before this was common, and at times a cape, recalling the Spanish outfits favored by Radclyffe Hall.

Not surprisingly, Mercedes became something of a public personage, based in part on her social position coupled with her unorthodox appearance, as well as on the people with whom she associated. Garbo was undoubtedly the most prominent, and her friendship with de Acosta was especially notable because the actress's reputation for unsociability was legend. Rebecca West could allude to de Acosta in a Los Angeles newspaper review of a stage play and assume that her readers would understand the reference (West 1932).[4] Perhaps the biggest boost to de Acosta's celebrity status was the success of her autobiography, *Here Lies the Heart*, which became a best-seller upon publication in 1960, with sales benefiting, no doubt, from the praise she received in influential newspapers like the *New York Times* (Todd 1960) and the *Herald Tribune* (Field 1960). *Newsweek* also devoted half a page to a photo feature on the book, captioned by a brief but tantalizing text: "Greta Garbo, the professional enigma, once spent a memorable six weeks alone with her on a tiny islet in a mountain lake. She has been a friend of Isadora Duncan, of Marlene Dietrich, of Stravinsky, of Cole Porter, and scores of others whose names are

Portrait of
Mercedes de
Acosta, by Abram
Poole, 1923. Santa
Barbara Museum
of Art, gift of
Mercedes de
Acosta in honor of
Ala Story.

now liberally dropped by her in her memoirs. Her own name: Mercedes de Acosta—poet and playwright" (*Newsweek* 1960). Maybe the best way to characterize Mercedes would be as a *minor* celebrity, just as she called herself a "minor poet" (de Acosta 1960, 102), but *avant-garde* lesbian celebrity might also fit. And to add to her credentials in this arena, she could be described also as an expert on celebrity culture in her time.[5]

THE IN CROWD

Although de Acosta recalled waiting with other children outside the stage door of a Broadway theater to receive a souvenir thimble from the legendary Maude Adams after a performance of *Peter Pan*, most of her early introductions to celebrities were made by either Rita or her mentor, Elisabeth (Bessie) Marbury. In fact, she first met Marbury, a playwrights' representative and theatrical impresario, through Rita. Both older women were members of New York elite society and hosted salons that drew prominent artists, writers, and other intellectuals of their day (one of their mutual friends, for example, was Sarah Bernhardt). Marbury was also a lesbian, almost forty years de Acosta's senior, and the younger woman profited from her friendship in numerous instances. For instance, it was Bessie who arranged Mercedes's first Hollywood screenwriting assignment in 1931, a script for Pola Negri entitled *East River*. Unlike Lydig, whose life was occupied with creating tasteful environments for herself and her guests, as well as assembling a peerless wardrobe, Marbury dedicated herself to a public life, building a theatrical agency and engaging in electoral politics in her later years. She adhered to utterly conventional bourgeois standards when it came to appearances although not in her very aggressive style of doing business. Her companion and lover for most of her adult life, Elsie de Wolfe, was similarly ambitious, although de Wolfe's métier was closer to Lydig's. She started out as an actress famous for the latest Paris fashions she wore as costumes but not for her acting ability and after leaving the stage became the one of the first and most influential interior decorators in the United States.[6]

   Thus, both Marbury and de Wolfe were early twentieth-century pioneers in what today we call image management or public relations. Both excelled in promoting spectacles for popular consumption. Marbury figured out that she could procure free advertising for her ventures by providing the press with attractive and plentiful photos, accompanied by interesting copy, while de Wolfe did the same on her own behalf (Lewis 2000; Marbury 1923; Smith

1982). They met in 1886, when Marbury was just beginning to represent such popular French playwrights as Jacques Feydeau and Victorien Sardou in the United States and de Wolfe was receiving respectable notices in the society press for her appearances in amateur theatricals. By the end of the nineteenth century Marbury was a powerful international broker of plays (one client was George Bernard Shaw) and later engineered various performers' careers (e.g., the dance team Vernon and Irene Castle), commissioned stage productions (including Jerome Kern's first musical), organized lecture tours (by, among others, Oscar Wilde and Count Robert de Montesquiou-Fezesnac, the model for Proust's homosexual Baron de Charlus), and was one of the first women to serve on the National Committee of the Democratic Party. De Wolfe, meanwhile, found employment on the professional stage, aided in large part by her lover's connections, but quit in 1905, when she embarked on her decorating career. Marbury came from a prominent New York family, whereas de Wolfe had a less secure foothold in high society, but both women were determined to become financially independent—and did. In fact, they both prospered and amassed considerable wealth. Yet, they were very different in one respect: Bessie excelled in promoting other people's reputations, while Elsie's renown came largely from cultivating her own and convincing others of her rightful claim as a trendsetter.

Marbury and de Wolfe made no secret of their relationship within their social circle. Apparently, they were called "the Bachelors" by their friends (Smith 1982, 50). How they represented themselves in more public contexts was another matter. For instance, in her autobiography, *My Crystal Ball* (1923), Marbury dwells on her close friendships with homosexual men like playwright Clyde Fitch (best known for the Broaday hit *Beau Brummell*) and actor Clifton Webb but never mentions their sexuality (although in Fitch's case, she does allude to this aspect of his character). She also takes pride in her association with Oscar Wilde and even boasts about selling his *Ballad of Reading Gaol* to the New York *World* when no British publisher would touch it.[7] At the same time, however, she distances herself from his highly public prosecution for sexual crimes, commenting, "His was a clear case of psycho-perversity . . . it would have been a more humane thing to have him placed under the care of physicians rather than to have delivered him over to jailers" (Marbury 1923, 99). It is not clear whether this comment was meant to quell speculations about her own sexuality or whether she regarded her love for de Wolfe as entirely different in kind from male homoeroticism. On the next page Marbury castigates Wilde not for his homosexuality but for his monu-

mental egotism and "lack of common sense" (100). Weighing these contradictory statements, it seems that her main complaint is that Wilde hadn't
been more discreet. As de Acosta recalled of her friend, Marbury loved a
"spicy" joke (de Acosta 1960, 71), and by her own account she was not a
prude.[8] On the basis of her exuberant autobiography, it is reasonable to sur-
mise that Marbury did not see herself as in any way prey to unnatural desires.

Furthermore, in her autobiographical discussion of her relationship with
de Wolfe, she makes no effort to disguise their intimacy. Indeed, she dedicated the book to Elsie, adding these words as an epigraph: "Together we sor-
rowed. Together we rejoiced. Together we failed. Together we succeeded. . . . "
Along with the insistence of these multiple "together"s and her fond portrayal of their relationship of thirty odd years, Marbury included a photograph of a sitting room in one of their homes bearing the caption "The
Marbury-de Wolfe Residence," a double portrait of the two women, and a
close-up image of de Wolfe, all testimony to her importance in Marbury's life
story. Nevertheless, Marbury seems compelled to explain why she never married. Her answer, though, is cursory, almost flippant: "I never had a really
good offer" (Marbury 1923, 35).

Marbury's memoir was published in 1923, when she was sixty-seven
years old; she died in 1933. Like her former lover, de Wolfe also wrote and
published an autobiography, in 1935, although by the time she did so the now
renowned decorator and taste maker had produced her own solution to the
inevitable marriage question and the suspicions that informed it. In 1926, at
age sixty, she married a British peer, Sir Charles Mendl. However, she notes
coyly, "[T]he marriage created something of a sensation at home and abroad.
For some reason or other . . . my friends . . . had never thought of either of us
as the marrying kind" (de Wolfe 1935, 217). From her friends' perspective,
the reason for astonishment is obvious, although de Acosta tells us that
Marbury was less astonished than heartbroken (de Acosta 1960, 207).[9] After
World War I, de Wolfe and Marbury spent very little time together and had
developed different interests, entertained different friends, and even preferred
to live in different countries (de Wolfe spent many months of each year at the
house in Versailles she and Marbury bought and renovated together), but
there had been no unqualified rupture. Nor does de Wolfe go to great lengths
to clarify for the reader's benefit the discrepancy between her decision to
marry and the many years she lived with Marbury. Writing about Bessie, she
recounts in detail their initial encounters and growing affection, as well as the
pleasures of setting up housekeeping together. She also paraphrases conver-

Bessie Marbury and Elsie de Wolfe
at home in New York City.

sations between them that include such endearments as "honey" and never
disguises the fact that they were deeply committed to one another.

Nonetheless, de Wolfe inserted an account, entirely fictional it turns out,
of a long-term but also long-distance love affair with an unnamed man, just
in case her marriage late in life would not adequately offset the impression
left by the descriptions of the Marbury–de Wolfe alliance. It is quite possible
that when she decided to tell her life story in public at age seventy, Lady
Mendl, née Elsie de Wolfe, might have wanted to refurbish her image by giving herself a long-standing heterosexual pedigree. A convincing interpretation of the fable has been provided by de Wolfe's biographer Jane Smith, who
describes this fib as "the first visible twinge of concern over her reputation"
(Smith 1982, 267).[10] Although an outright avowal of lesbianism in 1933
would have been too outrageous, even for the proudly unconventional de
Wolfe, this feint seems uncharacteristic of such an otherwise outspoken,
unapologetic woman. Most likely, she agreed with the prevalent belief that
great women who would be remembered for their contributions to culture

were not lesbians—Gertrude Stein, perhaps, being the exception but not one that de Wolfe regarded as worthy of emulation. And although de Wolfe's reticence about her sexuality could be compared to refusals to be relegated to an identity pigeonhole that are common today, the timing of her manufactured straightness must be seen in the context of specific historical circumstances quite different from the present. In the mid-1930s, the idea of lesbianism as a psychological disorder, as well as a form of social deviance, had become firmly entrenched in medical theories and practices, and accepted on a popular level as well. Lesbians might not have agreed with these judgments, but attitudes that condemned lesbianism remained practically unassailable in public contexts.

SOULS OF DISCRETION

The twelve years separating Marbury's and de Wolfe's autobiographies—the early 1920s to the mid-1930s—were a time of significant changes in lesbian (and gay) culture. This period also coincided with de Acosta's third decade of life, during which her associations with various celebrities were cemented and love affairs with several occurred—including her five years with Eva Le Gallienne and her liaison with Gladys Calthrop, Noël Coward's set and costume designer, who had been involved with Eva, too. De Acosta lived in the thick of the New York theater community, and her reflections on the era give a sense of the prevailing cultural climate, as well as her own approving attitude toward it:

> [D]uring these years the young . . . kicked over the last vestiges of
> Victorian influence which had circumscribed and inhibited their lives.
> They escaped from the influence of that old lady who had made hyp-
> ocrites of more than a generation. Now at last impulses concealed or sup-
> pressed were allowed to assert themselves, and young people of both sexes,
> thrilled with their new personal freedom, bounded out into the open.
> Who can blame them if they sometimes bounded a little too high and
> sometimes fell a little too low? (de Acosta 1960, 68)

For de Acosta, Michael Arlen's popular and controversial play *The Green Hat*, starring Katharine Cornell in the 1924 Broadway production, summed up the Zeitgeist: "It was a play in which the heroine was utterly reckless but always gallant. *Gallant* and *dangerous* were in a sense the passwords of the twenties. . . . At the end of *The Green Hat* Iris March gallantly drove her Hispano Suiza off a mountaintop" (de Acosta 1960, 128).[11]

One aspect of the free-spirited ambience in cosmopolitan cities like New York during the 1920s was the erosion of the previously well maintained boundaries between the homosexual subcultures—based mainly in Greenwich Village, Harlem, and the Times Square district—and fashionable society. Assuming the stance of a disinterested observer, in a draft of her memoirs de Acosta took note of the increasingly eroticized quality of urban life, in New York in particular (although she removed all the homosexual references in what she published):

> Everyone rushed up to Harlem at night to sit around places thick with smoke and the smell of bad gin, where Negroes "in drag" danced around with each other until the small hours of the morning. What we all saw in it is difficult to understand now. I suppose it was the newly found excitement of homosexuality, which after the war was expressed openly in nightclubs and cabarets by boys dressed as women, and was, like drinking, forbidden and subject to police raids, which made it all the more enticing. (de Acosta Papers)

She also wrote about similar themes in relation to a 1929 trip to Berlin, accompanied by Calthrop and "several young men," where they saw female prostitutes "on the streets [who] were actually men" and "women who dressed and looked exactly like men" (de Acosta Papers).

As these comments suggest, homosexual culture in the 1920s had attained a degree of conscious publicness, which, as historian George Chauncey Jr. has noted, contradicts received ideas about the furtiveness of gay lives prior to the 1970s (Chauncey 1994). Similarly, the temptation to read Marbury's or de Wolfe's autographic gestures towards heterosexuality as evidence of their being "in the closet" must be reconsidered as not only historically inaccurate but also reductive. When both autobiographies appeared, the metaphor of the closet that has become shorthand for the strategies adopted to mask homosexual desires and identities was unknown. Instead, Chauncey writes, in the first half of the twentieth century lesbians and gay men described themselves as living a "double life," which

> allowed them to have jobs and status a queer would have been denied while still participating in what they called "homosexual society" or "the

life." For some, the personal cost of "passing" was great. But for others it was minimal, and many men positively enjoyed having a "secret life" more complex and extensive than outsiders could imagine. Indeed, the gay life of many men was so full and wide-ranging that by the 1930s they used another—but more expansive—spatial metaphor: not the gay closet, but the *gay world*. (Chauncey 1994, 7)

"Coming out," too, had a different meaning when it was first coined. It was used in the context of the grand gay balls held in large halls in Harlem and midtown Manhattan, where an appearance in drag constituted a debut akin to a debutante's coming out into society.

Marbury and de Wolfe participated in a subdivision of the larger gay world that Chauncey writes about, an elite sector populated by members of high society and the entertainment professions, best exemplified by Marbury's close friend, neighbor, and partner in various charitable projects Anne Morgan, J. P.'s daughter, or de Wolfe's frequent visitors Cole Porter and Cecil Beaton. De Acosta kept the same or similar company. But by the late 1920s, the emancipated sexual mores de Acosta relished were under attack from various moral watchdogs, and rumblings of reaction began to stir. In 1927, the New York City police arrested the cast of Mae West's play *Sex*, as well as the actors in a Broadway hit dealing with lesbian love called *The Captive*. The Hearst newspapers campaigned for theater censorship using the latter play as justification. West's announcement that she intended to stage a play defending homosexuality, *The Drag*, on Broadway added fuel to the fire. Soon after, the New York State legislature passed an amendment to the state's public obscenity code that banned any plays "depicting or dealing with the subject of sex degeneracy, or sex perversion" (Chauncey 1994, 313). In the same year, threats of government regulation leveled at the major film studios to keep portrayals of sexuality—other than the hetero-and-destined-for-wedlock, or the already-married-and-monogamous kind—out of movie houses led to the establishment of the Hays office, a system of self-policing with little actual effect. Since no enforcement mechanism was implemented, what moralistic critics considered licentiousness continued and advocates of censorship persisted. In order to forestall legislation that would rein in on-screen sexuality the Hollywood studios agreed in 1934 to conform to a production code, which promised that the studios would censor themselves. The Code, as it was known, banned all sorts of explicit sexual expression and obvious innuendo in movies.

However, the most powerful factor in the chilling climate Chauncey cites as dampening homosexual expression in the United States and forcing lesbians and gay men into hiding from the early thirties to the late fifties did not involve new regulatory measures but was instead a consequence of the repeal of Prohibition. The apparently enlightened removal of the national ban on liquor sales proved less than felicitous for urban homosexual subcultures.When commerce in alcoholic drinks became legal once again in 1933, state control over public entertainments and amusements was asserted, very much to the detriment of lesbian and gay patrons. "Repeal made it possible for the state to redraw the boundaries of acceptable sociability that seemed to have been obliterated in the twenties . . . and literally criminalized much of gay sociability" (Chauncey 1994, 334–335). In many respects, the daily lives of Marbury, de Wolfe, and their friends were not nearly so constrained by social conventions and these changed conditions as were those of working- or middle-class lesbians. Still, the same standards of propriety expected of ordinary citizens applied to Elsie's and Bessie's public personae if they wanted to be taken seriously as social paragons. And they did, insofar as each woman presented her published life narrative as a template for an honorable career. Marbury, at least, did not invent a fictional male lover; she only tried to rationalize her unmarried status. In contrast, de Wolfe chose to publish her memoirs at the point when the closet was under construction (although the term itself wasn't used before the 1960s (Chauncey 1994, 6).

TATTLE TALES

Lesbians who were professional perfomers depended much more upon public esteem than either Marbury or de Wolfe and thus had to worry even more about having their names linked with what were regarded as abnormal sexual practices. For these actresses, dancers, and singers, celebrity required coming to terms with the segment of the publicity apparatus that often operated beyond their or their employers' control: the rapidly expanding profession of gossip writing, which matured, so to speak, with the media industries that disseminated it. By the end of the nineteenth century reports of goings-on in society circles became a staple of daily newspapers. In addition, *Town Topics*, a weekly paper devoted strictly to this kind of sensational journalism, first appeared in New York City in the 1880s and was augmented by two other gossip sheets, the *Tattler* and *Broadway Brevities and Social Gossip*. In their pages could be found news about the likes of Rita de Acosta Lydig and reviews of performances by amateur actors like Elsie de Wolfe. However, the attitudes toward press coverage adopted by the most prominent impresarios of the time, Broadway producers, differed considerably from those that are taken for granted today. Indeed, these showmen did not consider information about the private lives of their star performers a seemly focus for publicity. Discussing her experience with Daniel Frohman, the most powerful producer during this period (and one of Marbury's closest associates), the British music hall headliner Billie Burke commented, "[He] introduced me to New York quietly, avoiding publicity stunts, strictly forbidding me to appear in public or even see other plays. It was his Napoleonic principle that the illusions of the theatre would be shattered if the public saw too much or knew too much about the star" (Mosedale 1981, 31).

Frohman's wisdom was shared by respectable journalists and governed accepted practices until 1924, when Walter Winchell's popular column dishing out Broadway gossip first hit the streets. As Winchell's reputation grew, his stylistic innovations in reportage covering all facets of entertainment and high society also took hold. Certainly, his fingerprints can be found all over the pages of movie fan magazines, and his signature style of stringing together sentence fragments, spiced with slang and neologisms, separated only by ellipses, was copied by at least one, *Movie Mirror*. A few samples particularly relevant to the topic of lesbian celebrity provide examples of this feverish staccato style:

> Guess everything is hotsy-totsy again between Marlene (body-guarded) Dietrich and Joseph (Oedipus Rex) Von Sternberg [*sic*] . . . they attended the premiere together of 'Maedchen in Uniform' . . . Marlene wore that famous tailored suit once more . . . and lots of folks wish to gosh she'd start wearing dresses for a change and leave the pants to the men folk . . .

> . . . talking of that trip to Paris . . . Greta hit all the hot spots in Montmartre . . . even visiting a jernt where they have she-go-los to dance with the women tourists . . . but Greta didn't do any of tripping of the light fantastic. . . . (Busby 1933)

Hints of lesbian tendencies were not out of bounds for fan magazines, as this report of Garbo's consorting with "she-go-los" indicates, at least not in the early 1930s. Still, the easily deciphered allusion to lesbian culture in the item on Garbo is unusual, although the reported sighting of Dietrich in male attire is not.

The few references to de Acosta in such magazines are telling in this regard. Her presence in Hollywood, in Garbo's company, was duly noted, although the first time de Acosta was mentioned she remained an unnamed "woman companion" who went for daily hikes with Garbo in the Hollywood hills (*Modern Screen* 1931). It's unlikely that de Acosta's identity was a mystery to reporters keeping tabs on the movie star, whose every action was deemed newsworthy, but it may be that they were exercising caution when it came to trumpeting the name of someone who was not on the studios' promotional roster. Within a few months this reticence was abandoned, when the de Acosta–Garbo pair received less oblique coverage:

> Garbo has a new friend! And when Garbo becomes enough interested in anyone to have even a *rumored* friendship . . . it is news in Hollywood. This time it is Mercedes Acosta [*sic*] . . . a feminine writer imported from New York to write screen stories for Pola Negri. Miss Acosta is a very unusual lady . . . affecting Russian costumes . . . very white skin . . . strange and sometimes weird facial expressions. She was seen at Pola's beach party and her "different-ness" caused a great deal of excited comment. Her appearance is so distinctive that she can be compared to no one . . . perhaps that is what intrigues the never-so-friendly Swede. ("Film Gossip of the Month" 1931)

After another short interval they were again spotted together:

> [T]he lunchers at the Ambassador Hotel have been pleasantly surprised recently to . . . behold a very stylishly garbed young woman with a feminine companion laughing and gossiping at a nearby table. The young woman is none other than Aloof Garbo. . . . Her companion at luncheon was Mercedes Acosta [*sic*] and it is possible that they may have been talking about philosophy and such—but if so they must have hit on purely humorous angles, for they laughed considerably. (Bruce 1932)

Garbo's famous antipathy to fans' desires to know more about her (she reportedly burned unopened fan mail) has been interpreted in a variety of ways: cynics have wondered if her avoidance of publicity was a cunning public relations ploy intended to create an aura of mystery that elevated her above other glamorous but more accessible screen stars, while more recent commentators explain it as a frightened effort to keep her lesbian sexuality secret.[12] Clearly, Garbo's exceptional efforts to retain her privacy did not always succeed, although no publication mentioned a romantic or sexual component in her friendship with de Acosta.[13] As the report of Garbo's consorting with "she-go-los" indicates, however, hints about the star's lesbian activities managed to leak out.

Around the same time the fan magazines were getting off the ground, large circulation urban dailies introduced reports dealing with the movies. Louella Parsons, who was assigned to write a regular column on motion pictures at the *Chicago Herald-Record* in 1914, claimed to be the first full-time reporter working this beat. Eventually, through a series of relocations and the resolute patronage of William Randolph Hearst, Parsons became one of the primary sources and symbols of Hollywood gossip, rivaled only by her counterpart at the *Los Angeles Times*, Hedda Hopper.[14] Although ostensibly independent journalists, these writers relied as much on material fed them by studio publicists and press agents as on any other method of gathering the information that went into their articles. The author of a joint biography of Hopper and Parsons remarks, "[W]ithin the publicity departments of major studios such powerhouses as Hedda and Louella each had a man assigned to plant items at the top of their columns and another to place squibs at the bottom" (Eells 1972, 339). But these gossip writers were not passive mouthpieces for the studios, and could, if they chose, use their columns to attack a given star or studio production of which they disapproved. Hopper had no qualms about flaunting her power and was often remembered for a particularly wry remark about her home in Beverly Hills: "That's the house that fear built" (15).

In effect, the balance of power between Hopper and Parsons on one side and the studios on the other was a stalemate, with most actors caught between the two forces. Eventually, these two women came to stand for reactionary nationalism—both supported efforts to ferret out Communists and other "subversives" in Hollywood in the post–World War II period, much like the political direction Winchell took in the late 1940s—and they are remembered as "conservative, prudish, narrow-minded small-town women in an essentially conservative and prudish community, [who] used their gossip as a club to keep celebrities in line rather than as a needle to make celebrities scream" (Gabler 1994, 256). Nevertheless, Hopper was not above a bit of self-parody, like when she played herself as the archetypal rumormonger in the 1939 film *The Women*. Nor did either gossip columnist consistently use her privileged access to the public in order to simply enforce traditional morality.[15]

I began to question the power wielded by the gossip writers over terrified lesbian and gay Hollywoodites when I came across an intriguing line in

Here Lies the Heart. Recollecting a Christmas dinner she attended in 1932 at the Hollywood home of costume designer Adrian, de Acosta wrote, "I brought Marlene whom he had never met, and, together with Hedda Hopper and several other friends, we tried to evoke a Christmas spirit" (de Acosta 1960, 244–245). I wondered how Hopper, the consummate tattler, could attend this gathering without word about such queer goings on in Hollywood leaking to the public at large. But I couldn't find any evidence that it had. Or maybe the other guests were so adept at disguise that she would never guess. But further research contradicted both explanations. Hopper, it turns out, enjoyed the company of gay men, which explains her presence at Adrian's, whose homosexuality is now a matter of fact.[16] Moreover, as W. K. Martin writes, de Acosta and Dietrich "were unusually open about their affair. They entertained together, traveled together, and spent their days together when their schedules permitted" (W. K. Martin 1995, 95).

Martin interprets Dietrich's willingness to risk her movie career as testimony to her determination to resist a studio-imposed ideal of feminine propriety. The threat she faced was quite explicit. Dietrich, like every other actor working under contract for one of the Hollywood studios, was bound by a standard "morality clause," instituted in 1921. This clause mandated that "any actor or actress who commits any act tending to offend the community or outrage public morals and decency, will be given five days' notice of the cancellation of his contract" (York 1921). In practice, as it is now well-known, this meant not that actors refrained from activities that would violate the clause but that publicists were saddled with the task of keeping stories about such transgressions out of the press. Or they did their best to frighten lesser stars into excessive secrecy. Of course, if studio executives wanted to discipline a disobedient player, they could invoke the clause, but as far as major stars were concerned, this never happened. The studios had a greater interest in promoting the image of Hollywood as a wholesome, or at least law-abiding, community than in parading the misdemeanors of errant members before the public. For that reason, homosexuality was not only treated as a private matter but relegated to a realm of secrecy, in accord with the culture of the time. Of course, such acts of partition only ensured the public's fascination whenever the division between public and private knowledge became confounded, as often happens in celebrity discourse.

For de Acosta, the professional hazards of exposure were less onerous than for her actor friends and lovers, insofar as screenwriters who were not famous authors were virtually anonymous and therefore not newsworthy. On the other hand, with no husband or regular male escort in sight, combined with her conspicuous "different-ness," de Acosta's brazenness was perhaps more remarkable than Dietrich's. Quite deliberately, it seems, she projected an unambiguous lesbian image, which was met by equally willful oversight by the salaried traffickers in gossip. De Acosta's visibility therefore underscores Hedda Hopper's participation in the active production of "ignorance" about lesbians in Hollywood. As Eve Kosofsky Sedgwick points out, ignorance is never a blanket absence of knowledge—an absence that in sexual matters can easily be attributed to naïveté and remedied by infusions of enlightenment— but rather a structuring element in a particular regime of truth and power relations. Put simply, ignorance is an effect of power, and may also be an exercise of power (Sedgwick 1991, 4).

Apparently, de Acosta understood Hopper's power-knowledge game well if she dined in her company with her current lover (Dietrich, by all accounts, made little attempt to conceal her other sexual affairs, either). But the pact of secrecy between de Acosta, Dietrich, Adrian, and Hopper was meaningless without the collusion of various cultural apparatuses—the studios and theater producers, the press and press agents. And none of this would have worked without the participation of the celebrities themselves. Still, there is no doubt that de Acosta and her famous lesbian friends and acquaintances benefited from a sort of dispensation extended by the gossip press, whereby society women and very popular entertainers were allowed to be visible lesbians, as it were, without anyone ever using this word to describe them in a public forum. No moral or political commitment was required of gossip writers for them to embrace the code of silence. Above all, a self-imposed gag was professionally expendient at a time when scientific techniques of social regulation were gaining support in intellectual and political circles. In this context, mass culture was increasingly regarded as an important locus of social reproduction and therefore was called upon to foster cultural norms, which required condemnations of deviance and perversion. Gossip journalists working in this cultural climate acted, in effect, as public servants patrolling the borders of sexual morality by perpetuating the myth of normalcy.

SOCIAL CONTRACTS

The strategies adopted by the women performers in de Acosta's circle were rarely more drastic than keeping quiet about their sexual partners and activities whenever they thought this information might be broadcast. There is no evidence of widespread anxiety about being discovered or extreme efforts to create airtight heterosexual images. For instance, it is often assumed that these women married to avoid scandal, but even that implies a fear of exposure that remains unsubstantiated. De Acosta was married, in 1920, but said she did this to please her mother. From what she wrote about her relationship with her mother, as well as with her husband, this rationale is entirely plausible. Mercedes never assumed her husband Abram Poole's last name, nor did she live with him during most of the time they were married. She even spent her wedding night at her mother's house and wrote about this incident in her autobiography (de Acosta 1960, 115).[17] Honeymooning in Europe, she found time to cultivate new lesbian friendships, with British theater archivist Gabrielle Enthoven, for example (de Acosta 1960, 123–124). She also carried on affairs with Eva Le Gallienne and Gladys Calthrop quite publicly during the years when she shared living quarters with Poole in New York City immediately following their marriage.

Another unorthox marriage compact was Elsie de Wolfe's. Her private secretary Hilda West described how she and her boss consulted Burke's *Peerage* in search of a candidate for a titled husband who might be interested in marriage to a wealthy if not pedigreed American (Smith 1982, 223–224). The nominated peer, Sir Charles Mendl, turned out to be agreeable, although conjugal sexual relations played no part in the bargain.[18] Katharine Cornell and her husband, director Guthrie McClintic, seem to have been deeply devoted to one another, although her sexual preference was for women and his for men.[19] Eva Le Gallienne not only did not marry but also was named in divorce proceedings involving one of her lovers. She endured taunts in the press but shrugged them off and went on with her work.[20]

Another of de Acosta's actress friends may have used marriage to camouflage her lesbian activities and proclivities, but even in this case the circumstances are not entirely clear-cut. The actress in question was Alla Nazimova, who is now all but forgotten but was justly described by *New York Times* film critic Bosley Crowther (1967) as "the Greta Garbo . . . of the years around 1920." She became famous as the result of her widely acclaimed interpretations of classics of naturalist drama, Ibsen's and Chekhov's work in particular, and she was a national celebrity in the United States long before she made her first movie in 1916.[21] But Nazimova is largely remembered now, if at all, as an actress who played femmes fatales in silent films, epitomized by her performance in the 1922 film version of Oscar Wilde's *Salome*, which she also wrote, directed, and produced.

Bessie Marbury was friendly with Nazimova, and in 1915 gave de Acosta a ticket to see her in *War Brides*, an antiwar melodrama that drew record-breaking audiences to the Palace vaudeville theater in New York. De Acosta introduced herself to the star shortly thereafter, and the two became lovers for a brief period (and friends until Nazimova's death in 1945). Nazimova had numerous other lesbian relationships, most of these after the dalliance with de Acosta, including affairs with Le Gallienne and both wives of Rudolph Valentino. In 1916, a substantial offer from Metro Pictures—$13,000 a week—lured her to Hollywood, where she did little to stifle publicity that contained allusions to her lesbian tendencies. Nor did she hide her sexuality from her employers. In the early 1920s she proposed making a film based on *Aphrodite*, a novel by Pierre Louÿs, author of the lesbian classic *Bilitis*, in which she planned to include lesbian scenes as part of the movie's depiction of pagan culture in pre-Christian Alexandria (the studio canceled the project when they figured this out). And her women-only parties at her Hollywood home—which, in another gesture that underscored her exotic image, she named the Garden of Alla—were legendary. According to biographer Gavin Lambert, "In the flamboyant early days of her stardom in silent movies, Nazimova enjoyed dropping hints about her bisexuality, which became one of Hollywood's best unkept secrets" (Lambert 1997, 13).[22]

During this period, from 1912 to 1925 to be precise, the public was repeatedly reminded that Nazimova was married to actor Charles Bryant. Certainly, this distracted attention from her sexual relationships with women, and other men. For Bryant, the association with the star offered him great professional and financial opportunities. In the production credits for *A Doll's House* and *Salome*, as well as in most film indexes, Bryant is named as director, although Nazimova did the actual work. She also wrote the screenplays for both films but used a synonym, Peter M. Winters, to disguise this aspect of her contribution. And, with consequences that later came to haunt her, Nazimova signed an contract assuming responsibility for Bryant's taxes. However, the marriage was phony. Nazimova had married an actor named Sergei Golovin in Russia in 1904 and never divorced him. Her house of cards crumbled in 1925 when reporters got wind of Bryant's marriage to a young woman from Connecticut. Since the press had never been apprised of his divorce from Nazimova, they demanded an explanation of the couple's legal relationship. Nazimova was disgraced by the disclosure of her sham marriage and tried to repair the damage by inventing an equally fictitious divorce. Ignominiously, she was saddled with paying Bryant's tax bill at a time when

Alla Nazimova in
Salome, 1922.
Billy Rose Theater
Collection, New York
Public Library.

her own earnings had greatly diminished because the studios cut her loose after several failed experiments in film production, including the financially and critically disastrous *Salome*.

Nazimova's story may read like a wacky, semitragic variation on the coverup strategy—evidence of at least one celebrity closet *avant la lettre*—but this one has a few more twists that call for a different interpretation. Although scandal ensued upon the discovery of Nazimova's unmarried status, it was not about lesbianism. And, instead of taking the opportunity to chide the star for her immoral ways and reveal even more damning information, the Hollywood gossip industry presented a united front in her defense. In fact, they had done so for years. Louella Parsons was aware of the fact that Nazimova and Bryant were never married but "deliberately falsified it—and others followed her lead" (Bodeen 1972, 596). Even after the lie became public, Parsons and other authorities on stars' private lives continued to repeat the falsehood. The only article printed about Nazimova while she was alive that did not echo this untruth was a profile written by Djuna Barnes (1930), a lesbian who may have been uninterested in propping up the actress' wifely facade. Amazingly, the spurious story managed to survive in spite of its refutation, to the point where Parsons's obituary of Nazimova (1945) reproduced again the discredited information.

The lesson to be gleaned from this episode—in addition to the obvious affirmation of Parsons's authority—is not about the enforced invisibility of lesbians but concerns a much broader effort to make celebrity narratives conform to very narrow social norms, to the point of disregarding facts when they interfered. The gossip press rescued Nazimova from ignominy because she was a big star, acclaimed as a great actress—not above rebuke, but almost. And she was also part of a system of image production that was predicated on creating fictions that were accepted as real. The result was a body of knowledge about entertainment favorites that could not incorporate a story as aberrant as Nazimova's and, therefore, erased any information that violated the axioms of normalcy.

MERCEDES REDUX

Up to this point, I have proceeded as if the missing narratives of lesbian celebrity could be assembled from the fragments and hints left behind by the women whose names I've cited. I have used their own writings or followed their biographers' tracks to lend credence to ideas concerning the parameters of lesbian celebrity in the pre–gay liberation period. But in doing this I have been performing a kind of intellectual violence, applying a descriptive term, lesbian celebrity, to these women when it would have been, for them, nonsense. Ultimately, this effort is bound to fail. These women *were* celebrities. They *were* involved sexually with other women. They may have even recognized themselves and each other as lesbians. And they, along with myriad other stars, were surely objects of fans' lesbian fantasies.[23] But lesbian sexuality was rarely discussed openly, and lesbian identity was never ascribed to celebrities—certainly not in the media that confirmed and amplified their fame—in the terms it has been since the late 1960s. Until then a famous performer's heterosexuality would be taken for granted unless an unambiguous proclamation was issued. Of course, this was never done, because, from the late-nineteenth century onwards—amplified significantly in the 1930s—the language of moral depravity and mental illness were the only intelligible concepts of lesbianism available in the United States.

In fact, by the time de Acosta set out to write her autobiography in the late 1950s, lesbian culture was in the midst of a period of intense surveillance and censure, the culmination of the reaction against sexual diversity and tolerance that began with the repeal of Prohibition. As Chauncey has noted, gay life became "*less* tolerated, *less* visible to outsiders, and *more* rigidly segregated [from straight culture] in the second third of the century than the first" (Chauncey 1994, 9). What *was* visible by the late 1940s, thanks to the media, was the campaign to demonize homosexuality as politically dangerous, an innate condition that rendered all lesbians and gay men psychologically deficient, morally deformed, and inherently untrustworthy. At the same time, the logic of the celebrity system as it developed over the century created a demand for intimate narrative accounts about stars' private lives, as the editors of fan magazines realized by the end of World War I. This required coherent stories about families, shopping and dining habits, vacations and pastimes, and, most importantly, romances. The occupation of a celebrity watcher, both journalists and fans, consisted of filling in these details and keeping up with new developments in the stars' lives.

Thus, by mid-century, the lesbian autobiographer was faced with a choice between producing a very sketchy account of sexual matters or hoping that willful ignorance would prevail. This is where de Acosta's autobiographical project becomes particularly interesting, not for its contribution to lesbian history but for what she didn't, or couldn't, publish in 1960. She had set herself a difficult task. It wasn't just that she would have to write about lesbian attractions and attachments if the book was to have any claim to authenticity. Many of the people she would name in this context were well-known, several of them were major stars, and a number of them were still alive. And if she did refer to herself or any of her friends as lesbian or use an equivalent expression, she would then be compelled to address the topic within the terms available at the time—as a disease.

The motto de Acosta adopted as her insignia, and had embossed on her personal stationery, was "Verdad y Silencio" (Truth and Silence). In fact, *Here Lies the Heart* often performs a delicate balancing act in an apparent effort to reconcile these two values that would usually be deemed incompatible for a writer. On one hand, her book offers a study in discretion, never once mentioning the word "lesbian" or naming anyone a homosexual (although she does use the word "homosexuals" once, in a list of the diverse house guests of an eccentric sculptor). On the other hand, its sexual "truths" are everywhere implied. In many respects, she had much in common with her friend Janet

Flanner, whose "Letter from Paris" columns between 1925 and 1939 in the *New Yorker* (1971) were full of news about lesbian cultural figures without drawing attention to the recurrence of this motif.[24] De Acosta needed to tread very carefully, and caution led her to tidy up and pare down her memories of love and sex with women in the retrospective account of her life she made public.

If successful, the complicated work that goes into this sort of revisionist project should remain inconspicuous, or at least that is the author–editor's hope. Judging by her book's critical reception, she achieved this aim. Detractors did not accuse her of fabrication but instead faulted her for being unorthodox and elitist. Such headlines as "Aberrant Hedonist Writes All" (S. M. A. 1960) and "Writer 'Drops Names' Through Autobiography" (W. G. R. 1960) sum up the contents of these pieces. Another review, "Greta Garbo's Pal Has Much to Tell," dismisses de Acosta's social circle as "the greatest collection of psychos outside Bellevue" (Buffington n.d.) but doesn't question the truth of the tale. And those who recommended the book praised it, in the words of one reviewer, "as a historical document, as an authentic social history" (McLaughlin 1960). *Women's Wear Daily* promoted the book's veracity, too, when it repeated de Acosta's fanciful story about convincing Dietrich to don trousers (in fact, the Berliner had worn this apparel long before she landed in the United States and to publicity parties in Hollywood soon after she arrived, causing some raised eyebrows [Busby 1933; W. K. Martin 1995, 60]).[25]

Professional book reviewers may have been willing to believe her, but de Acosta had her own reservations about candor and was willing to say so publicly. In an interview with Joseph Wershba of the *New York Post* promoting the book, she told him,

> I don't think any person can write an absolutely truthful autobiography. You can't tell about situations involving other people—except perhaps after your death. You can't do it because of libel and because of your own good taste. You can tell the truth up to a certain point. Beyond that, you hurt people. (quoted in Wershba 1960)

In private, de Acosta also grappled with this dilemma but came up with a somewhat more convoluted, less confident answer. The first draft of her autobiography, which is remarkable for its radical dissimilarity to the published version, contains this passage in its opening pages:

[I]ntelligent lies are many times nearer the truth than unintelligent truth, and in many cases more stimulating. I understand that many truths are only half truths, and that in many cases—for the comfort and happiness of everyone at large—it is clearly each person's duty to occasionally cultivate falsehood.

And yet, even after this discovery, I found it very difficult to lie and still find it so.

Am I truthful because of a deep desire for the Truth? Or am I just a coward? (de Acosta Papers)

De Acosta seems to be urging her imagined reader to accept her story as true, but she plants seeds of doubt in these initial paragraphs, which undermine her case.

However, the muddiness of the reasoning here says one thing rather clearly: there are some events she was uncomfortable putting into print. To solve this problem, she employed a tactic that at first proved disastrous: she omitted all references to anyone with whom she has been involved sexually, with the exception of Isadora Duncan—no Nazimova, no Dietrich, no Hollywood dinner parties or house guests, no Calthrop or Maria Annunziata Kirk (known as Poppy, Mercedes's last long-term lover); not even her husband is mentioned. The most stunning absence is Garbo, who becomes the main attraction in the published version of *Here Lies the Heart*.

And there is another, more fascinating discrepancy—the antithesis, in a sense, of her oversight of various lesbian lovers—between de Acosta's initial effort and the authorized autobiography: passages in the former which illustrate how and why, until she was seven, she was raised as a boy. In her first draft of the book she writes,

[M]y mother decided I was to be a boy .... She ... sometimes called me Raphael, a name she apparently had in mind for me had I been a boy, and one which I have all my life since regarded as more my own than the one with which I was christened. (de Acosta Papers)

She then describes at length the "tragedy" that disabused her of this idea when several male playmates gave her a lesson in the anatomy of sexual difference after she claimed to be a boy:

"Prove you're not a girl", they screamed.

I put my poor little hand down on my body hopelessly seeking for something which was not there. In that one brief second everything in my young soul turned monstrous and terrible and dark. . . . When . . . it was finally admitted that I was a girl I fell into a delirium. For three days I raged in bed and ran a high temperature. (de Acosta Papers)

A few pages further on in the manuscript, she returns to this theme. Even after acknowledging that she is not a boy she continues her adamant declarations about not being a girl, telling a nun who disputes this fact, "'I am not a boy and I am not a girl, or maybe I am both—I don't know. And because I don't know, I will never fit in anywhere and I will be lonely all my life'" (de Acosta Papers).

Having offered these illustrations of her transgender identity and sexual ambiguity, de Acosta's story then veers toward a more reflective tone strikingly reminiscent of *The Well of Loneliness*. She reflects upon how she subsequently interpreted her childhood confusion and the theory of sexuality she developed as a result:

And perhaps even this childhood tragedy, with its roots of despair, has since flowered into a beautiful tree and while, at some moments, it has shadowed my life from the sun, that very shade under which I have lingered has cooled my spirit and enabled my eyes to see deeper and further than the people who travel always in the blazing sun. It has made me see and understand the half-tone light of dawn and twilight, whose vibrations are ever the most mystical and romantic, so too have I come to regard these half tones of life and the people who walk in their rhythm, as the most beautiful. . . . To the outward form of sex which the body has assumed I have remained indifferent. I do not understand the difference between a man and woman, and believing only in the eternal value of love, I cannot understand these so-called "normal" people who believe that a man should love only a woman, and woman love only a man. . . . I believe in many cases this is why the "normal" people are usually much less inspired, seldom artists, and much less sensitive than the "half-tone" people. (de Acosta Papers)

The rhetorical appeal to nature as a support for homosexual desire is what calls to mind *The Well*. But, in her commentary on these issues de Acosta employs ideas about lesbian sexuality that mix notions of gender inversion similar to Radclyffe Hall's with Freud's theories about sexuality as an unconscious disposition shaped by early childhood experiences. In addition she writes about having a "mother complex" (de Acosta Papers), all of which indicates that she was familiar with psychoanalytic language concerning sexual identity. She then erases any residual notions of pathology that either school of thought might encourage by subordinating both to precepts of various Eastern religions she had studied. In other words, she adopted many of the attitudes toward homosexuality prevalent in the mid-twentieth century, with a dab of mysticism thrown in to temper the homophobia that medical concepts of homosexuality foster.

Other than dwelling upon knotty questions about truth, gender, and sexuality, de Acosta's first draft consists of a series of chapters on famous people she had met and conversed with but were not close friends—Sarah Bernardt, Eleanora Duse, and Anna Pavlova, for instance—as well as some space devoted to anecdotes about her childhood and family. If published, this book would have been a timid product for someone with de Acosta's ability to deliver a firsthand account of the mid-twentieth-century theatrical and film communities in New York and Los Angeles. It may have been an editor or de Acosta herself who noticed the dearth of gossip-quality information about celebrities in what she had written and decided that a new approach was necessary. In any case, she returned to her typewriter and produced a fresh manuscript that became the blueprint for the published autobiography.

Her second draft for *Here Lies the Heart* included many of the stories about family and famous people reported in the first, although reorganized to fit into a more coherent chronological sequence. To this she added a wealth of recollections about her career and myriad friends—including, as I mentioned before, various lovers not identified as such—and elaborated the social and historical contexts where she encountered this sizable cast of characters. Curiously, the musings about sex and normalcy quoted above disappeared completely (although she retained the "mother complex" rationale to explain her lack of enthusiasm for marriage). The story about being raised as a boy and her confusion about her true gender appeared in subsequent drafts but reworded and whittled away as she worked over the manuscript, with the sole remaining paragraph on the topic being penciled out on the galley proofs— that is, just before the book went to press.

Placing these two versions of de Acosta's life story side by side, a number of other contrasts emerge. Words that might be interpreted as signs of lesbianism in the first draft are nowhere to be found in the published work. Still, she let stand a number of references to individuals and situations with homosexual overtones. Pairs of men are regularly named as companions, for instance, *New Republic* editor Stark Young and architect Bill Bowman, diet doctor Gayelord Hauser and his companion Frey Brown. Women couples are also mentioned, including a few with male nicknames: Gabrielle Enthoven and Cecile Sartoris, G. B. Stern or "Peter—as G. B. is called by her friends" (de Acosta 1960, 244) and Diana Wynward. And several descriptions of people she knew contain attributions of masculinity to a woman or femininity to a man. Bessie Marbury "had the brain of a man, well balanced and keen, lodged in a massive, masculine-shaped head" (72). On first meeting Nazimova, de Acosta was surprised that the great actress "seemed like a naughty little boy" (74). Clifton Webb "was slender and willowy and had a flair for wearing clothes" (77), while Quinton Tod "dressed to perfection and was neatness itself" (262). Even if such remarks could be interpreted as affectionate observations, de Acosta's characterization of John Barrymore's "feminine character" and what she saw as his "need to be dominated" (de Acosta Papers) might have set off more than a few alarms, but she deleted these observations prior to publication. However, she did not revise her portrait of Barrymore's wife, Michael Strange, who wore "velvet jackets which she had made in the style of Alfred de Musset . . . a Walt Whitman shirt . . . heavy leather riding gloves with wide cuffs . . . 'the type of glove George Sand wore' [and] . . . a man's soft hat, generally one of Jack's" (de Acosta 1960, 194).

In addition to subtle allusions to transvestite or transsexual temperaments and homosexual culture, the final version of the book includes various anecdotes that implicate de Acosta as a participant in this queer milieu, either directly or by association with people she befriended. For instance, she tells about an incident at a convent school she attended, where she acted as a go-between for two nuns in love with one another (36–37). She describes star gazing on Fifth Avenue with her best school friend as an adolescent; they pursued the Barrymores, John and Ethel, and Mercedes says *she* "swooned" over Ethel while her friend preferred John (42). Living in New York as an adult, she fell in with a group of British show business lesbians—including the celebrated musical comedy actress Teddie Gerard—and their gay comrades, one of whom amused them all by being evicted by his hostess, Mrs. Cornelius Vanderbilt, because he and a second butler failed to appear at an important dinner party. About this misdemeanor de Acosta writes, "[I]t was not difficult for Mrs. Vanderbilt to conclude that wherever these two missing young men were, they were together" (125). And, in much more serious vein, she dispenses plentiful hints about the sexual nature of her most enduring relationships with women—Le Gallienne, Dietrich, and Kirk—never with explicit statements but still giving the impression of the passion that was involved. For instance, she recalls, "I suddenly had a letter from Poppy saying that she wanted to return to Paris [where de Acosta was living] and suggesting we share a flat together. I put in a call to Mexico City and we decided she would fly to Paris as soon as I found an apartment" (343). Kirk left her husband behind in Mexico.

Other women who were short-term lovers are treated more coolly. Ona Munson, for example, conducted an ardent transcontinental affair with de Acosta in the mid-1940s. De Acosta writes in detail about their first meeting in 1932 at the home of Ernst Lubitsch, Munson's lover at the time, but when the narrative moves on to later years, de Acosta has little to say about Munson other than that the actress "often came to spend the night when she was shooting at Republic Studios in the San Fernando Valley" (305). Similarly, about the start of her affair with Calthrop, she recalls, "That enchanting and beautiful person, Gladys Calthrop, had boarded the *Majestic* at Southampton. We spent most of the trip together and had a very pleasant crossing," followed by a couple of sentences describing the designer's work (182). After this fairly prosaic description Calthrop vanishes until she is mentioned in relation to a fire in a house de Acosta and her husband were renovating. De Acosta had already set up a work room for herself, and Calthrop, she notes off-handedly, was living there at the time (201).

It is easy enough to gloss over these apparently insignificant details, although a close reading of de Acosta's prose does suggest a decoding strategy of sorts. Between the references to Calthrop, for instance, de Acosta departs from her usual list of travels, social encounters, and sketches of the people she knew to recount an anecdote about her theft of an exotic black tulip from a hostess's flower arrangement. This recollection begins with the sentence, "Flowers have at times moved me the way certain beautiful and enchanting women have moved me" (199), echoing the words "beautiful and enchanting" used to describe Calthrop a few pages earlier, implying that this woman, like the tulip, was also an object of her desire.

Amid the parade of more or less obvious lovers in de Acosta's memoir, Garbo was a special case. As I have already pointed out, their "friendship" was publicly acknowledged. Even de Acosta's obituaries mentioned it, as did the previously cited gossip columnists and reviewers of *Here Lies the Heart*. For Garbo, though, publicity was anathema, an attitude that deeply violated the tenets of celebrity culture. Her refusal to give interviews was so inconceivable for the Hollywood press that reporters referred to it incessantly and took to referring to any such actions on the part of a star as "pulling a Garbo" or "going Garbo" (York 1932).[26] The one thing that was guaranteed to alienate the antisocial star was the publication of anything about her that claimed to be based on intimate knowledge. Yet, having recast her staid autobiography as a chatty memoir, de Acosta must have realized that she would have to deal with Garbo. As it turned out, after the book was published Garbo never corresponded with or spoke to de Acosta again. Although predictable this must have been painful, since it is clear from how de Acosta writes about her—replete with superlatives—that Garbo was the most important woman in her life, except, perhaps, her mother and her sister Rita.[27]

The texture of the prose de Acosta uses to describe Garbo is extremely adulatory, as well as fervent, conveying a grand passion, at least from Mercedes's perspective. Contrary to her reputation for melancholy and hauteur, Garbo in de Acosta's rendition is kind, warm, cheerful and fun loving, not to mention one of the greatest artists who ever lived. And de Acosta supplies descriptions of time spent in Garbo's company that are decidedly romantic. One such scene is set in 1931, soon after they met, when Garbo invited de Acosta to spend six weeks alone with her on an island in Silver Lake in the Sierra Nevada: "How to describe the next six enchanted weeks? . . . Six perfect weeks out of a lifetime. This is indeed much. In all this time there was not a second of disharmony between Greta and me or in nature around us" (de Acosta 1960, 224). And in 1935, several years after de Acosta and Dietrich had become steady if not monogamous lovers and the affair with Garbo appeared to have cooled off, Mercedes received a cable from Greta upon returning to New York from Europe: "I will meet you for dinner a week from Tuesday at eight o'clock at the Grand Hotel [in Stockholm]" (269). De Acosta booked passage on a ship leaving the next day, kept the appointment, and spent (at least) a week with her beloved.

This last endearment is not de Acosta's but seems quite appropriate given the adoration she lavished on Garbo. But de Acosta worked very hard to make sure that the sexual relation with Garbo, or any other woman for that matter, remained offstage in her autobiography. That work is evident on the manuscript pages de Acosta produced as she shaped the book's final form. In the second and third drafts, as well as the galley proofs, those sections of the text dealing with early encounters between the two women are heavily emended, as if the author had to struggle to get the tone just right. Most interesting in this regard are the short but significant deletions that removed hints of intimacy. Recounting her first visit to Garbo's house de Acosta deleted phrases that mention Garbo taking her hand at two different moments. When she tells the story about Garbo's impulsive return from Silver Lake to pick her up so they can vacation together, she shortened the words attributed to Garbo—"I'm on my way back for you"—by crossing out "for you." And that night, before they depart for the lake, de Acosta had written, "I put her to bed on the porch, although we were both too excited to do much sleeping," but decided to remove this sentence, too (de Acosta Papers).

These items are just a sample of the many adjustments made by de Acosta where Garbo was concerned, but she was similarly engaged in purging other material that might imply a lesbian perspective—literally, in the sense that she might reveal too much about how she looked at women. For instance, an appreciative passage about Garbo's legs was removed. Her description of Teddie Gerard was shortened by eliminating the observation that the actress "had a beautiful body" (de Acosta Papers). Additional editorial work involved the removal of hints of masculine identifications, her own and others. Again, her representation of Garbo was most heavily scrutinized. De Acosta first altered the concluding words in a sentence about a script she hoped to write for her lover, "She had told me she longed to have a part in which she could dress as a man," to " . . . dress in men's clothes" but reconsidered and crossed out the entire sentence. She also removed a line that read, "She was more like a naughty boy than a great film star." In the section dealing with the time spent on Silver Lake, she changed her appraisal of Garbo's rowing ability from "like a man's" to "superb." Similarly, she excised the description of an incident involving Dietrich's order of "sixteen complete men's outfits" from de Acosta's tailor and appearance at the studio dressed in "an entire man's suit." Why she demured in this instance is unclear, since Dietrich's fondness for masculine attire was well-known. Discussing the early days of her affair with Kirk, she wrote, "That night Poppy cooked dinner for me and I invited her to come and stay with me. I then understood why Rodin married his cook!" but later reconsidered and deleted this analogy of their relationship to a marriage. About herself, she mused in the penultimate draft, "[W]ho of us are only one sex? I, myself, am sometimes androgynous. When I consider all these complex problems, I have to put aside this book for a bit so as not to end by just throwing it out of the window" (de Acosta Papers). Instead, de Acosta resolved her dilemma by throwing out these several sentences.

In one of her later revisions de Acosta added a curious story about conversations with the socialite Mabel Dodge Luhan, who during a stay in Hollywood as Adrian's guest encouraged Mercedes to write an autobiography about "personalities she had known," just as Luhan had done in her *Intimate Memories* ([1933–1937] 1971). In what could be interpreted as an indirect expression of misgivings about the autobiography she was in the midst of preparing for publication, de Acosta recalled her discomfort with Luhan's suggestion that she portray friends and acquaintances "with a certain amount of malice, some suggestion of scandal. . . . Look at the number of people you know intimately," de Acosta remembered Luhan telling her. "You could begin with Adrian" (de Acosta Papers). But if Luhan's own willingness to make her sexual life public—as she had done by writing about her love affair with D. H. Lawrence—was to serve as the example for de Acosta, to "begin with Adrian" would mean giving a candid report of the costume designer's homosexuality, which would expose his much publicized marriage to Janet Gaynor as a charade and almost certainly ruin his career. Instead, de Acosta tried out the method on Luhan herself, who, she remarked, "had written, in many instances, quite cruelly about a number of people who had crossed her path—or perhaps more precisely—whose path she had crossed, for Mabel is always the aggressor." Curiously, this is the sole instance where de Acosta or her editors expressed a concern about the possibility of legal action, writing in the margin, "Libel? I'd cut now" (de Acosta Papers). The entire section on Luhan was deleted.

Indeed, de Acosta seems to have been uninterested in using her autobiography as an opportunity to settle past grievances. The notable exception is Elsie de Wolfe, the only person subjected to spiteful appraisal in the book. De Acosta describes de Wolfe as an "an exceptionally untalented actress" and, as an interior decorator who never "did anything really creative or original" (de Acosta 1960, 73). De Acosta also insinuates that some of the French antiques de Wolfe imported were fakes and that the income de Wolfe produced for France by selling bogus Louis XIV and Louis XV furniture was the reason she was awarded the French Legion of Honor, rather than her work as a nurse during World War I, which was the official justification. (This swipe at de Wolfe's business practices was included in one of the drafts but subsequently omitted from the published version.) Why de Wolfe was singled out for this kind of contemptuous treatment is not absolutely clear. Perhaps de Acosta sought revenge for her long-dead friend Bessie Marbury, who de Wolfe effectively repudiated when she married Charles Mendl. More likely, though, these nasty comments were intended as a symbolic evening of the score with de Wolfe, who sued Rita Lydig in 1927 in an attempt to recover $12,000 the bankrupt socialite owed her. Otherwise, the few unkind comments that de Acosta allowed herself to articulate in various drafts—for instance, an aside that mentions Nazimova's lack of a "harmonious blend of great art and great soul" (ibid.)—were eliminated in the final version. Yet even with all de Acosta's efforts to sanitize her memoirs, it is difficult to imagine that she could have foreseen the trial her character would undergo when stories about her affairs with eminent actresses moved from subcultural folklore into history.

WHO'S WHO

De Acosta's transition from relatively obscure social gadfly to lesbian icon is fairly recent—it began in 1990. That year, the unwritten rule that proscribed any mention of lesbianism in relation to renowned, glamorous performers in the press or writings on the lives of stage and screen personalities began to break down. Previously, a few references to lesbian actresses had appeared in popular literature on Hollywood, most notoriously in Kenneth Anger's campy gossip tomes *Hollywood Babylon* (1975) and *Hollywood Babylon II* (1984). The first drops names like Janet Gaynor, Lili Damita, and Claudette Colbert, along with Dietrich, Nazimova, and the two women he claims she introduced to Rudolph Valentino and who, Anger says, were also lesbians— Jean Acker and Natacha Rambova.[28] Significantly, 1990 was also the year Garbo died.[29] The renewed interest in this supremely reclusive movie star occasioned by her demise unleashed a spate of new biographies, all of which acknowledged her lesbianism, with de Acosta credited with providing much of the evidence. For example, Antoni Gronowicz's *Garbo: Her Story* (1990) purports to be a verbatim account of conversations between the author and Garbo, in which she freely discusses her affair with de Acosta, although the anecdotes differ significantly from those recounted in *Here Lies the Heart*. In an appendix to another Garbo biography, published five years after Gronowicz's, Barry Paris catalogues the myriad factual errors contained in *Garbo: Her Story*. In his own *Garbo*, Paris convincingly challenges Gronowicz's claim of authenticity, using de Acosta's autobiography as the basis for much of his counterargument (Paris 1995, 555–563).

In these two books de Acosta remains a secondary character, but in two additional contributions to the post-1990 Garbo literature—*Loving Garbo,* by Hugo Vickers (1994), and *Greta and Cecil*, by Diana Souhami (1994), both dealing with Cecil Beaton's infatuation with the celebrated beauty—de Acosta is accorded a more central role, since she and Beaton formed a bond based on the suffering each endured as Garbo's devoted but repeatedly frustrated lover. Both Vickers and Souhami use de Acosta's papers, not just her published autobiography but also the preparatory manuscripts for the book, as well as her correspondence with Beaton, to document the triangular relationship. In addition, Beaton's letters and diaries provide these writers with plentiful comments about de Acosta, often sarcastic remarks he made for Garbo's benefit.

Second in importance to Garbo in the celebrity ranking of de Acosta's lovers is Marlene Dietrich, who was the subject of at least five published biographies (in English) prior to the 1990s, none of which mentioned de Acosta, or other female lovers for that matter. Since then, however, Dietrich's lesbian involvements have been discussed and analyzed by Donald Spoto (1992), Steven Bach (1992), Dietrich's daughter Maria Riva (1993), and W. K. Martin (1995), not to mention various books that remark upon her lesbianism in a broader context. Then there's Eva Le Gallienne, who published two autobiographies (1934; 1953), neither of which discussed de Acosta, in spite of their fiery affair that lasted over five years. However, Robert Schanke's (1992) and Helen Sheehy's (1996) biographies of the distinguished actress contain a great deal of information about this chapter in Le Gallienne's life, along with details concerning relationships with other women she lived with and loved. Yet another example is Alla Nazimova, whose career is chronicled in Gavin Lambert's biography (1997), the only book-length study to date of the once-famous actress. Again, de Acosta appears, as Nazimova's lover for a brief period but also as her friend. De Acosta also puts in a brief appearance in Michael Morris's *Madam Valentino: The Many Lives of Natacha Rambova* (1991), which quotes de Acosta's recollection in *Here Lies the Heart* of seeing Rambova and Valentino dance in 1923, as well as her statements about the lasting friendship they developed on the basis of their shared interests in Eastern religions. But because one of the main purposes of Morris's project is an affirmation of Rambova's heterosexuality, he treats de Acosta's professed friendship as suspect.

It is no coincidence that this revival of de Acosta's memory comes at a time when the lesbianism of movie stars from Hollywood's heyday is under scrutiny, and her celebrity stock has definitely appreciated as a result. And in Axel Madsen's *The Sewing Circle*, subtitled *Hollywood's Greatest Secret: Female*

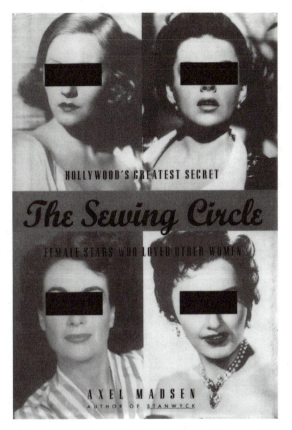

Book cover of
The Sewing Circle

Stars Who Loved Other Women, she at last achieves star status in her own right. In keeping with the book's promise of unmasking a conspiracy of silence, its dust jacket sports a set of lavender-tinted portraits—Tallulah Bankhead, Judy Garland, Joan Crawford, and Barbara Stanwyck, all easily recognizable in spite of the large black rectangles that obscure their eyes. To find de Acosta in this company one need read no further than the book jacket, which dubs her "a lover to the stars" and repeats an anecdote attributed to Alice B. Toklas: "Say what you want about Mercedes, she had the three most important women of the twentieth century" (Madsen 1995, 71), although opinions vary on who, in addition to Garbo and Dietrich, Toklas had in mind.[30] The book's survey begins with a sketchy biography of de Acosta, and her erotic adventures are the subject of several chapters and passages in others, granting her a mythic quality in the process. In this spirit, Madsen reiterates a quip credited to Truman Capote, who is reported to have invented a game that challenged players to "connect people sexually through as few beds as possible," and for which, he maintained, "the best card to hold was Mercedes, because 'you could get to anyone—from Cardinal Spellman to the Duchess of Windsor'" (Madsen 1995, 71).[31]

As an antidote to secrecy and gossip, *The Sewing Circle* promises revelation and substantiated truth, but the opposite is what Madsen actually produces, since he inflates and invents "facts" that are routinely contradicted by more rigorously researched historical records. The errors are too numerous to list. To offer an example: in one short paragraph I spotted five inaccuracies, in addition to several exaggerations.[32] For the most part, these mistakes bespeak sloppy research and do not affect the overall narrative, but more egregious is the author's failure to offer references for much of the sensational information he presents. In a number of instances, Madsen's litany of de Acosta's sexual conquests appears to be based on a reading of *Here Lies the Heart*, which assumes that any woman mentioned by de Acosta as a friend—Maude Adams or Katharine Cornell, for instance—must have been a lover, even when there is no information offered (or, as far as I know, available) to support this conclusion.[33] The combined effect of this factual mishmash, absence of citations, and breathless tone of scandal insinuates that the entire topic of lesbian sexuality and relationships is unworthy of serious treatment. And that seems quite consistent with what Madsen set out to accomplish, despite his proclamations about the importance of this book by touting it as an exposé of "Hollywood's greatest secret." When dealing with lesbian celebrities, Madsen warns us in his introduction, we're confronted with women who willfully obscured the truth and found that "[s]taying in the closet was altogether satisfying, sometimes even intensely romantic" (Madsen 1995, xv). In effect, Madsen's careless attitude toward history says that it doesn't matter whether or not these events happened; what matters is that an aura of hypocrisy and craven hedonism surrounds the women he names.

Nonetheless, *The Sewing Circle* seems to satisfy the requirements for a history of lesbian accomplishments desired by advocates of visibility, as does a volume of interviews by Boze Hadleigh entitled *Hollywood Lesbians* (1994). Indeed, Madsen's and Hadleigh's books were mentioned as inspiration for a photo-text feature in the gay and lesbian monthly *Out*, which praised them as "not a requiem but an homage . . . recalling what the credits never revealed" (Als and Turner 1995). But the kind of testimonial offered may produce effects quite different from those usually associated with homage. Although different in form and only somewhat redundant in content, both books share the style of an eager busybody who believes lesbians are inherently scandalous—not very different from the tone adopted by reviewers of de Acosta's memoir in 1960 but now made overt.[34] What has changed are the opportunities for holding this discussion in public, or for using the racy subject matter openly to market one's wares. The appeal of these books is not unlike that of representations of lesbianism in most pornography, potentially engaging for heterosexual male consumers and lesbians, as well as for anyone interested in any configuration of stars' sex lives. But that is not how these volumes are advertised (compared, say, to promotion of Kenneth Anger's *Hollywood Babylon* diptych [1975; 1984], which was quite frank about the books' voyeurism). Instead, the authors and publishers claim to present reality: newly discovered unvarnished truths.

Curiously, Madsen's cavalier use of de Acosta as a lesbian lodestone is mirrored in several of the aforementioned, generally more circumspect biographies. As I have pointed out, de Acosta's own account is cited liberally as a source of information, but in a number of cases the reliability of her version of events is questioned. Usually de Acosta's credibility is undermined by repeating the views of someone she knew who had developed an antipathy to her and, therefore, dismissed *Here Lies the Heart*. Sheehy does this, quoting Le Gallienne's assessment—"so full of lies that it's positively incredible!" (Sheehy 1996, 429). Vickers employs a similar strategy, although he grants that "the stories have stood the test of time" (Vickers 1994, 254). Spoto, too, notes such opinions, although he tacks on a defense of de Acosta's probity: "Friends who resented her frankness tried to deny the most torrid romantic revelations, often referring to the book as 'Here the Heart Lies.' But . . . the basic truth of de Acosta's book (if not the accuracy of every detail) is indeed unassailable" (Spoto 1992, 105). Perhaps one of the most vicious assessments of her character, though, is Dietrich's daughter's, who recalls that de Acosta was "creepy" and that she "looked like a Spanish Dracula" (Riva 1993, 153), a comment that has been reproduced by several other Dietrich biographers, as well as by Madsen.

After reading these repeated aspersions about de Acosta's honesty and references to other disagreeable aspects of her personality, I was not surprised to read in Vickers's book that Janet Flanner "loathed" her (Vickers 1994, 160). Just one more strike against her, I thought, and there were already so many. Moreover, there is nothing in de Acosta's own chronicle that suggests that this may not have been the case. In *Here Lies the Heart*, de Acosta describes Flanner merely as a friend who paid a visit in 1941. Everyone she wrote about was a "friend," so it is not difficult to imagine that this may be overstatement. Therefore, I was quite surprised to find a lighthearted, poetic,

amorous letter to de Acosta from Flanner, the lines of which form the outline of a tulip, among her personal papers. Written in 1928 after one of
Mercedes's visits to Paris, the letter-poem is an unmistakable expression of
endearment. One line reads, "She ate daintily; consuming a sweetened crumb
like a singer taking a high note. She ate flesh talking of flowers and flesh"
(reminiscent of de Acosta's musings on flowers and women, occasioned by
the anecdote about theft of a tulip). The rest of the poem consists of similar
tender tributes to Mercedes.[35] Vicker's willingness to maintain Flanner's dislike of de Acosta, although a minor matter, again leaves an impression of
Mercedes as an untrustworthy character. And what is the source for Vickers's
information? As it turns out, it's a conversation between the author and a
friend of Poppy Kirk's, who might easily have harbored unkind feelings for
Poppy's overbearing lover.[36] Ah, gossip.

Gossip, it becomes plain, has been the linchpin of histories of lesbian
celebrities, because they are presumed to be, by nature, dissemblers. It may be
the case that gossip presents problems for those interested in uncovering historical facts, but that should not automatically disqualify it as reasonable conjecture (nor should it be treated as *more* reliable, simply because lesbians are
involved). Moreoever, tracing the convolutions of gossip's transmission and
reception may provide insights into the production of knowledge about lesbians. This may be why gossip is precisely what Michael Morris (1991)
attempts to put to rest in his biography of Rambova. His main target is
Kenneth Anger, whose statements concerning the lesbian relationship
between Nazimova and her dearest friend (as well as Valentino's homosexuality) are the subject of an impassioned rebuttal in his book's final pages. It
may be that Morris is concerned about how such stories endure as cultural
myths, reinforced by such representations as Ken Russell's kitschy 1977 film
Valentino, which portrays Rambova as an ambitious, ruthless, domineering
woman who cavorts with Nazimova while exploiting her hapless husband.[37]
But Morris's furious rejoinder to allegations that either Valentino or
Rambova, or both, had homosexual relationships ultimately produces more
curiousity about the rumors than conviction about their falsehood.

The question of Rambova's sexuality is not confined to the anti-Anger
postscript in Morris's book. He repeatedly interrupts the narration of
Rambova's life to dispell any suspicions that might arise from her associations
with various lesbians: Elsie de Wolfe, whose brother married her mother;
Nazimova, of course; and de Acosta. Regarding *Here Lies the Heart*, he
accuses de Acosta of misrepresenting her acquaintance with Rambova as a

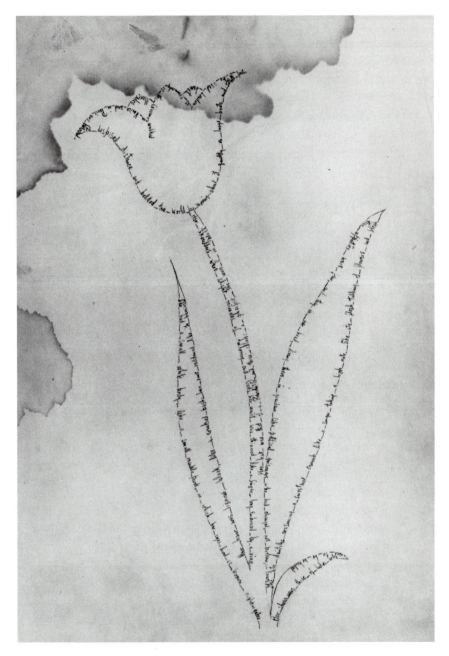

Poem written by Janet Flanner for Mercedes de Acosta. Courtesy Janet Flanner Estate, Rosenbach Museum and Library.

friendship, as if any connection to a known lesbian like Mercedes would weaken his claim that Natacha was *not* a lesbian (Morris 1991, 131). Again, letters to de Acosta from Rambova leave a very different impression, indicating that they corresponded frequently, maintained a cordial friendship, and even planned to collaborate on a dramatic script (de Acosta Papers). Correcting Morris more pointedly, Lambert offers gay director George Cukor as an irreproachable authority affirming that Rambova and Nazimova were lovers and reproduces a photograph of the two women lounging about in pajamas that can be interpreted as support for this declaration (Lambert 1997, 235).

Rather than attempt to decide, once and for all, whether Morris or Lambert has uncovered the ultimate truth about Rambova and Nazimova's relationship, it might be more productive to consider what their debate is about. In particular, the recent crop of exposés about lesbian goings-on in Hollywood that lavish attention on de Acosta seem eager to use her authentic lesbianism as a master key that will unlock the door to a mysterious world, which might be exciting or loathsome, depending on the reader's perspective. More importantly, these rewritten histories of de Acosta and her friends should caution us against interpreting the possibility of recovering lesbian celebrities as an unequivocal sign of progress. The fascination with lesbian stars can just as easily underwrite an authoritarian, censorial morality that regards lesbians as inherently corrupt, devious, and deceitful.

SCENE CHANGES

Garbo's death in 1990 coincided with heated debates over the practice of "outing" in the gay press and elsewhere (Mayne 1993, 157–167). In that context, disclosures about the de Acosta–Garbo affair could be conscripted to bolster lesbian visibility. Granted, knowledge of Garbo's homosexuality had circulated in lesbian culture for many years, thanks largely to de Acosta's autobiography. De Acosta's efforts to disguise their relationship as a close friendship had not fooled those predisposed to read between the lines, as a letter about *Here Lies the Heart* published in a 1960 issue of the lesbian monthly the *Ladder* confirms: "Your readers will not want to miss Mercedes de Acosta's autobiography. . . . She devotes a large portion of the last half of the book to her long intimacy with the enigmatic and bewildering Greta Garbo, and for many this will be the most interesting part of the book" (B. G. 1960). The knowledge implied by this squib did not yet qualify as truth.

Andy Warhol's invitation for the party for Here Lies the Heart. © 2003 Andy Warhol Foundation for the Visual Arts / ARS, New York, Rosenbach Museum and Library.

That had to wait for the feminist and gay liberation movements of the seventies to chip away at the barriers separating unauthorized lesbian gossip from what qualify as real, or even plausible, representations in celebrity culture. When that became possible, de Acosta was ready for resurrection, although not for unambiguous celebration.[38]

There is no contemporary figure comparable to Mercedes de Acosta (although she could be considered a forebear of Cuban-born nightclub impresario and scene-maker Ingrid Casares). She might, however, be brought up-to-date by means of a retro-chic maneuver, embraced as a rediscovered camp icon, a status confirmed by her friendships with Truman Capote and Andy Warhol in the mid-1950s. With Warhol, in particular, she shared an interest in glamour, fame, Garbo, and her sister Rita's shoes.[39] A signature Warhol butterfly decorated the invitation to the book party for *Here Lies the Heart*, held at his favorite Upper East Side hangout. This connection also suggests another interpretation of de Acosta's significance regarding lesbian celebrity. Like her friend Andy's life and work, Mercedes's story—as she told it and others have retold it—directs attention to the theatricalism of celebrity, its affinity to stage management and showmanship. But rather than dismissing her or anyone else's celebrity as politically suspect because too superficial, too illusory, we might consider how the staging of lesbian celebrity brings otherwise unacknowledged contradictions between cultural ideals and social practices—including sexual ones—into focus.

CHAPTER SIX

POPULAR MECHANICS

ADVANCED TECHNOLOGIES OF
LESBIAN CELEBRITY

In 1985, at age twenty-nine, Martina Navratilova had an image problem. This wasn't a crisis concerning her body image, a case of suffering the damaging effects of "beauty culture" that so many feminist critics write about: girls who starve themselves because they don't look like fashion models or Barbie, young women who take fatal combinations of diet pills, mature women who have liposuction to reduce their dress size, older women who undergo expensive surgery to eradicate the signs of sagging flesh. No, this was a different kind of image problem, a problem with the media's assessment of her character. She had a reputation for indulging her whims (she devoured junk food and expensive jewelry, and owned a fleet of expensive cars); her fashion sense was questionable. She played aggressively but was known to cry when she lost an important match, and she associated with controversial people. Nevertheless, less than a decade later Navratilova had attained worldwide eminence on a scale few in her profession ever achieve, with members of the press leading the applause.

Certainly, Navratilova's prestige was based on her record-setting number of tournament victories, and other major accomplishments in her sport, something that is not directly influenced by unflattering press coverage. But a significant feature of her reputation was that she represented, in a variety of very public arenas, the realization of full-fledged lesbian celebrity—not a star who is secretly lesbian nor a lesbian who becomes famous within the ambit of lesbian culture and may be called upon to act as its delegate to what is called the general public. But because this type of celebrity had been practically impossible until she achieved it, her fame did not come without chal-

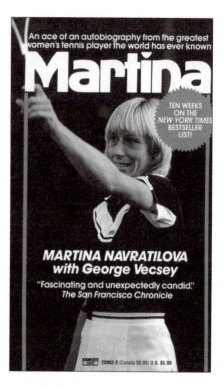

Photograph © Carol L. Newsom

lenges, conflagrations, reproaches, and embarrassments. Perhaps this was the price paid for being one of the first, if not *the* first, lesbian superstars, but these events may also contribute to an understanding of lesbian celebrity that goes beyond a single success story. Navratilova reached and retained iconic status by staking her claim to fame on practices of self-fashioning and self-conduct that have become familiar features of contemporary Western culture. Thus, her lesbian celebrity becomes a case study in the constitution of the new kinds of personhood such technologies of the self produce.

In many respects, Navratilova's history as a courageous seventeen-year-old defector from Communist Czechoslovakia and her often successful performance on the tennis courts should have made her a darling of the sports press. At this point in her career, she had been ranked number one on the professional women's tennis tour for six years, had won the coveted Grand Slam, and the greatest amount of prize money in her sport to date. But these accomplishments did not seem sufficient to counteract the media's nagging attention to what they perceived as her shortcomings. In addition to extravagant spending and eating, the media frequently noted her emotional volatility, inadequate femininity, and, not least of all, her homosexual alliances. How could she solve these image problems? She could afford to hire someone to help her navigate the shoals of public scrutiny, and she did. She was a client of Peter Johnson, a top business agent at the International Management Group (IMG), the largest firm in the business of representing star athletes and other notables. (In 1982, their client list included the Pope.) And she could publish an autobiography that would address all the embarrassing issues routinely mentioned in press coverage of her outstanding athletic achievements, and she did, with the help of *New York Times* sportswriter George Vecsey (Navratilova 1985).[1] At the top of the list of her image management projects was redressing the fallout from her lesbian reputation.

NEWSMAKERS

The reason that references to lesbians and lesbianism were a regular feature of press reports about Navratilova was no mystery. Her affair with Rita Mae Brown that lasted from 1980 to 1981 presented the press with an invitation to add this episode to the stock of knowledge they routinely retrieved from the archive of her individual idiosyncrasies.[2] This was an offer they couldn't refuse, because it added a spicy element to any major story on her. She even cooperated, after a fashion, when she expressed fears that she would be judged adversely because of her association with Brown during an interview in 1981 with a reporter from the *Daily News*. A naïve Navratilova asked him not to publish these remarks, but the paper judged the information too juicy to pass up, although the reporter was considerate enough to delay the publication of the revelation for a few months, until she had been granted U.S. citizenship (Navratilova 1985, 235; Zwerman 1995, 93). But sports journalists had not waited for Navratilova to say publicly what they already knew and peppered their stories with allusions to her sexual relationship with Brown well before the *News* made it official, so to speak.

When she first became involved with Brown and was besieged by reporters for the British tabloids at Wimbledon in 1980 Navratilova denied the affair outright, announcing at a press conference, "I find it offensive and ridiculous that anyone should think that I am gay" (Blue 1994, 96). However, evidence that she not only traveled with the well-known lesbian novelist but also that they had bought a pricey house in Virginia together piled up so fast that, without applying the L-word to Navratilova herself, sportswriters (and presumably readers) were able to connect the dots (Lorge 1981a; Pileggi

1981). Around the same time there was a flood of publicity concerning lesbians on the women's tour in the wake of Marilyn Barnett's lawsuit against
Billie Jean King, the grand dame of women's tennis, in which Barnett claimed
that she should be compensated financially for seven years of devotion to her
ex-lover.[3] When that story first broke, Navratilova and Brown had already
split up, but both were either interviewed or mentioned in articles published
in the national press (Andur 1981; Boswell 1981; Kirshenbaum 1981; Lorge
1981b). The views of Nancy Lieberman, who had little to do with professional tennis but was Martina's newest girlfriend, were also solicited,
although their amorous relationship was never mentioned in these articles.

So in 1981 Navratilova was out, but not really. Brown may have exaggerated her own importance as the only public lesbian in the United States at the
time, but she was indeed a public figure—more so outside the tennis world
than the not yet indomitable Navratilova—due to the success and notoriety of
her first novel, *Rubyfruit Jungle* ([1973] 1977).[4] Therefore, no one would
imagine that the liaison with Brown was not sexual and the tennis player was
not a lesbian. But when Brown told a reporter from the *Washington Post* that
Navratilova had left her for Lieberman, her ex promptly denied it (Mansfield
1981). For the most part, though, Navratilova didn't bother disclaiming a
romance with Lieberman, since Nancy was all too ready to do that for her.
Lieberman was adamantly *not* out. She crafted a semi-credible story that she
was a straight admirer and fellow jock who would rescue Navratilova from a
potentially career-ending slump in her game, which she blamed on Brown's
harmful influence. Navratilova repeated the same account. The sports press
accepted the story and reproduced it endlessly, perhaps because Lieberman
was also an established professional athlete, known as Lady Magic to fans of
women's basketball. Even if they knew Lieberman's story was as fictitious as
Brown's novels, they now had an excuse to look the other way.[5] According to
accounts of a press conference that the new couple held at their home in
Dallas shortly after they became "roommates," Navratilova announced that,
with Nancy's help, she intended to concentrate on improving her tennis, and
Lieberman said that she planned to introduce Martina to potential boyfriends
(Brown 1997, 354; Pileggi 1982). Bisexuality became Navratilova's official
alibi, just like it was for King when she held a press conference to admit the
affair with Barnett and explain her version of events.

Subsequent press coverage of Navratilova and Lieberman's discreet liaison endorsed this rendition of the two women's arrangement, even when
descriptions of their intimacy seemed to indicate otherwise. For example, *Life*

magazine reporter Brad Darrach observed, "They work out together, travel to tournaments together, have screaming fights and hysterical giggles together, visit Nancy's mother together"; he also noted that they shared a bedroom (Darrach 1983). It was years before Lieberman acknowledged that their relationship was sexual. She made this confession in her 1992 autobiography as testimony to the sinful life that preceded her transformation into a born-again Christian, wife, and mother (Lieberman-Cline 1992). Navratilova only discussed Lieberman as a past lover after this disclosure (Navratilova 1993).

Long before "don't ask; don't tell" became shorthand for official U.S. government policies intended to enact a compromise between gay rights advocates who demanded that homosexuality not disqualify men or women from military service and their homophobic opponents, the same principles governed a tacit bargain struck between the sports press and lesbian or gay athletes. Navratilova (and undoubtedly countless others) went along with the strategy, because it allowed them to keep in check nosy, scolding members of the press, or at least those who always treated homosexuality as a sensational topic. Indeed, this was what pundits assessing the King debacle recommended for lesbian tennis players. For instance, a *New York Times* story, "Homosexuality Sets Off Tremors" (Andur 1981), cites the expertise of a psychologist who worked as a consultant for various major sports teams and "advocated anonymity for homosexual athletes" (presumably anonymity *as* homosexual athletes).

Still, for Navratilova the rules of this particular game were never strictly enforced but not suspended either. Shortly before the breakup with Brown, and just weeks after the news of the suit against King leaked out, a *Washington Post* sportswriter remarked that Navratilova had committed "the cardinal sin of athletic superstardom. She's labored to become a person but hasn't yet gotten around to working on a palatable image" (Boswell 1981). Given the context, by palatable he meant an image where Brown, or any other lesbian lover, wasn't in the picture. During the Lieberman years, she managed to keep most inquisitors concerned with revelations about her sexuality at bay, although the press never let readers forget about the past association with Brown. And when she and Nancy parted in early 1984, the image problem flared up again when Judy Nelson appeared on the scene. Nelson's professional identity at the time was mother, which meant that she could not masquerade as a trainer or workout buddy as Lieberman had. By 1984, Navratilova was close to unbeatable, and sports reporters couldn't simply ignore her. Therefore, they couldn't ignore Nelson either. Besides, neither woman seemed especially eager to conceal the fact that they were lovers. Still, sports writers and editors chided Navratilova for refusing to answer questions about her private life.

The press duly reported the appearance of the "newest traveling companion" and "best friend" of the 1984 Wimbledon champion, but more extensive remarks about Nelson were often nasty. She was described as an opportunistic hanger-on in Navratilova's entourage, who was seen making inappropriate gestures—blowing kisses and sending notes to Martina during a match. A reporter for *Sports Illustrated* even blamed Navratilova for his and other members of the press's mean-spirited coverage of Nelson because the tennis star "flaunted her private life." The reproof goes on: "Besides, she selects generally newsworthy friends—professional athletes [Lieberman], a lesbian writer of *romans à clef* [Brown]—and now the blonde Texas mother of two whose heretofore unrevealed talents for publicity put her on the short list with Zsa Zsa Gabor, Ed Koch, Hollywood Henderson, and Pia Zadora" (Deford 1984, 16).

Pete Axthelm, a tennis reporter for *Newsweek*, echoed these sentiments in a column entitled "The Curse of Unlovable Champs" (there were only two unlovables mentioned; the other was tennis's tantrum-throwing bad boy John McEnroe), where he opined that Navratilova "alternately brandishes her unorthodox life-style and recoils from those who seek to explore it, [and therefore] remains a remote figure and a force more readily marveled at than loved" (Axthelm 1984). Axthelm had previously authored a feature article for *Newsweek*, a cover story no less, which was a generally flattering profile of the tennis player and described Navratilova as "complex," "fascinating," and "*honest*" (Axthelm 1982, 45, emphasis added). The story also dealt with Lieberman on her terms—replicating the best-friend-who-is-not-a-lesbian character sketch when he most certainly knew otherwise. This may account for his pique when several years later Navratilova withheld choice soundbites and thumbed her nose at his and other sportswriters' expectations concerning the protocol to be observed by homosexual athletes—a code to which she had previously adhered.

In the final pages of her autobiography, Navratilova deals with the needling from the press she received when Nelson's company became conspicuous in 1984. Beyond that, she is extremely reticent on the subject. She outlines their courtship and her move to Fort Worth to be near Judy, but love, sex, or that her new house was inhabited by both of them are never mentioned (Navratilova 1985, 308–310). In the book, she also downplays lesbianism routinely but nevertheless mentions attractions to women—mainly crushes on female teachers and other tennis players—several times. At one point she says that she came to realize that these feelings had not been "just a phase." In addition, the Brown episode receives ample space—an entire chapter and various comments elsewhere. Navratilova's regrets about the affair are evident but these have more to do with having been distracted from her calling by Rita Mae, who cajoled her into going to museums and theaters instead of the practice courts, than with having her love life made public (Navratilova 1985, 213).

Perhaps the attention Navratilova devoted to Brown in her autobiography was meant as a public response to the novelist's continued efforts to convince her to come out unambiguously. Brown pursued her campaign for full disclosure in her novel *Sudden Death* (1983), which details the fierce rivalries and underhanded dealings that go on behind the scene on the professional women's tennis tour. The book features an up-and-coming tennis pro, Carmen Semana, who ditches her older, intellectual girlfriend when the exposure of their homosexual relationship by an unscrupulous reporter threatens her career. Carmen gives in to pressures exerted by her agent, her professional organization, tour sponsors and promoters, and marketing executives, who urge her to end the relationship or disgrace women's tennis and ruin her chances for product endorsements. As a kind of divine retribution, Carmen is then consumed with guilt and loses the cherished Grand Slam, the prize she had imagined would be won by giving in to the representatives of institutionalized homophobia. The book presented a credible moral dilemma, no doubt, but it did not prove prophetic. By the time it appeared Navratilova's ascent to tennis superstardom was well underway, and she won a "little" Grand Slam in 1984.[6]

Although it is difficult to determine how much and with what results the reports about Navratilova's love life in the press affected her popularity with tennis fans, these stories were the major available sources of information about her. Thus, what was printed and what was omitted pretty much circumscribed the fans' knowledge. Portrayed as a sometimes lesbian, with other less-than-perfect features such as being a junk food junkie and overweight as a result (in her early twenties), as well as an Eastern European, bred and trained under Communist party auspices, she appeared for years in the press in an unflattering light to tennis fans, most of whom, not surprisingly, did not greet her warmly or cheer her very heartily when she won. However, in her own estimate, the real image problem did not stem from her disfavor with fans but from the press that influenced them and, subsequently, the sports-wear and other manufacturers who did not engage her to endorse their wares.

PACKAGE DEALS

Image problem number one—lesbian Martina—led directly to image problem number two—uncommodifiable Martina. Or, rather, criticisms of her handling of the Brown affair and repeated references to this episode in the press overflowed into the multidimensional universe of professional sports, which she needed to navigate. And a significant dimension of that universe was the sphere where players' agents negotiated endorsement deals with product manufacturers. In the case of top players, the income from these contracts might surpass greatly the prize money a player won. Indeed, it was—and still is—not uncommon that a promising new player, if deemed photogenic and wholesome or heterosexy, could benefit more from endorsement contracts than many of her more seasoned and accomplished elders.[7] An instructive example is described by John Feinstein in *Hard Courts: Real Life on the Professional Tennis Tours*. In 1990, he writes, "[Zina] Garrison, the fourth-ranked player in the world, didn't even have a shoe or clothing contract," compared with not-quite-fourteen-year-old Jennifer Capriati, who in the same year signed endorsement contracts for $4.5 million even before she turned pro (Feinstein 1992, 121). In this case, the explanation for the enormous disparity has nothing to do with sexuality or nationality, but race. Garrison is African American, and Capriati is white. Racial identity no longer affects endorsements so decisively, as can be seen in the plentiful product promotions involving Venus and Serena Williams, the African American sisters who rose to the top ranks of women's tennis at the end of the 1990s, but it clearly did earlier in the decade.

Navratilova indicates that her image problem—she uses the phrase—hurt her mightily in this branch of the business, a theme she returns to consistently in her assessment of her career. Recalling her plans for a comeback in 1981, she writes in her autobiography, "I was really concerned about my image—not so much who I thought I was, not so much what the public thought, but what the gnomes and the gremlins in the business world thought. The unseen 'They' who decides what the public feels" (Navratilova 1985, 236–237). Almost a decade later, she expressed similar rancor to Feinstein: "[Monica] Seles is making more money from Yonex [the racket manufacturer] than I am. . . . It isn't a matter of needing the money; it's other people putting some kind of value on you" (Feinstein 1992, 390). And as recently as 2000, in an interview for the *Advocate*, Navratilova reiterated her disappointment about this injustice (Navratilova 2000).

Navratilova may have hoped that as her career picked up steam in 1981 endorsement contracts would follow, but Billie Jean King's experience the same year provided sobering evidence that this was not likely. The taint of lesbianism could scotch any impending deal and preclude others in the future. In her book on various scandals in women's sports, Mary Jo Festle lists the economic fallout of the so-called galimony scandal that affected King directly:

> Negotiations for a Wimbledon clothing line deal [she had won the women's singles there five times] worth $500,000, which had virtually been finalized, fell through after the news came out. She also lost endorsements with a Charleston hosiery company, a Japanese clothing company, and a blue jeans contract worth $300,000. She took for granted that over the next three years she lost at least $1,500,000. She took for granted that many other companies would not renew their contracts with her once they ran out and doubted that new products would sign her. In fact, a year later, she was the only major player in the world without a clothing endorsement contract. (Festle 1996, 239)

Navratilova, who was spared the kind of public embarrassment King endured, was not denied all endorsement contracts, but manufacturers rarely offered her lucrative deals, a development she interpreted as punishment for her sexual preference. She wasn't poor, however, although unlike many other players of her stature her fortune was built mainly on prize money won over the years—over twenty million dollars at the time of her retirement from singles competition in 1994.

In fact, Navratilova was the first female athlete to win over one million dollars in one year, 1982, for which she could again thank King, although this time the effects of King's actions were more welcome. In 1970, King had led a boycott of the professional tennis tour by women players who wanted to demonstrate their unwillingness to accept the disparity between the prize money handed out to men and women in their sport, as well as the unequal number of tournaments and matches within major tournaments like the U.S. Open, which likewise whittled away their potential earnings. However, the argument put forward by King and other supporters of equal pay and treatment by professional organizations was not that women claimed to be athletically equivalent to men in their sport but that they were as good, if not better, *entertainers.* They produced a show to which spectators flocked. Arguing the case, King claimed, "For two years we've outdrawn the men at Forest Hills [the former site of the U.S. Open] by whatever criteria they've used, but this year the men's money was two and a half times the women's" (Kirkpatrick 1972).

This is not a position Navratilova was eager to defend, since she regarded herself as an athlete who deserved the same opportunities as men on that account alone. Moreover, she was critical of other players she suspected of being more interested in celebrity than in athletic accomplishment (Navratilova 1985, 60). But Feinstein, who presents an in-depth study of the sport from the perspective of a conscientious journalist, concurs with King and comments that "box-office appeal counts just as much, if not more, than on-court ability" in determining the amount a player might be offered as a guarantee, which is the hefty fee paid to a popular player for merely showing up for a tournament and a source of considerable income for top-ranked players like Navratilova (Feinstein 1992, 99). Once she became one of the most successful players in the world—she was ranked number one for 223 weeks over eight years—she could count on receiving offers of such guarantees, but high-paying and image-enhancing endorsements still eluded her.

The entertainment factor in women's tennis had further repercussions for players, which involved unofficial influence exerted by entertainment entities like television networks on supposedly unbiased decisions made by tennis officials. For instance, Feinstein reports, "The U.S. Open is run by CBS. The USA Network, which does the weekday cablecasts, has some say, but CBS is clearly in charge. CBS is so much in charge that agents will call the network to find out what court their clients are being assigned and even when to lobby just a bit for a spot on a show court" (Feinstein 1992, 381–382). For Navratilova to truly ignore how entertainment values increasingly governed her sport would be disingenuous and impractical, not something a successful professional athlete in the late twentieth century could really afford. This brings us to image problem number three.

LIKE A WOMAN

In her own assessment, Navratilova's biggest image problem was not lesbianism per se, nor was it the negative effect of advertisers' disregard, although this may have been the effect that she dwelled upon long after she had amassed a good-sized fortune.[8] The major problem she describes in her autobiography is femininity or, rather, her shortcomings in that department. The book opens with an anecdote about being mistaken for a boy at age twelve, which she informs the reader was quite common and led to worries about being abnormal (Navratilova 1985, n.p.). Throughout the text she returns to similar questions, noting how she eventually came to realize the importance of cultivating a feminine appearance and how, under Lieberman's tutelage, she began to take steps in this direction. A lesson in makeup at the Vidal Sassoon salon in New York in 1981 is mentioned, related to her decision to lighten her hair and have it styled more fashionably (Navratilova 1985, 238). Tellingly, the section of photographs included in the book begins with a glamorous head shot, not one of the images of the athlete at work or snapshots from the Navratil family album that also appear in the book.

The press responded favorably to the renovated Navratilova. Articles published in 1982 continued to refer to previous times when she seemed dowdy, chubby, and awkward, and they delighted especially in recalling the epithet coined by the dean of tennis commentators, Bud Collins, to describe pudgy post-defection Martina: the Great Wide Hope. But they also mentioned approvingly her new streamlined look. Axthelm's story in *Newsweek* made much ado about her makeover and quoted the champion as saying, "I've been growing into [my body] and the last few years I've felt more like a woman than ever before" (Axthelm 1982, 48). This may be a slightly inaccurate figure of speech, since one of the most frequently mentioned improvements in Navratilova's appearance was that she lost some twenty-odd pounds. The author then added that this newfound femininity was assisted by cosmetics but that such superficial touches are only the outer manifestation of "a bright new inner Martina" (45).[9]

However, the cover photo that announces the feature article does not picture a particularly feminine Martina, but instead shows a very muscular and aggressive tennis player in motion, as does the first photo of her inside the magazine. If anything, Navratilova's concern with her appearance may have been a canny attempt to placate the professional organization that governed her sport, the Women's Tennis Association. Anxious about rumors and evidence of lesbians in their ranks, the WTA tried to encourage femininity among younger players, instructing them in its 1986 edition of the *Guide to Playing Professional Tennis*,

> Whether you are glamorous, athletic, businesslike, or intellectual, make sure your image is one that the press will latch on to in a positive way.

Two photographs that accompanied a
Newsweek story on Martina Navratilova
in 1982. The picture on the right was
captioned "'The Great Wide Hope' playing in 1976." Photo by Melchior
DiGiacomo. The one above was
described as "night life with Rita Mae
Brown." Photo by Art Seitz.

> Take time over your appearance. Select tennis clothes carefully and pay
> attention to what you wear at player functions. . . . How you conduct
> yourself *off* the court may have more significance to your career than any-
> thing you ever do *on* the court. (quoted in Festle 1996, 243)

At a time when she was intent on becoming the best player in the history of her sport, Navratilova would have been unwise to make enemies among those who controlled it.

It is easy to read the extravagant anxiety Navratilova expressed in her autobiography about not being considered sufficiently feminine as an attempt to deflect attention from questions about sexuality or as a coded discussion of the same. To some degree, this seems justified. On the other hand, it may be helpful to remember that the tension between women's athletics and defini-tions of femininity have not always involved homosexuality. From a histori-cal perspective, the more persistent problem is gender, although sexuality always figures in reasons given about why women should not engage in sports. Susan Cahn makes this point in her historical study of the changing views regarding women's participation in sport in the United States from the nineteenth century until the end of the twentieth. Common to the entire epoch, Cahn explains, were worries about erosion of masculine values, which could be sustained on the basis of claims of men's physical superiority exhib-ited in athletic contests (Cahn 1994, 20). However, when women first demanded admittance to playing fields and ball courts opponents expressed fears that physical exertion would damage the athletes' reproductive organs, not that they would become become one anothers' lovers.

Then, as now, women who excelled at sport were apt to be accused of being "mannish," but for many decades this adjective was associated with any sort of sexual appetite, which was widely believed to be a masculine trait. Since a characteristic of true femininity was assumed to be a lack of interest in sex, and these sportswomen were assumed to be heterosexual, the earliest female competitive athletes were accused of being oversexed. The presuppo-sition that sports lead to and/or foster deviant female sexuality arose only in the 1930s, when medical expertise became the arbiter of the discourse con-cerning a number of sexual practices, especially homosexuality. "Between 1900 and 1930," Cahn writes, the

> sexual debate in sport centered on the problem of unbridled heterosexual
> desire, the prospect that "masculine" sport might loosen women's inhibi-

tions toward men. But by the 1930s female athletic mannishness began to connote failed (rather than excessive) heterosexuality. . . . The impression of heterosexual "failure" contained a further possibility as well: The amazonian athlete might be not only unattractive but unattracted to men— she might prefer women. (Cahn 1994, 165)

Lesbianism replaced licentiousness as the danger awaiting women who ventured into this masculine domain.

Many women interested in sport were not discouraged by the rhetoric meant to deter them, and counterarguments in favor of the benefits of physical exercise eventually prevailed. In addition, a compromise of sorts was struck that eased women's entry into what was generally perceived as male territory when female sports competitions were presented as entertaining spectacles, designed to attract spectators interested primarily in ogling women's bodies. As early as the 1880s, enterprising promoters of women's sports in the United States recognized this possibility, while the women who participated by displaying their athleticism in ways that were deemed unseemly were accused of being prostitutes (Cahn 1994, 14). Cahn reports that in the 1920s, sports tournaments for women often included beauty contests, and press reports on athletic displays by women frequently concentrated on participants' faces and figures.[10] Of course, the tradition lives on, after a fashion, in *Sports Illustrated*'s annual swimsuit issue and athletes' recruitment as models by fashion vendors.[11] At the height of her career in 1985, Navratilova, too, could be found posing in various designer outfits in the pages of *Vogue* (Strand 1985). This culmination of her hope for feminine validation was then repeated when she opened the doors of her Fort Worth home to a photographer from *Architectural Digest* the next year (Bryan 1986).

Navratilova was not the first female sports star to embark on a campaign to counteract a masculinized image by consciously undertaking a makeover. Decades earlier, Babe Didrikson, perhaps the most accomplished of all twentieth-century American women athletes, devised a similar strategy of image management and effected a more drastic metamorphosis than Navratilova's. After she first received notice for her two gold medals and one silver in track and field events at the 1932 Olympics, Didrikson was routinely described by the press as "boyish," although they might as well have said "butch," since the androgynous look of the 1920s flapper had by then gone out of style and muscular, flat-chested women with cropped hair like young Didrikson had become associated with sexual deviance. She made little effort to appear otherwise until once established in the national spotlight. Then she remade her looks from head to toe—prettied up with longer, permed hair and makeup, wearing only skirts in public—and she even acquired a husband to complete the transformation. She also changed the sport in which she competed to the more ladylike game of golf, which she then dominated for several decades. Apparently, the press and public never questioned her "mannishness" again, and she managed to conceal a long-standing lesbian relationship with one of her protégées until after her death in 1955 (Cayleff 1995).

Compared with Didrikson, Navratilova's newfound femininity entailed rather minor adjustments. But the more substantial makeover she underwent took her in what appears at first the opposite direction genderwise. Around the same time that she was doing her best to look pretty at key PR moments, Navratilova was also engaged in a rigorous workout and training program in order to rebuild her body into a powerful physical instrument. Her athletic talent, often described as natural, had begun to dissipate, a decline she attributed retrospectively to a lack of discipline: too little practice and too much rich food. Lieberman was the instigator of the new regimen, although Navratilova's dedication to maintaining a strict diet and a carefully planned program of strenuous exercise and practice lasted long after their breakup in 1984. She assembled a staff comprising several coaches, a nutritionist, a trainer, and various others hired to maintain peak performance of the champion's body. The group was dubbed Team Navratilova by members of the sports press, who had never seen a similar congregation of physical expertise in a female athlete's employ.

By 1983, the descriptive language used by the press in articles on Navratilova began to shift from descriptions of the usual list of performance highlights and characteristic on-court maneuvers to her impressive anatomy. *Life*, for example, described her as the "F-15 of tennis . . . [who] embodies the state of the art, the ultimate in technical refinement and combat performance" (Darrach 1983, 20). *Time* quoted Virginia Wade, the British tennis champion: "'So fit, so fast, so quick off the mark, so athletic, so confident. To me, she's like a finely tuned sports car, a Ferrari really'" (Callahan 1983). *Vogue* sounded the same note, commenting that "her physique is intimidatingly muscular" (Strand 1985, 343), and even ran a sidebar that detailed her training program for readers who might be aspiring tennis pros, although they omitted instructions for weight lifting (J. Kaplan 1985). Perhaps this aspect of her workout was deleted because, despite the feminization cam-

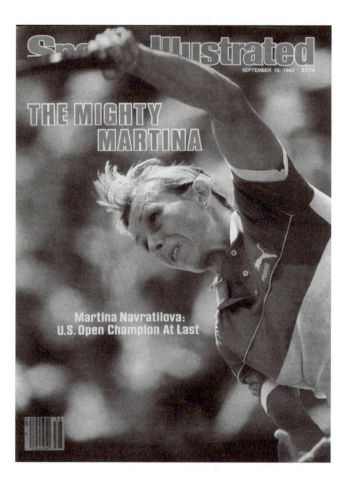

A remodeled
Navratilova in
1983. Sports
Illustrated.

paign abetted by *Vogue* itself, her fitness routine produced a body that evoked alarming visions of marauding amazons. The *Life* article was the most explicit in this regard:

> Her neck is a woven column of muscle. Her arms and legs are sinewy,
> powerful, roped with big veins. She has hands like a workman and her
> belly is a washboard of flexible ridges. Except for the small breasts and
> shapely hips, her superbly conditioned physique might be that of a man.
> (Darrach 1983, 20)

She was testing and pushing gender boundaries in a sport that always prided itself on the ladylike comportment of its players. As one concession to this tradition, Navratilova, just like all of her fellow competitors, still wore a skirt while engaging in ferocious battles for titles, prize money, and fame. Despite this symbolic concession to traditional femininity, for a long period of time—from 1981 to 1987—she won numerous titles and scads of money, which gained her a reputation as almost superhuman.

CYBORG LOGIC

The mechanical imagery applied to Navratilova did not stop at the fascination with her newly streamlined body. The computer programs designed by both her nutritionist and a strategist hired to help analyze her own and opponents' playing styles and weaknesses supports the contention of a writer for *World Tennis* that she had mutated into a cyborg—part human, part machine (Kalyn 1983). The cyborg has become a favorite metaphor among analysts of the forms of subjectivity characteristic of postmodern cultures. Perhaps the best known proponent of this approach is Donna Haraway, whose "Cyborg Manifesto" explains the utility of this figure for understanding social relations between subjects in advanced industrial societies. These mongrel creatures are, for Haraway, "monstrous and illegitimate" but also capable of modeling radical political possibilities (Haraway 1991, 149–154).

At the outset of her essay, Haraway makes clear that her cyborg is a myth, although not therefore disqualified from political discourse, since, as she argues effectively, the concepts governing all social identities are similarly fictional. In other words, she embraces the antiessentialist theoretical frameworks developed by feminist, postcolonial, and queer theorists for whom the appeal to any natural identity or difference is inherently oppressive, as in the case whenever the idea of "woman," for instance, informs restrictive and pernicious policies and practices. Cyborgs embody certain kinds of knowledge, which include, among other things, innovative ideas about human capabilities. Although a cyborg may seem an exotic entity, most are extraordinarily mundane. Cyborgs should be understood as novel but increasingly familiar kinds of subjects, "new ways for people to be" (Hacking 1986, 223) and new categories that identify such people. Ian Hacking proposes that such new identities are effects of social change but adds that although a particular category may be linked to programs for social control it may also introduce new possibilities for how people may be described or what they may do.

In her quest for self-realization, Navratilova became a cyborg. Her ambitions led her to venture beyond the established formula for athletic success: talent, combined with dedication and intelligent coaching. The transforma-

tion began in 1981, when Lieberman, whose experience in professional basketball taught her that an athlete must achieve optimum conditioning if she
is to reach the top of her game, encouraged Navratilova to adhere to a serious exercise regimen. In 1982, she embarked on a radical new diet. The
results were evident immediately. That year she won ninety out of ninety-
three matches, eighty-six of eighty-seven in 1983, and six consecutive Grand
Slam titles beginning with Wimbledon in 1983. In 1984, her fellow players
on the women's pro tennis tour acknowledged her dominance when they
composed and sang a ditty to the tune of Michael Jackson's "Beat It" at a
party during the Eastbourne tournament in England:

> Martina, you're too good./Just give us a break./You're beating us so
> bad./It's too hard to take./Quit eating that food./And lift no more
> weights./Stop it! Stop it!/Have some more sex./Have some more booze./It
> doesn't matter if you win or lose. (quoted in Deford 1984, 14–15)

By all accounts, the seemingly indomitable player altered forever the criteria
for fitness in women's tennis. Ultrafemme Chris Evert, for example, began to
lift weights in an attempt to remain competitive with her chief rival
(although her efforts ultimately failed).

Navratilova's conditioning was not limited to conventional methods used
to improve performance, adding techniques previously unknown in her sport.
She engaged the services of Robert Haas, a specialist in sports medicine, who
regulated Navratilova's diet based on computer analysis of her blood chemistry. Haas also had a hand in writing the computer program that evaluated
the condition of her muscles at a given point so that exercises could be tailored appropriately, as well as a computerized scouting program for devising
a game plan to be used when playing a specific opponent. Of course, such
attempts to apply rational calculation in athletic arenas were undertaken well
before then by managers and coaches in a variety of team sports, where players are instructed to enact maneuvers much like pieces on a chess board.
However, tennis, more than team sports, demands spontaneity on the part of
the individual player, who is on her own while on court (consultation with
coaches during a match is forbidden) and must be able to adjust her playing
strategy to counter an opponent's action at a moment's notice. Discipline
becomes particularly crucial during preparation for the game, which in
Navratilova's case was approached as a process of scientific measurement and
regulation of her physical and mental reflexes.

"The Brave, New Martina" in
World Tennis, 1983.

One of the most striking representations of Martina-as-cyborg appeared in the April 1983 issue of *World Tennis* magazine. The cover features a smiling Navratilova, with electronic circuit boards embossed on her forearm and hand, while the opening photo depicts her standing with arms angled away from her torso, like a paper doll, against a background pattern that resembles an integrated circuit. Could the association with the rational technologies of self-control be any more explicit? The article quotes Haas: "She is the first tennis player to put herself in the position to be scientifically manipulated to enhance her performance." He then predicted, "She will be the first example of what I think will be a new breed of athlete . . . the first bionic tennis player"(Kalyn 1983, 58).

Speaking for herself, Navratilova disclaimed remarks that attributed her near unbeatability to some kind of cybernetic engineering, finding these insulting. Her published comments indicated that what peeved her most was the implication that her excellence was not her own achievement, not that she used specialized mechanisms to enhance her game. For example, she told a reporter for *Time*, who introduced the topic with a reference to "counselors and coaches, who peck at computers as she plays, as though they were operating her by remote control," by informing him, "The computer has done nothing for my tennis but wonders for my diet" (Callahan 1983, 40). But despite her insistence on the minimal influence of measuring, calibrating, and statistical analysis on her accomplishments, she took an active part in promoting an approach to the game that was thoroughly technological, insofar as she adopted a raft of rational strategies with the aim of cultivating the body and mind of a champion.

WITH AUTHORITY

Navratilova may have poo-poohed the importance of scientific calculations when interviewed about the secrets of her success while it was happening, but in later years, when her career was winding down, she extolled these methods and their underlying premises. The platform she found for promoting her physical fitness ethic, as well as a general philosophy concerning the benefits of conditioning, was unusual. She did not embark on a second career as a coach of younger players or a writer of advice columns in sports magazines.[12] No, she became a writer of detective fiction, coauthoring three novels between 1994 and 1997. At one level, these books seem an obvious public relations gimmick intended to keep her name in circulation, but they can also be read as a retrospective assessment of her career, as well as commentary on her celebrity. All the novels are set in locations familiar to any fan of women's tennis—Wimbledon, the French Open, Hilton Head—and feature characters who bear resemblances to well-known individuals in that profession. And the plots provide multiple opportunities for the protagonist in all the novels, a former tennis player, to confront and comment upon a variety of problems that have plagued the sport—exploitation, greed, and celebrity itself—with the notable exception of homosexuality.

Writing mystery novels may have appealed to Navratilova because, as Julian Symons comments, the genre is akin to sport: a game with a set of rules established by its earliest practitioners, Edgar Allan Poe and Arthur Conan Doyle. Those who compose such stories adhere to the principles faithfully, and those who read them participate as players in the game. One rule, for instance, is that the criminal should be introduced early and cannot be the detective or a professional crook. Another is fair play: no clues can be fraudulent. When the criminal's identity is finally revealed, the reader should be surprised but not because she was given deceptive information. "Starting from the assumption that the detective story was a game," explains Symons, "the rules had two purposes, first to describe the nature of the game and then to show how it should be played. . . . [C]lues had to be provided, and it was necessary that the detective should draw from them rational and inevitable conclusions" (Symons 1972, 105). Another analyst of the form, Marxist economic and political theorist Ernest Mandel, also points out the mechanical quality of these novels: "[T]he classical detective story is a formalized puzzle, a mechanism that can be composed and decomposed, unwound and then wound up again like the works of a clock" (Mandel 1984, 18). In this respect, he finds detective fiction the apt counterpart of other mechanized cultural forms introduced in the mid-nineteenth century, photography, for instance.

Navratilova and her coauthor, Liz Nickles, stay well within the boundaries of the classical form in their collaborations, staging three elaborate criminal schemes for the protagonist, Jordan Myles, to untangle over the course of the three novels. An additional level of intrigue is added, though, when Navratilova's celebrity persona hovers over the pages of these otherwise unremarkable texts. Like all novels in the genre, the main character in the Navratilova–Nickles concoctions is the detective who solves the mysteries, with the help of a sidekick, a former police detective who is more knowledgeable about the nuts and bolts of detection and provides Jordan with advice as well as occasional protection from murderous criminals. But, despite whatever one might expect, this amateur PI is decidedly not a fictionalized Martina Navratilova. Instead, she is a formerly promising, but never triumphal, tennis professional who suffered a debilitating accident and became a physical therapist, now employed at a state-of-the-art sports clinic. Her sexual involvements are heterosexual, and she has dark hair.

Still, Navratilova is not entirely offstage. The dust jacket for the second novel, *Breaking Point* (1996), features a photograph of the tennis star with her laptop instead of a more typical pictorial rendition of the main character or an emblematic scene. Her face also adorns the jacket for *Killer Instinct* (1997), the third novel, against a blood red image of a dead tennis player. In the first of the series, *The Total Zone* (1994), Navratilova does not appear on the cover but is neatly integrated into the text, insofar as her name comes up repeatedly in conversation among characters chatting about the tennis world. Moreover, another character in that book, Mariska Storrs, is an undisguised Navratilova

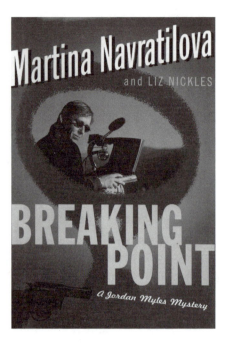

Photograph by Jeffrey Aaronson

near-clone: defector from the Soviet Union, lesbian, who speaks words about the longevity of her career that can be found in biographical portraits of the real Martina.[13] In *Killer Instinct*, another top-ranked émigré champ named Seranata Aziz is referred to by a younger player as "the Lege" (as in "legendary"), which in tennis lore is what teen phenom Jennifer Capriati dubbed Navratilova in 1990 (Navratilova and Nickles 1997, 6). Jordan Myles, too, is allotted snippets of the author's biography. For example, she prefers to drink her bottled water without ice, which hard-core fans will recognize as one of the Lege's quirks, and she goes to work as a part-time television commentator at major women's tennis tournaments, as Navratilova did for CBS and HBO after her retirement from singles competition (3). And, just like her famous creator, one of Jordan's friends from her days on the tennis tour is Billie Jean King (194). Such self-conscious references satisfy the fan, whose interest in the novels is likely to stem from interest in the tennis star, and simultaneously remind the reader of the author's insider status when it comes to commentary on the inner workings of the pro tennis scene. There is an additional dimension to the confusion between the author's identity and that of the protagonist: it produces a compelling mystery for the reader—finding the true Martina—and thus pleasure in the game of solving it, even if never gratified.

Detective fiction may offer another lure, in addition to that of pursuing clues, involving the writer's display of expertise, which Mandel understands as a way to "endow one's commodities with additional use value" beyond mere thrills and escape from everyday concerns (Mandel 1984, 78). The author's specialized knowledge may be the result of extensive research, but Mandel points out that it may also be acquired during a previous career, and he cites a number of examples, from Michael Crichton to Umberto Eco. Clearly, detective novelist Navratilova belongs in this category and, as such, presents retrospective commentary on social relations within professional tennis. Not surprisingly, the media and its power to produce celebrity is a common topic in these pages. *The Total Zone*, Navratilova–Nickles' initial effort, introduces our hero as she negotiates the crowd gathered at a massive media event, a gala awards presentation honoring outstanding athletes at Madison Square Garden, no doubt similar to many such affairs Navratilova attended. Jordan quickly becomes involved in a scuffle with the paparazzi, who muscle her out of their way to get a shot of a major sports star. Lesson number one: the media are dangerous, and if there is any mistaking this implication it is dispelled by the appearance of security guards on the scene. Lesson number two: the media and professional sports are a symbiotic pair.

At one point in the novel, an old tennis hand (modeled on the legendary tennis expert and aficionado Ted Tinling), who has seen all the great players in action, instructs Jordan in the similarities between great competitive athletes and great movie actors: "Kelly [a Chris Evert stand-in] created a persona the fans liked, and she acted the part totally. The media knows what the public wants to read—and if they want to sell stories that's what they'll give them. If she had worked in Hollywood, Kelly could have won an Oscar" (Navratilova and Nickles 1994, 97). As things turn out for a young tennis starlet who is a client at Jordan's clinic and commits suicide in mysterious circumstances just before the Wimbledon tournament, the pressure to perform both athletically and theatrically can be deadly. In the end, however, the media does not emerge as the true culprit. Rather, it is an obsessive fan and a manipulative father who share the blame for the young woman's death. However, the twisted psyches of both villains can be attributed to the media-related phenomenon of celebrity worship: The fan stabs a player who might defeat his idol in an important match (shades of the Steffi Graf fan who stabbed Monica Seles to eliminate her from competition). The father forces his daughter to be a tennis celebrity even though she would rather not (shades of too many tennis fathers to mention).

The second novel is less concerned with the media, concentrating instead on the evils of unscrupulous sports managers and promoters. Still, spectacle is what these bad guys bank on, and therefore the media is always a handmaiden to their schemes. By book three Jordan has become a full-fledged member of the press contingent at the big matches. Her new position allows her to contemplate the unblinking gaze of the camera eye, which "enhances each [player's] move as if you are a specimen under a microscope" (Navratilova and Nickles 1997, 4). But she manages to overcome her reservations and eventually becomes something of a celebrity as the host of a magazine show called *Women/Sport*. In this capacity she once again encounters the effects of unscrupulous wheeler-dealers who want to make megaprofits in the business of pro sports. In this case, Jordan is courted by an ambitious firm interested in enlisting her to do an infomercial for a sports drink and related products designed to increase an athlete's endurance. The entire enterprise becomes the site of heinous acts, everything from deception by Jordan's lover and colleague at the clinic, who invented the new products and tries to browbeat her into accepting the endorsement deal, to the string of dead bodies poisoned inadvertently by the drink. After Jordan assembles the evidence, she figures out that the formula for the high-tech brew contained quantities of vitamin A and potassium that are toxic for anyone with a slightly defective heart—the familiar twentieth-century story of science run amok, although science also provides the clues that allow Jordan to figure out the mystery.

In her sideline as a television personality, Jordan risks colluding in these atrocities by promoting the drink, although media institutions are again exonerated. In fact, it is her TV job that allows her to stake out a position independent of her lover, who is so busy trying to capitalize on his chemistry experiment that he becomes careless and callous. Jordan's post-tennis identity brings her fame, and therefore freedom, that surpasses what she achieved during her fleeting career on the courts. No longer under the microscope or a mere spectator, she is now aligned with the media's power. One could speculate that Navratilova used her fictional heroine as an imaginary attempt to claim some of the media's power for herself. But her diminished ire might also be interpreted as Navratilova's assertion of mastery over that power, on her own terms.

BODY POLITICS

The changing interpretation of the relationship between media and sports that occurs over the course of the three mystery novels may indicate how author Navratilova revised her thinking about this complex issue after she had spent time in the press booth at Wimbledon and elsewhere. But the treatment of the second major locus of power that emerges—scientific technologies of the self—remains consistent in the books, as well as consistent with Navratilova's own history. In addition to providing the perspective of an insider in the professional tennis milieu, Jordan is portrayed as a credentialed proponent of the sort of disciplinary methods Navratilova mastered in order to achieve international athletic stardom—diet and fitness programs complemented by techniques designed to improve mental conditioning, so that the athletic body can achieve peak performance in an individual sport like tennis, where optimum mind/body integration and functioning are necessary for competing against top players. In this respect, Jordan *is* the star's alter ego. This is the pervasive theme in the Jordan Myles novels and suggests a more extensive critique of Navratilova's attitude toward herself, in addition to a reading of these books as an authoritative gloss on professional women's tennis.

What Navratilova tapped into and took advantage of as an athlete is best described in terms of the modern political framework that Michel Foucault calls bio-power and the related concept bio-politics. As Foucault defines it, bio-politics involves the concentration of political power in the administration of life, as compared to power wielded through systems of punishment and death-threatening obligations, such as public torture and compulsory military service. Foucault argues that bio-politics, more specifically what he calls the "anatomo-politics of the human body," is a modern formation "centered on the body as a machine: its disciplining, the optimization of its capabilities, the extortion of its forces, the parallel increase of its usefulness and its docility, its integration into systems of efficient and economic controls" (Foucault 1978, 139). This abstract description resonates particularly well with Navratilova's formula for human achievement as she put it into practice, inscribed it on her body, and reinscribed it in her detective novels. Although Navratilova's project at first appears aimed at mobilizing timeless and universal human capacities, it is in fact related directly to a particular set of social, historical conditions.

The premises and practices at the Desert Spring Sports Science Clinic where Jordan works, as well as those adopted by Navratilova in the 1980s, offer an excellent example of how bio-power is constituted. Consider, for example, Jordan's introductory description of her workplace and the roster of her profession colleagues:

The lushly landscaped grounds included fifteen tennis courts with Deco
turf, hard Har-Tru, red clay and grass surfaces, rebound Ace and even an
indoor Supreme court; a regulation basketball court; a baseball and soft-
ball field; a soccer field; a 500,000-gallon superpool; and a new eighteen-
hole golf course. We drove past the cutting-edge fitness center that also
housed physical-therapy facilities and the technical core for computerized
nutritional profiling and tracking and video motion analysis of golf swings
and tennis strokes. The staff buildings, next to the parking lot . . . contained the offices of the cream of the crop culled from all aspects of medicine, including sports psychologists, rehabilitationists, acupuncturists,
homeopathic specialists, licensed nutritionists, an osteopath, and a visiting
professor of kinesiology and bioengineering. (Navratilova and Nickles
1994, 26)

Details about what some of these technicians actually do are sprinkled
throughout the texts, as are examples of how athletes apply their expert
advice in their daily lives. For instance, Malik, a basketball star who wants to
transform himself into a tennis champion, exhibits for the clinic staff his self-
monitoring diary:

"I keep a record of everything. . . . I got in here what I eat, the supple-
ments I take, how much I sleep, the stretches I do, and my complete
training program, of course; my log from the gym, aerobic and anaerobic,
number of reps, amount of weight, number of strokes on each machine."
(Navratilova and Nickles 1997, 91)

The brother of another client in another novel reviews the potions in his sister's refrigerator: "[E]vening primrose oil. Flaxseed oil. Vitamin E—four
hundred units. Vitamin C. Beta-carotene. Choline" (Navratilova and Nickles
1994, 68). The list goes on for an additional ten lines or so. These and similar passages leave an impression of endless possibilities for improvement of
the body-machine, ample fuel for a bio-mechanic's dream of building a better person. Of course, the prototype is Navratilova herself.

Presented in these programmatic terms, the bio-engineering of
Navratilova's body might seem at odds with her commitment to improving
her image. But these two aspects of Navratilova's reinvention of herself need
not be taken as contradictory, especially if we consider that the self-fashioning
practices involved in producing a desired self-image are always exercises of

bio-power, too. A few additional words from Foucault may clarify: bio-power, he explains, brings "life and its mechanisms into the realm of explicit calculations and [makes] knowledge-power an agent for the transformation of human life" (Foucault 1978, 143). For Navratilova, going blond and putting on blush were as much calculations as building muscle, since she could see the earnings side of her bank account swell with every visit to the hairdresser or dab of the makeup brush as she made herself more marketable. In addition, it seems fair to take at face value Navratilova's statements that her attention to grooming made her *feel* better, allowed her to think more clearly, more strategically, since she no longer needed to fend off snide comments about her eating binges and could get on with collecting prizes and praises for her on-court skill. In addition to the income she received from winning, she garnered the pleasures of championship.

MIXED REVIEWS

Curiously, Navratilova's biography, so packed with details of her self-fashioning, lacks a concomitant lesbian self-invention chapter. This is particularly remarkable since the Navratilova saga refers consistently to the importance of self-knowledge, which is the typical rationale for coming out. For many years, long after the Brown affair and during the time when she made no effort to conceal her sexual relationship with Nelson, statements about Navratilova's sexuality—by her as well as by the press—remained ambiguous. Not until the breakup with Nelson in 1991 and the publicity generated when Nelson sued her for half her earnings during the years they were together, which added up to multimillions in prize money alone, did Navratilova say what everyone knew already. In fact, in an interview with Barbara Walters on the newsmagazine TV program *20/20* that many consider her formal coming out, Navratilova did not mention the word lesbian, although she said quite explicitly that their relationship involved sex, as well as love.[14]

Before long, she began lending her name, and sometimes more, to various lesbian and gay political campaigns—criticizing public policy on AIDS, appearing at benefits for AIDS organizations, becoming a plaintiff in the American Civil Liberties Union's challenge to Colorado's constitutional amendment that prohibited gay rights legislation in the state in 1992, as well as sundry other contributions. In the spring of 1993, she appeared as a featured speaker at the national lesbian and gay March on Washington. Still, she never *came* out in the sense usually associated with the term. For many years she refused to discuss the matter. Then, without fanfare, she *was* out, calmly replying to a question from a gay reporter, "Do you think it helps that people look at you and say, 'The best woman's tennis player of all time is a lesbian?'" with the response, "I can only hope so" (Bull 1991, 40).

Lesbian celebrity should have been a picnic for Navratilova after years of hounding by the press about her refusal to talk about her sexuality. But her protracted waffling was not always easily forgotten or forgiven by some who resented her stubborn refusal to declare her lesbian identity during the period when she was so often in the public eye. When the *Advocate*, the flagship of the U.S. gay/lesbian press, published its first Martina cover story in the October 5, 1993, issue, several readers took the opportunity to excoriate her in letters to the editor. For example, one correspondent took her to task for denying her lesbianism during the interview with Walters (at least, that was the letter writer's interpretation). Another scoffed at her for playing lousy tennis at the 1993 U.S. Open and complaining about Nelson's gold-digging behavior. Yet another condemned her as a "has-been in more ways than one" and used the conflict with Nelson as grounds for a political denunciation of everything Navratilova represents: "Blindly defending the antics of a lesbian icon like Navratilova who uses people and discards them sets all of us back and sends a message of approval for her celebrity selfishness" (Germano 1993).

The editors of the *Advocate* also seemed to have doubts about holding Navratilova up as a representative of the "community." Their ambivalence was signaled by their choice of a cover photo depicting her as an avenging Fury, grimacing at her unseen opponent with a look of meanness and aggressive determination that was extremely unflattering—as if to rebut all the banal images of Navratilova used in other publications in the early 1990s.[15] Although the expected reaction to her willingness to stop mincing words would be a welcoming embrace by her "community," she was instead greeted in these quarters with suspicion (and maybe envy), coupled with the inevitable recognition of her stature as a major sports star.

In a reversal of what might be the typical reception given a lesbian celebrity, the mainstream press proved much kinder. For instance, *Newsweek*'s tennis reporter gushed, "Navratilova has turned into far more than merely one of us. She is mentor, conscience, role model, our own World Icon." He added a comment on her abandonment of feminine pretense—"yet another radical Martina makeover." In another apparent about face, he does not use her preference for less femme garb as an opportunity to disparage her: "But

The *Advocate*'s first Navratilova cover, 1993. Liberation Publications.

if this is accentuating some lifestyle manifesto—*Hey, this is me. I don't care*—Navratilova has got it all wrong. It's we who don't care any more. Acceptance is history; her public shows up now with honor and respect abounding." He even repeats a quip she made in response to the persistent questioning of her sexuality: "Reporter: 'Are you still a lesbian?' Martina: 'Are you still the alternative?'" (Kirkpatrick 1994). At an earlier time, this kind of playful banter would have produced a minor scandal; now it was amusing.

What may have offended *Advocate* readers was that Navratilova's claim to fame wasn't based on a particular identity, a conventional lesbian identity, but instead relied on protean strategies that risked being deemed grotesque. After she more or less retired from playing the high stakes games of professional tennis, she retained her willingness to flaunt her remarkable musculature in public, as in the promotional image used to advertise the Rainbow credit card, a so-called affinity card designed to attract lesbian and gay customers, where she posed in an updated, transgendered version of Lewis Hine's famous *Steamfitter* photograph.[16] The man pictured by Hine is a white, working-class hunk, circa 1920, who applies his strength to adjust a bolt on an enormous piece of machinery that fills the frame—an idealized modernist, humanist image of industry's promise for human betterment. The Rainbow Card ad features an almost identical emblem of mechanical power and Navratilova in an almost identical pose. As quotation, however, the photo proposes an appropriation and displacement of its classic referent, while it also wryly acknowledges the cyborg myth Navratilova so diligently cultivated as she battled her way to the top of her sport. But the image is more than slightly goofy; it is also somewhat sinister, with Navratilova dwarfed by antiquated machinery reminiscent of scenery in *Metropolis*. This dystopian intimation may be why the advertisers quickly ditched the picture in favor of more benign pictures of the Lege without such arty touches or complex historical references.

SOCIAL MOBILITY

It would be easy to conclude that Navratilova's status as the world's most famous lesbian in the 1990s demanded that she fit the mannish mold.[17] That, heterosexual gender ideology instructs us, is the only way a lesbian can be recognized—seen and appreciated. Case closed. If there is to be a lesbian celebrity then she must represent triumphant female masculinity. Although the femme variant may seem to provide a challenge to such categorical

Initial promotion for the Rainbow Card. Do Tell, Inc.

The Steamfitter (1920), by Lewis W. Hine. Courtesy George Eastman House.

claims, this involves a simple reversal of the same old binary terms and therefore may endorse the entire system or render this type of lesbian celebrity
indistinguishable from her hetero-femme counterpart (See chapter 2 for a
more detailed discussion of this issue). However, all such debate about the
significance of gender for lesbian celebrity may be too hasty when we consider Navratilova's image problems and how she solved them by cultivating
an image that was not particularly masculine—for example, she employed
tried and true feminine cosmetic techniques—but not at all feminine either.
Her training methods required that she ignore the idea that physical strength
and agility, or competitiveness for that matter, are essential masculine characteristics. Indeed, gender had little to do with the persona she produced
through various applications of technological expertise: physical and mental
discipline, career management, and public relations. Moreover, although she
spent a great deal of time trying to solve her image problems by mastering
the signifiers of femininity, she gave up this project once her stardom was
guaranteed. That's when she abandoned once and for all the traditional tennis skirt.

Again, Navratilova's star image conforms to a feature of the cyborg-subject
in late capitalist, advanced industrial society that Haraway describes: "a crea-
ture in a post-gender world" (Haraway 1991, 150). Now, post-gender could
be interpreted as a questionable political epithet. However, Haraway argues
emphatically that it is entirely political. Since the unnatural cyborg "skips the
step of original unity," it prefigures the possibility of undermining and over-
turning fantasies of mastering nature and the awful consequences of the
self/other dichotomies that underwrite systems of domination (ibid.). But
how cyborgs might be incorporated into lesbian and gay politics is not immediately clear.[18]

This is where Navratilova's brand of lesbian celebrity comes in, which is
quite different from measuring her political effectiveness in terms of her viability as a role model—a questionable concept, given that we could hardly
begin to describe what role she would be modeling—or a standard-bearer for
the problematic ideal of visibility. She has certainly been visible, but what she
represents—her image—entails much more than appearances on television
screens and magazine pages with the identifier "lesbian" appended in a caption or bit of commentary. Nor is her political activism the issue. She may
speak at hundreds of gay and lesbian rallies or at none, but the import of her
celebrity would remain unaltered. The most radical political effect of
Navratilova's fame has been produced by her experiments using technologies

of self-transformation that ignored gender, which guaranteed her celebrity. For over a century, heterosexual definitions of gender have been inseparable from celebrity (discussed in chapter 3) and arguably more powerful since movie stars set the standard. Navratilova's challenge to compulsory gender identity and behavior during her latter years on the public stage exposed the false claims of normalized gender in this domain.

A final comment is necessary. Navratilova did not invent lesbian celebrity, nor was hers an individual accomplishment, even if her personal resolve to create an image that suited her is taken into account. Just like Jordan Myles in her detective novels, Navratilova is the singular hero of this story, but the genre has its conventions to which the story faithfully adheres and which circumscribe the hero's actions. One of the formulaic components of celebrity is the uniqueness of the star, and celebrity is often cited as evidence of the ephemeral quality known as charisma. But Navratilova would never have been a celebrity without an entire ensemble of social institutions and cultural practices. The most obvious is the field of professional sports and her own particular branch, women's tennis. In a more general sense, institutionalized spectacle—elaborate entertainments playing to huge audiences—must also be counted as a precondition for any contemporary athlete's rise to prominence. Of course, media institutions are crucial, since without the press and broadcast industries professional sport would never have become a platform for international fame and astronomical earnings, as it did in the late twentieth century. Perhaps most significant in Navratilova's case, however, was the array of physical and mental conditioning techniques and expert technologies that govern what is now regarded as a healthy body, or even better, a successful body, and enabled her to become a superstar. In short, her celebrity combined and mobilized these various social practices, and in the process contributed to their popularization.

At the same time, the image problems that troubled Navratilova's position as a public figure were not produced by individual idiosyncrasies but can be traced in every instance to uneasy encounters with another set of social institutions and ritualized cultural practices—primarily those involving definitions of gender and sexuality. During the formative years of her career, she did not epitomize any feminine or heterosexual ideals. But she also did not fit the image of a lesbian, liberated or otherwise. She was not closeted, but she did not risk condemnation by proclaiming her lesbian identity. She embodied the possibility of a new kind of person: a powerful but not "mannish" lesbian. And by 1991, with all the pieces in place, Navratilova had put together a new celebrity image, a lesbian celebrity. Others followed soon after, in other entertainment sectors—music, television, fashion, theater—confirming Ian Hacking's observations concerning the production of new subjectivities:

> When new descriptions become available, when they come into circula-
> tion, or even when they become the sorts of things that it is all right to
> say, to think, then there are new things to choose to do. When new inten-
> tions become open to me, I live in a new world of opportunities. (Hacking
> 1995, 236)[19]

Celebrity emerges as a cultural site where such new descriptions may take shape—not new faces and names but new kinds of people.

Because Navratilova's stardom poses remarkable challenges to hetero-sexual norms, it may be tempting to interpret these accomplishments as just rewards for her determination to achieve full self-realization and thereby break free of constraining sexual and gender categories. However, this famil-iar fable about self-awareness and self-fulfillment must also take into account the new self that replaced the less disciplined, more capricious, and less cal-culating Martina Navratilova. Recall, for instance, Foucault's words concern-ing the body's "optimization of . . . capabilities" within "anatomo-politics," that allows "its integration into systems of efficient and economic controls." These phrases may suggest that we should regard Navratilova's self-fashion-ing strategies as unwitting collaborations with oppressive forces. But her biography tells otherwise. She did manage to use her well honed body and acute intelligence to become a distinguished individual, less subordinate than most of us to others' demands on our time, attention, and resources. However, her metamorphosis indicates the precarious position of the kind of personhood produced as an aggregation of entrepreneurial mentalities; dis-courses of health, bodily discipline, and regulation; and bids for emancipation from onerous social categories.[20] This predicament is not Navratilova's alone but is shared by all of us who must craft and embody a self appropriate to life in a world where self-management and self-control, not to mention self-invention and self-promotion, have become practical and moral imperatives.

CHAPTER SEVEN

AFTERWORD

If a portrait gallery of lesbian celebrities were assembled it would include many more individuals than I have been able to profile (or even name) in this book. But my intent was never to produce an inventory of glamorous, courageous, and talented women who can be paraded as evidence of lesbian accomplishments and serve as inspirations to ordinary lesbian folk. Nor will I now conclude with a blanket characterization of the transformations of popular culture that the public figures who would be included in such a pantheon might effect. After describing diverse encounters between lesbians and celebrity culture, a retreat to generalizations seems not only unwise but also would require revision almost as soon as they were pronounced. Indeed, the only conclusion that seems justified is that lesbian celebrity is, mercifully, unpredictable and variegated. This does not imply, however, that no common motifs recur when the topic is studied. A number of these have been examined in preceding chapters, and these concluding comments will deal with connections between several that are dealt with in different contexts.

First, consider the question of melodrama, discussed in chapter 3 as a cultural form that prompted denunciations from the guardians of high culture when it first came to dominate theater in Western cultures during the nineteenth century, due to its emphasis on intense feelings. Such condemnations were often linked to disdain for cultural attributes seen as feminine, as well as characteristic of the supposedly unrefined tastes of working-class audiences, like sentimentality and irrationality. The condescending attitude found in such criticisms of melodrama therefore echoes familiar expressions of a gender hierarchy, where masculinity eschews base feminine emotionalism while claiming the supposedly superior domain of rationality for itself. And this dichotomy, I argue in chapter 3, parallels the discourse on entertainment celebrity, similarly dismissed by social critics as a frivolous diversion ruled by idolatry, prurient appeal, and gossip.

This attitude has not changed much since the time when such ideas were first articulated, as various commentators on the Warholization of American culture quoted in chapter 2 demonstrate. The evocations of Warhol in this context routinely refer to his work as a symptom of moral decay—capitalizing on superficial sensationalism, highlighting appearance rather than substance—just like entertainment celebrities. Of course, Warhol's repudiation of heroic masculinity in both his art work and persona, along with his own iconic status, makes him an ideal candidate for the detractors of celebrity culture. Indeed, Warhol appears several time throughout this study as a curious accomplice of lesbian celebrity: His name serves as shorthand for the decadence of celebrity culture outlined above, including the recently admitted lesbians within this milieu. Also, by means of his friendship with Mercedes de Acosta, he provides a link between what could be called the modernist era of lesbian celebrity discussed in chapter 5 and more recent permutations dealt with in chapter 6. Warhol may be only a tangential figure in this study, although his effectiveness as a signpost at various stages suggests that he deserves a citation as an honorary lesbian celebrity. However, few major cultural figures in the twentieth century have displayed a less melodramatic affect than Warhol, so let us not dwell on him further and return to the question of melodrama.

As I explain in chapter 3, the persistent antipathy toward melodrama—and its first cousin, spectacle—can be interpreted as unease with its staged battles against repression, since the prototypical melodrama is resolved by triumphant efforts to uncover and speak truths about protagonists' desires and identities, with all the impassioned, uncomfortable confrontations that may involve (Brooks 1984). Later, in chapter 4, I explore how the rationale for coming out developed within U.S. gay and lesbian culture and its relationship with ideas about self-realization. When these two phenomena are juxtaposed the correspondence becomes unmistakable. I mention the coincidence in the review of the features of contemporary entertainment celebrity in chapter 3, although it can be spotted as well in recent media spectacles. Take, for example, Martina Navratilova telling Barbara Walters on *20/20* that Judy Nelson was indeed her lover, that is, before they broke up and Nelson sued her. Tearful during that interview, Navratilova later talked about the greater sense of self-worth this revelation gave her (Navratilova 1995, 51). Or consider Ellen DeGeneres, who used Oprah Winfrey's TV show and the covers of *TV Guide* and *Time* magazine as platforms to announce to the world that she is gay and proud of it, while speaking at length to reporters, as well as Oprah, about the agony that remaining silent has caused her. She, too, cried on camera.

Writing these descriptions of these very public enactments of the coming out ritual, I am aware that words like "spectacle," "tearful," and "agony," or mentioning Walters and Winfrey may summon cynical dismissals of the sentiments expressed, as well as the forums in which these took place. However, I do not intend to question either Navratilova's or DeGeneres's sincerity, or Walters's and Winfrey's for that matter, but instead want to draw attention to the melodramatic structure of coming out stories in general. Accounts of the same rite of passage by less famous lesbians are just as melodramatic, sharing the common themes of confusion and crisis, followed by revelation and contentment (Cruikshank 1985; Penelope and Wolfe 1989).

But there is another way in which melodrama infuses representations of lesbian celebrity and becomes, in effect, one of its defining features: coming out stories dealing with famous performers concocted posthumously. This occurs most frequently in the retrospective biographies of entertainment celebrities that have proliferated during the past decade and a half, which I discuss in chapter 5. Indeed, several more appeared after I finished writing that section, and one deserves particular attention. In *The Girls: Sappho Goes to Hollywood* (2000), celebrity biographer Diana McLellan repeats many of the now familiar anecdotes with more or less the same cast of characters— Nazimova, Garbo, Dietrich, de Acosta, among others. However, her chronicle of careers shaped by lesbian desires and affiliations ups the ante in the scandal-mongering sweepstakes. Not only does she assert as fact what are, at best, inferences about various sexual encounters, she invents a torrid affair that ended in enmity between Garbo and Dietrich in Berlin in the 1920s. This exercise in wishful thinking (done much better, it should be said, by Cecilia Barriga in her delightful 1991 video *Meeting of Two Queens*) then becomes the foundation of an elaborate imaginary edifice of lesbian intrigue.[1] In this instance, as well as elsewhere in her book, when documentary evidence remains scarce McLellan attributes the gaps to an indelible pattern of mendacity among lesbians.

This much isn't new, although the book is perhaps more egregious in its portrayal of lesbians as exceptionally furtive than previous examples of what has become a cottage industry in the field of celebrity biography. More than its predecessors *The Girls* demonstrates the compulsion to represent lesbianism as a fundamentally esoteric and perhaps sinister condition, where the promise of revealing secret knowledge propels the story and exposure of lesbian "truths" provides the payoff. And since, according to this scenario, the clandestine lives of lesbians serve as a basic requirement for intelligibility of such stories, the promise to shed light on what was going on behind closed doors aligns these fanciful histories with the agenda of visibility politics. Does political success as an effect of visibility presuppose a melodramatic framework for lesbian politics? There is nothing wrong or bad about a fondness for this sort of storytelling, but recognizing the formal parameters of melodrama, its scripted quality, should raise questions about the claims of authenticity associated with the expression of repressed lesbian desires and identities, including fundamental truths, associated with the act of coming out.

But when examined from a different perspective, which need not dispense with melodrama altogether, reflections on lesbian celebrities of the past may suggest other interpretations, especially when considered alongside their more recent counterparts. Radclyffe Hall, Mercedes de Acosta, and Martina Navratilova—several of the major players in preceding chapters—offer various configurations of another consistent theme in this book: self-fashioning. And, returning to the denizens of show business in chapter 5, as well as the flamboyant Jill Johnston in chapter 4, another motif appears: theatricality, which is not necessarily formulaic and often improvised. Combine these attributes, and the resulting subjectivities—theatricalized, eccentric, innovative, queer—offer significant resources for lesbian political imagination. At the very least, the trope of self-invention presents the possibility of lesbian politics not straightjacketed by the invisibility/visibility playbook and the production of moralistic positive images—a more imaginative and protean range of choices.

The idea that any dimension of celebrity culture might serve as a political resource may seem wrongheaded to critics who point to the entanglements of celebrities with commercial media and the cultural marketplace as evidence of their complicity with capitalism's commodity fetishism. The mere fact that celebrities are produced nowadays by marketing and publicity (when were they not?) and should therefore be analyzed (or, more frequently, dismissed) as products manufactured by various branches of the culture industry, implies that they automatically become agents of capitalist exploitation.

This market is driven, or so the argument goes, by calculations of how best to take advantage of fans' desires by cooking up schemes to produce *new* desires. What's missing from this equation is an acknowledgment that markets are cultural as much as economic sites, and not all of their features are explained adequately by the arithmetic of balance sheets. Similarly, although there certainly have been economic repercussions of the explosion of sexual and gender politics in the late twentieth century, these do not account for all, or even most, of the effects of these social movements.

However, one need not join critics of commodification in order to question the political valence of lesbian celebrity. At the conclusion of chapter 2, I argue that lesbians anointed as bona fide celebrities in American culture may easily support a normalizing agenda. Others may contend that normalization can contain seeds of social change, in so far as the transformation of lesbian and gay outlaws into honorable burghers requires expansion of social institutions—new kinds of family, for example, or reconfigurations of the concept of marriage. But inclusion of lesbian and gay participants in these social structures and rituals often upholds the nuclear family and the insular couple as centerpieces of intimate life. Of course, those who would conscript lesbian celebrities for visibility politics are less worried about their effective support of normalcy, if the gay press, which offers an ongoing parade of gay (or gay-friendly) celebs, is any measure. Thus, celebrity discourse in the context of contemporary lesbian culture generally produces a two-sided debate: either moralistic hand-wringing about the dangers of seduction by media imagery or, conversely, about the need to project praiseworthy, exemplary lesbians in popular media.

These tensions appear at various points in this book, not only in the analysis of visibility politics in chapter 2 but again in the discussion of theories of celebrity in chapter 3, as well as in chapter 4's review of the anticelebrity positions common in the gay and women's liberation movements of the late 1960s and early seventies. Although these disputes seemed the most intriguing aspect of lesbian celebrity when I began this project, my attempt to explore how representatives of both sides have disagreed eventually led me in a direction very different from that taken by any of the critics of celebrity described so far. Specifically, I began to explore questions about the politics of self-invention that emerged when practices of self-fashioning became a important factor in the making of lesbian celebrities. Once again, though, I anticipate protests, because mentioning this dimension of lesbian culture, as well as celebrity culture, as a political activity implies that self-invention can be harnessed to political projects. But, of course, it already has been, as a consequence of strategies mapped out by the liberation movements. Coming out, claiming a new identity, and the related enterprise of self-realization became a condition for liberation. And in chapter 6 I describe how the contours of such a trajectory defined Martina Navratilova's lesbian celebrity image.

The kind of self-fashioning that Navratilova and other recent celebrities embody and enact is quite different from that observed during earlier eras. Historical figures from the early twentieth century like Elsie de Wolfe and Bessie Marbury, important pioneers in image management and celebrity promotion discussed in chapter 5, were connoisseurs of self-expression (which is why I referred to them and their contemporaries previously as modernists). Nowadays the techniques used to produce selves are primarily rational practices; theatricality is frowned upon. Self-possession, not emotional expression, has become the ethical model proposed by most branches of lesbian culture, as well as the governing concepts of lesbian subjectivities. Indeed, the demand for positive images in recent years articulates not only something the media is expected to provide; every lesbian is expected to produce a positive image of and for herself. The rationality that informs current concepts and practices of lesbian identity may also explain the success of the recent crop of lesbian celebrities in gaining acceptance, often applause, for their forthright self-presentations. They epitomize the rewards of a life lived as a creative work of personal awareness and self-development.

Like a positive self-image and outlook, coming out, too, has become practically obligatory. Where celebrities are concerned, this decisive moment then reshapes the entire star image—verbal as well as visual. Still, the meaning of such declarations may be changing (not that it ever remained static). Recall the acclaim *Newsweek* gave Navratilova for having attained the status of "mentor, conscience, role model" (Kirkpatrick 1994) after she came out— *because* she came out. Now contrast this embrace of a star, who had previously been disparaged for flaunting her lesbian relationships (in other words, for not being secretive), with Rosie O'Donnell's parallel career move about a decade later. The headline for a *People* magazine story on O'Donnell's lesbianism (like Navratilova's or DeGeneres's, an announcement that surprised very few) read, "Oh by the Way . . ." (Tauber 2002). A report on O'Donnell's coming out in the *New York Times* similarly emphasized the blasé quality of her announcement: "She's Out of the Closet. Now What?" (Kuczynski 2002).

In many respects the treatment of O'Donnell's public lesbianism in the press retreads familiar territory. For instance, on the cover of *People* O'Donnell is credited with taking a "brave step," repeating the melodramatic clichés about the difficulty of either knowing or revealing lesbian proclivities one more time. But this is not what the articles emphasize. Instead, O'Donnell's nonchalance and her fans' ready acceptance became the story, along with testimony from friends that her homosexuality was never a secret anyway (Tauber 2002, 82). According to the *Times*, "[T]he news caused hardly a stir, and that in itself is eyebrow-raising" (Kuczynski 2002, 1). What's more interesting, though, is that in this account the most news-worthy aspect of O'Donnell's announcement was the coordination of public appearances—talk show interviews, magazine articles, a book tour for her autobiography, a guest appearance playing a lesbian mom on the gay sitcom *Will and Grace*, an aside during her standup comedy act. A celebrity's coming out may have provided the premise for this coverage but the substance of the story was how she and her advisors engineered the disclosure.

By all reports, the performance was masterful. Just as impressive was how O'Donnell's rational approach to self-invention became more noteworthy than her avowals of sexual identity. The news told us about the success of her managerial strategies—Rosie as an unabashed entrepreneur of her self. Her objective: a fully realized invidual, one who is successful, happy, and healthy (with a few physical problems acknowledged, although she's working on these, too), as well as a productive social agent, producing her own well-being along with working hard at crafting an entertaining persona for her fans. Martina Navratilova's lesbian celebrity seemed to indicate a shift from iden-tity politics to the politics of self-control in the service of self-fulfillment. Rosie O'Donnell's takes further steps in that direction. More significantly, O'Donnell's public representation of lesbian personhood confirms once more lesbians' expertise in self-invention, not just as exemplars but as trailblazers, too. But as innovative as this may appear, self-fashioning projects nowadays have become the norm. The injunction to take charge of, discipline, organ-ize, and plot a destiny for oneself has become compulsory. Which prompts a final question: will lesbians trade in imaginative assaults on normalcy for these well-made, well-managed, reasonable selves?

NOTES

CHAPTER ONE: INTRODUCTION

1. Before embarking on this project, I wrote several essays that pondered the political implications of visibility: Gever 1989; 1990; 1991; 1994.

CHAPTER TWO: VISIBILITY NOW!

1. Although Bono left GLAAD soon after *Daily Variety* printed a story quoting her opinion that *Ellen* had become "too gay" during the 1998 season following the famous coming out episode, Bono denied that she spoke these words although not the sentiment and vowed to remain an activist for lesbian and gay visibility (Bono 1998).

2. Additional text in the Bono's fund-raising letter reads: "I came aboard GLAAD because I knew it was the best way I could help make a difference in the way lesbians and gay men are reflected in the mass media—*as well as the way we're all treated in society at large*" (emphasis added).

3. In her autobiography, Gingrich quotes her brother as telling the press: "'I'm glad Candace has a day job. I have another sister, Susan, who's a member of the Christian Coalition. You don't see Hollywood glorifying her, you don't see TV shows calling her up'" (Gingrich 1996, 160).

4. Joan W. Scott describes how this operates in accounts of lesbian and gay history: "History is a chronology that makes experience visible, but in which the categories appear as nonetheless ahistorical: desire, homosexuality, heterosexuality, femininity, masculinity, sex, and even sexual practices become so many fixed entities being played out over time, but not themselves historicized" (J. W. Scott 1993, 400).

5. This distinction, made by Gayatri Chakravorty Spivak among others, is an important one. Spivak notes Marx's differing use of two words both commonly translated into English as "representation": "speaking for," as in politics (*darstellen*), and "representing," as in art or philosophy (*vertreten*); rhetoric-as-persuasion versus rhetoric-as-trope. The problem that arises when these two meanings are confused, Spivak argues, is that the conflation of these two meanings by intellectuals "forecloses the necessity for counterhegemonic ideological production" (Spivak 1988, 275).

6. Among the developments that Gross cites are ruptures in the code of silence imposed on homosexual practices of public figures, which was seriously undermined by revelations concerning the homosexuality of actively antigay right-wing politicians and political operatives—Rep. Robert Bauman and Terry Dolan, in particular—in the 1980s. This then motivated various gay political strategists to call for exposure of others who campaigned against gay and lesbian rights while secretly carrying on same-sex relationships.

Now, it is entirely possible that the newer standards of openness may satisfy a kind of voyeurism that in no way results in diminished social censure of homosexuality. Or such revelations may be cited to affirm pernicious ideas about the inherent characteristics of homosexuals. For example, Douglas Crimp discusses how Roy Cohn's homosexuality has been offered as an explanation for Cohn's duplicity and cruelty once this became public knowledge following his death in 1986 (Crimp 1994, 308).

7. As Dyer's title *Heavenly Bodies: Film Stars and Society* (1986) indicates, his analysis is devoted to movie stars, but many of his observations and statements about celebrity phenomena in general can be applied to other forms of stardom, as I argue in chapter 3.

8. As far as professional sports are concerned, there is a long tradition of celebrity players, although in this cultural sector, too, the stakes continue to be raised, as signaled by the enormous salaries paid to big name stars. Perhaps the best example of how this is understood is provided by press coverage of Michael Jordan's celebrity, although Michael Eric Dyson's metacommentary on this phenomenon (Dyson 1993, 64–75) is considerably more thoughtful than that offered by the popular press.

9. I have used the *New York Times* as a primary source for commentary on celebrity culture because it is widely regarded as the newspaper of record and therefore immune to the sensationalism characteristic of celebrity gossip and adulation, but this image may be changing. In 1998, the paper instituted a regular column of celebrity news and flattering profiles of public figures in its local daily edition.

10. Although concerns about increasing space devoted to entertainment celebrities in the press is nothing new (see, in this regard, my overview of this issue in chapter 3, as well as the discussion of the development of movie fan magazines in the early twentieth century in chapter 5), reporters' and editors' willingness to allow stars and their representatives approval of texts and photos prior to publication has come under scrutiny recently. For example, following a review of differing perspectives on the issue Robin Pogrebin (1998) concludes, "The bottom line is that neither magazines or stars can live without each other." It may be telling that the *Times* chose to run this story on their front page, indicating again the embrace of celebrity journalism by this pillar of respectability. And again, on May 3, 1999, the *Times* featured a story about the machinations of Pat Kingsley, publicist for Ellen DeGeneres among others, on the first page of the Arts section.

11. GLAAD honorees with no primary lesbian or gay commitment have included obvious choices, like the television series *Thirtysomething*, which broadcast an episode featuring a gay male couple in 1989 (i.e., before the inclusion of gay and lesbian characters on network television became widespread), and major Hollywood films with gay themes and central characters like *Philadelphia* and *In & Out*. But they also have been awarded to less likely candidates like *20/20*, *Geraldo*, and *Entertainment Tonight*, presumably in recognition of their airing of lesbian and gay perspectives without too much moralizing. A full list of all GLAAD Media Awards recipients is available at: www.glaad.org/glaad/media-awards/past-winners.html.

12. The first three items in this litany of pro-visibility arguments have been articulated by Larry Gross (1989). The role model is a familiar feature in writings on lesbian and gay celebrities, living and dead, and a typical expression of this can be found in Martin Duberman's text "On Being Different," which introduces the various volumes in the biography series for teenage readers, Lives of Notable Gay Men and Lesbians, he edited for Chelsea House Publishers (New York). The same rationale is also offered by defenders of "outing," whose arguments are amply documented and supported in Gross (1993).

13. The historical literature on sexuality in the United States since the mid-nineteenth century suggests a similar dynamic tension between lesbian forays into public culture and increased scrutiny and strategies for containment. This double movement is discussed in Chauncey (1982–83), but is also evident in the broader history traced in D'Emilio and Freedman (1988).

14. I do not want to give the impression that de Lauretis accepts Foucault's interpretation of the discourse of sexuality and its relation to power uncritically. Several times in this collection of essays, she points out how his inability to incorporate gender constitutes a crucial oversight, with implications for feminists interested in related questions.

15. The authors do not say what year these figures represent but from related information, I assume that it is 1992. As a counterpoint, they cite economist Lee Badgett's study showing that the earnings of gay men and lesbians are significantly *lower* than those of heterosexuals.

16. Interestingly, this article in an upscale magazine bemoans the embourgeoisment of gay male culture, which according to the author has lost its transgressive edge as a result.

17. An excellent overview of this area of feminist research and theory can be found in J. W. Scott (1990).

18. This aspect of the theory of sexual difference is not Irigaray's, but that of Jacques Lacan, whose emendations of Freud's ideas provided feminist cultural theorists with key concepts that they then employed to craft their critique of the psychic structures of patriarchy.

19. Freud's definition of a psychosexual fetish is: "a substitute for the woman's (mother's) phallus which the little boy once believed in and does not wish to forego . . . for if a woman can be castrated his own penis is in danger" (Freud 1963, 215).

20. Judith Mayne (1991) cites this and other iconic lesbian images from the Hollywood archive, as well as the stunning oversight of this aspect of female spectatorship in what have become classic texts for 1970s and 1980s feminist film theory.

21. I should point out that in her oft-reprinted and cited essay, Mulvey limits her observations to classical narrative cinema, that is, Hollywood movies produced during the years when the studio system dominated the industry—the 1930s through the 1950s—although the analysis she works through in this article has been applied by others to a wide range of representational practices and different historical periods.

22. For an extended discussion of how feminist film theorists tend to reinstate binary gender in discussions of lesbian desire, see Roof (1991, 37–66).

23. Kaplan qualifies the idea of the male gaze, in an attempt to rid her analysis of any essentialist connotations, but is not entirely successful, as the context for the quote indicates: "The gaze is not necessarily male (literally), but to own and activate the gaze, given our language and the structure of the unconscious, is to be in the 'masculine' position" (E. Kaplan 1983, 30).

24. Judith Roof points out the heterosexual bias in the analyses of female subjectivity produced by Mulvey et al., which "tends to conflate biological gender with the activity/passivity stereotypes it finds operant in cultural expressions of sexual difference" (Roof 1991, 46). Teresa de Lauretis (1991, 1994) also uses psychoanalytic frameworks to make the argument that lesbian desire is not merely a secondhand version of the heterosexual male variety.

25. Dennis Rodman was the other celebrity employed by M.A.C.

26. Marshall Sahlins (1976) makes this point eloquently and convincingly in his analysis of the modern Western fashion system.

27. Perhaps the most mundane, but nevertheless exemplary, instances of this process are the consumer practices concerned with eating rituals: customary and proscribed foods, the organization of menus and mealtime schedules, and the like. Of course, styles of adornment, and clothing in particular, also classify consumers according to culturally specific regimes that bespeak social statuses and relations.

CHAPTER THREE: CELESTIAL CONFIGURATIONS

1. Hall's second novel, *The Unlit Lamp* (1924), received good reviews and gained Hall admittance into the ranks of the British literary elite. Her fourth, *Adam's Breed* (1926), received both the prestigious Prix Femina and James Tate Black Prize for best literary novel of the year and sold well. Hall's previous novels also included *The Forge* (1924) and *A Saturday Life* (1925).

2. Sales figures are from Baker (1985, 246 passim) and Weeks (1977, 111). Baker notes that publisher Jonathan Cape almost rejected *The Well* due to the "taboo subject matter" but accepted it because he saw opportunity for profit, calling it "a good piece of publishing property" (204).

3. On this point Terry Castle writes, "[S]ome of the matchups in *The Well* are close enough to

suggest the roman à clef. Valérie Seymour, the sophisticated lesbian hostess who takes Stephen under her wing in Paris after Stephen leaves home, is patently modeled on the charismatic Natalie Barney, whose salon on the Rue Jacob was a haven for lesbian writers and artists between the wars. Along with her lover, the painter Romaine Brooks, Barney became one of Hall's and Troubridge's good friends in the 1920s. Other characters, especially those who appear in the Paris chapters, resemble homosexual men and women Hall knew on both sides of the channel in the postwar years—Mimi Franchetti, Adrien Mirtil, Violette Murat, Ida Rubenstein, and Lily de Gramont, the Duchesse de Clermont-Tonnerre" (Castle 1996, 39).

4. The fact that the professional journal of sexual science that published Jennifer Terry's research devoted two special issues to articles critical of the medical discourses on sexuality and gender is a good indication of the changes that have occurred as the result of challenges from lesbian, gay, and feminist activists and scholars.

5. Bonnie Zimmerman comments, "Valérie [Seymour] offers a welcome relief from the tortured self-hatred of the hero, Stephen Gordon, that wounded male soul trapped in a woman's body. It is ironic that Hall, a writer of modest talents compared to her illustrious contemporaries [Djuna Barnes, Collette, Virginia Woolf, Gertrude Stein et al.], should have created the novel and hero that have had the most profound and lasting influence on modern-day notions of lesbians" (Zimmerman 1990, 7).

Maybe because I am of the same generation as Zimmerman, I too found *The Well* a disappointing read and for many years dismissed it as irrelevant to contemporary lesbian issues. More recently, though, I find myself repeatedly returning to the novel to satisfy a variety of interests, including my curiosity about the discrepancies between Hall's public persona and that assigned to her fictional ideal of a lesbian self.

6. It may well be the correspondence between Hall's support of the medical model of homosexuality and the narrative resolution she devised for the misfit Stephen that allowed later commentators to assume that Hall shared her protagonist's fate as a social exile. The blurb reprinted on the cover to an edition of *The Well* published as recently as 1990 by Anchor Books informs us, incorrectly, that the book "is the thinly disguised story of Radclyffe Hall's own life" and that its publication "almost ruined Hall's literary career."

7. Ironically, Brummell was interested in the reification of sexual difference by eliminating what he saw as decadent effeminacy in bourgeois men's dress and manners.

8. Even famous opera divas of the early twentieth century like Mary Garden were enticed by the promise of substantial fees to appear in movies made by an industry capable of producing only silent films.

9. Like Daguerre, Disdéri started out as a theatrical scenery painter and tried his hand, unsuccessfully, at producing a panorama as paid entertainment. He set up his first studio in Paris in a building owned by Houdini's brother-in-law, also a professional magician.

10. Nadar effectively quit the photography business in the mid-1870s, but his son continued to make prints from his father's negatives or rephotographed the old portraits and even used photomechanical printing processes to publish large editions of these images until his death in 1939. Meanwhile, Disdéri was unable to sustain his dominance in the *carte de visite* industry, eventually filing for bankruptcy in 1872 (Hambourg, Heilbrun, and Néagu 1995, 251–255; Keller 1995, 81–83).

11. Brady was unable to readjust his business practices to meet the requirements of *carte de visite* production, nor was he temperamentally suited to head a photographic company that dealt in mass produced images, and he was forced into bankruptcy as a result. His extensive documentation of the Civil War, upon which his enduring reputation is based, was also financially disastrous.

12. On this note, see McCauley's description of the attitudes of Napoléon III, a frequent subject of French celebrity photographs, who appears to have appreciated the propaganda value of circulating images of himself and his family via the popular *carte de visite* medium (1985, 82–83).

13. Dietrich posed with husband Rudolf Sieber and daughter Maria for a series of press photos when Rudi arrived in the U.S. Since Dietrich and studio publicists were eager to downplay the scandal, photos from the series appeared in a variety of contexts, but their intended purpose is best illus-

trated by their publication in movie magazines around the time when the lawsuit was also being covered (see, e.g., Fletcher 1932, 280).

14. Incorporation of speculation about celebrities' extramarital sexual adventures took somewhat longer, since this happened only when more liberal attitudes toward sexuality became prevalent. For an overview of changing sexual mores and institutions in U.S. culture, see D'Emilio and Freedman (1988).

15. William Henry Fox Talbot experimented with the method as early as 1853, and it was used by a commercial printer in New York in the 1880s (Ivins 1981, 189).

16. An annual subscription for these traditional papers cost over fifteen dollars, at a time when the average daily wage was eighty-five cents. This and subsequent data on the economic impact of penny papers is taken from Schudson (1978).

17. Frank Luther Mott reproduces in full a police court report from an 1833 issue of the *Sun*, two items of which give a sense of the tone and content of the popular innovations in news reporting found in penny newspapers: "Margaret Thomas was drunk in the street—said she never would get drunk again 'upon her honor.' Committed, 'upon honor.' . . . Patrick Ludwick was sent up by his wife, who testified that she had supported him for several years in idleness and drunkenness. Abandoning all hopes of a reformation in her husband, she bought him a suit of clothes a fortnight since and told him to go about his business, for she would not live with him any longer. Last night he came home in a state of intoxication, broke into his wife's bedroom, pulled her out of bed, pulled her hair, and stamped on her. She called a watchman and sent him up. Pat exerted all his powers of eloquence in endeavoring to excite his wife's sympathy, but to no purpose. As every sensible wife ought to do who is cursed with a drunken husband, she refused to have anything to do with him hereafter—and he was sent to the penitentiary" (Mott 1962, 223–224).

18. For a more complete description of the foundation and early years of the *Daily News*, see Mott (1962, 667–668).

19. The tabloids launched in the 1920s and 1930s that survived wars of competition and episodes of mismanagement, including a number in major cities across the U.S., developed into more respectable papers by the 1940s. Although today's supermarket tabloids resemble these early forebears in their willingness to participate in creating the scandals they report, as well as their emphasis on gruesome and fantastic events, the latter day tabloids have largely grown out of publishing experiments in the 1950s and innovations in the genre made during the 1970s. See Bird (1992) for a fairly comprehensive account of this history.

20. Mosedale (1981) writes that in 1940 the newspapers that carried Winchell's column numbered 1,000 and estimates his radio and newspaper audience at fifty million Americans, over a third of the country's total population at the time.

21. The sole exception I discovered in my survey of movie magazines published between 1915 and 1933 was a 1931 cover of *Modern Screen* with Clark Gable *and* Greta Garbo, timed to coincide with the release of *Susan Lenox: Her Fall and Rise*, in which they costarred.

22. Again, Dietrich's affair with Joseph von Sternberg, which they made little attempt to hide, was one of the most closely watched sexual relationships in Hollywood. A typical item is this snippet from *Modern Screen*'s "Inside Stuff" column in the February 1933 issue: "Marlene Dietrich is now carrying her 'mannishness' so far as to wear the same cut of trousers, when she affects that masculine attire, as Director Joseph von Sternberg. What would you call it—a brother-act or sister-act?" (24). The simultaneous reference to Dietrich's adulterous affair with a man and her lesbianism may seem odd at first, but may indicate how the meaning of the von Sternberg liaison was exoticized—therefore represented as atypical of Hollywood or American marriages in general—by annexing it to Dietrich's star image as a sultry, seductive, *foreign* libertine.

23. Joan Crawford was featured in a story in *Modern Screen* (September 1932) about how she risked destitution by rejecting a producer's sexual advances while employed as a chorus girl. This infusion of cautionary tales about the downfall awaiting credulous aspiring ingenues has not disappeared but resurfaces in the present-day equivalents to the fan magazines—TV celebrity interviews.

Interestingly, one such item, on model agencies that make false promises to young wannabees was aired on the *20/20* program that followed the infamous *Ellen* coming out episode.

24. The leftist and liberal critical literature that treats entertainment celebrities as instruments of capitalist manipulation is extensive and too lengthy to list. A few examples, in addition to Morin, are T. B. Harris (1957), Eckert (1990), and Parenti (1992).

25. Gustave Le Bon, whose late-nineteenth-century writings on the social psychology of crowds is still frequently cited, wrote, "Crowds are everywhere distinguished by feminine characteristics" (Le Bon [1895] 1981, 39).

26. Huyssen's chapter title from which this passage is taken summarizes this phenomenon well: "Mass Culture as Woman."

27. Gledhill concurs with Thomas Elsaesser's (1987) contention that all cinematic genres, not only domestic, family-centered narratives usually classified as such, can be understood as variants of melodrama.

28. Movie viewing, Blumer wrote, has the "conspicuous tendency . . . to dull discrimination" (1933, 198) and "dissolve moral judgment into a maze of ambiguous definitions" (199–200).

29. For an extensive treatment of the defining features of melodramatic performance style, see Brooks (1984). For a discussion of the connections between melodrama and film stars, see Gledhill (1991). But the point can also be illustrated by recalling any performance by a Method actor trained at the Actor's Studio, the young Marlon Brando, say, or by a member of the cast of one of Douglas Sirk's splendid Hollywood melodramas (e.g., *Magnificent Obsession, All that Heaven Allows, Written on the Wind, Imitation of Life*), or, for that matter, any performance on a television dramatic program, to understand its basic features.

30. I realize that voyeurism is believed by a number of feminist theorists to be a male or masculine perversion, but I find this absurd, or another way to interpret lesbian subjectivity as an "inversion" or a misguided denial of sexual difference. The effect of all such explanations is a refusal to consider that the binary concept of gender is not immutable.

31. That Hall's novel conjured up an image of lesbians as martyrs was both widely recognized and rejected by the author. A cartoon on this theme published shortly after *The Well* scandal erupted, which depicted a crucified Hall, infuriated the author, who found it intolerably blasphemous, and she refused to speak about it for years (Baker 1985, 257).

CHAPTER FOUR: GOING PUBLIC

1. For gay men, media celebrity seemed less dangerous for those singled out, perhaps because public lesbians were often associated with the women's movement and feminist issues, which attracted much more press attention than gay and lesbian political organizing and action in the late 1960s. At times, however, condemnations of gay male activists who were featured in media reports could be just as nasty.

2. The epithet "pig," frequently used in the writings of radicals in this period, was borrowed from the Black Panther Party. For a discussion of this influence, see D'Emilio (1992, xxxv).

3. For a description of the entire sequence of events, see Abbott and Love ([1972] 1985, 119–125).

4. In support of this assessment, I offer the evidence of *Gay's* routine neglect of feminist activities and viewpoints, save a regular column by pseudonymous lesbian Lily Hansen (Lilli Vincenz), who wrote almost entirely about her personal life (family, girlfriend, dog). The only exception to such gestures toward lesbian inclusion were *Gay's* infrequent profiles of lesbians who became famous long ago and were either dead (Radclyffe Hall) or living in obscurity (Djuna Barnes). Pieces by men in *Gay* often evaluated their female peers in terms of their attractiveness and were disdainful of any who were old, overweight, unfashionably dressed, or otherwise not glamorous. It's not too difficult to figure out why lesbians deserted the gay movement to form separate organizations. In one issue (March 1, 1970), they illustrated the token lesbian column with a soft-porn type image of a naked woman,

which prompted a public protest by Martha Shelley at a panel on gay liberation and the media. For *Gay*'s rebuttal to Shelley see Ogren (1971), which avers that women's liberation and gay liberation share no common ground. In another issue of *Gay*, art critic Gregory Battcock (1970) expressed support for the Panthers, the anti–Vietnam War movement, and opposition to police harassment while refusing expressly to support women's liberation. The pattern continues in Sorel David's lukewarm review of Johnston's first book, *Marmalade Me* (1971), a selection of her dance and art criticism from the *Village Voice*, where the critic states, "I used to like Jill Johnston, but that was before she became a professional lesbian." *Gay*'s disinterest in lesbian issues can be contrasted with coverage in *Come Out*, the publication of New York GLF. Significantly, *Gay* was affiliated with the Gay Activist Alliance, formed by (mostly male) members of GLF who objected to the original group's gestures of solidarity with the Black Panthers and its sympathy with and support for women's liberation.

5. Johnston's views on this topic can be found in the two *Voice* articles cited previously (1971a and 1971b), as well as in *Lesbian Nation* (1973). One difference between her position and Shelley's was that she didn't condemn other feminists who were singled out for media attention. In addition, her first two books were published by established presses like Dutton (*Marmalade Me*) and Simon and Schuster (*Lesbian Nation*), which was unacceptable for the strictest adherents of the radical (lesbian) feminist code of conduct in relation to the media.

6. The cover story on Martina Navratilova in the June 30, 1982 issue of *Newsweek* does not contradict this observation, since it appeared during the period when she vociferously denied that she was a lesbian. (See chapter 6.)

7. See, for example, two articles on gay liberation that appeared in mass circulation magazines in 1971, both of which included photographs of Johnston: "The Militant Homosexual" (1971) in *Newsweek*, and "Homosexuals in Revolt: The Year that One Liberation Movement Turned Militant" (1971) in *Life*. In the former, Johnston is the only woman depicted, and she is one of three lesbians who appeared in the eight heavily illustrated *Life* magazine pages devoted to the new gay movement.

8. During the past decade or so, "coming out" and "the closet" have become generalized metaphors applicable to an increasingly broad range of situations and people. Nowadays, one can "come out" as a previously "closeted" wife beater, depressed person, National Rifle Association supporter, you name it. But, I would argue, associations with being closeted and coming out as a homosexual remain embedded in these expressions.

9. From the outlook of 2003, when "rights" is the word generally associated with gay/lesbian politics, the assumption is that this movement arose out of African-American struggles for civil rights and related campaigns for social justice. Such precedents are not irrelevant, but the first gay liberation groups self-consciously aligned themselves with socialist revolutionaries in the Third World and more militant supporters of the Black Power movement in the U.S., who believed that equality and justice would result only after the edifice of capitalist imperialism was demolished. This perspective can be gleaned from the numerous writings from this time that contain idiomatic spellings like Amerika, a rhetorical trademark of the Black Panther Party, and closed with the slogan, "All Power to the People!" See, for example, Chicago Gay Liberation ([1970] 1992) and Third World Gay Revolution ([1971] 1992).

10. Lesbian-feminism developed in a number of directions and survives as a distinct cultural formation in enclaves around the country. In addition, successful agitation for recognition within the women's movement offered a more agreeable environment for work on lesbian issues and ideas for many lesbian activists. Still, a goodly number of lesbians remained allied with gay politics and have been particularly prominent within it since the AIDS epidemic erupted in the early 1980s.

11. I use 1968 as the temporal demarcation of gay politics' decisive turn away from the homophile political model, based upon programs designed to promote tolerance and acceptance, toward a more defiant stance, not 1969, when the Stonewall uprising took place. Although the latter is an important landmark, the forces that it has come to represent had already taken root, as the formation of groups at various colleges in 1968 indicates.

12. Rose defines identity projects in this way: "Contemporary individuals are incited to live as if

making a *project* of themselves: they are to *work* on their emotional world, their domestic and conjugal arrangements, their relations with employment and their techniques of sexual pleasure, to develop
a 'style' of living that will maximize the worth of their existence to themselves" (N. Rose 1998, 157).

13. Others have challenged the premises and substance of role theory. Among these critics are
Urry (1970), who points out how social position and behavior understood in terms of roles leads to
the reification of social identities, and Coulson (1972). Wrong (1957) critiques socialization and role
theory from a psychoanalytic perspective, observing that these paradigms overvalue normative commitments and neglect such psychodynamic factors as inner conflict. Also J. Rose (1986) employs psychoanalytic theory to challenge feminist sociological studies that update structural-functionalism to
forge a theory of gender socialization and sex roles (e.g., Nancy Chodorow). For these feminist soci-
ologists, Rose writes, "the internalization of norms is assumed roughly to work, [and] the basic premise and indeed starting-point of psychoanalysis is that it does not" (90).

14. The media provide innumerable examples of how statistics are understood by gay and lesbian
political analysts as an accurate reflection of reality. For example, the statistic produced by the 1948 Kinsey
report on male sexual behavior, which found that approximately ten percent of American men were
exclusively homosexual for at least three years between the ages of 16 and 55, has been cited routinely by
gay rights organizations to bolster claims for minority status. When much lower figures—as low as one
percent—were produced by subsequent surveys these numbers were interpreted as a threat to the gay
rights movement. The *New York Times* even featured one such story on its front page (Barringer 1993a),
but ten days later, followed up with an interesting counterpoint (Barringer 1993b). However, the latter
item did not seriously question the validity of statistics as a measure of social phenomena. The gay/les-
bian media participates actively in the same devotion to statistical data, as evidenced in the monthly survey results published by the *Advocate*, the largest circulation gay or lesbian magazine in the U.S.

15. Perhaps the most sustained narrative of this kind in print is Duberman (1992). Shorter but
similar tales of attempted cures for homosexuality can be found in such collections of lesbian coming
out stories as Penelope and Wolfe (1989) and Cruikshank (1985). See also, the myriad autobiographical pieces in the gay and lesbian press. The first widely distributed film documentary inspired
by gay and lesbian liberation, *Word Is Out* (1977), contains a searing account of a young lesbian's hos-
pitalization and electroshock therapy.

16. See, for example, the sidebar that accompanied *Time*'s "Homosexuality in America" cover
story, "Discussion: Are Homosexuals Sick?" (1969). A similar piece, "Is Homosexuality Normal or
Not?" (1971), appeared in *Life*.

17. One can find evidence of these splits in the different gay liberation newspapers that appeared
in New York City in 1969. *Come Out* was put out by a cell of GLF that belonged to the politically
oriented faction and took a political line consistent with the group's radical left orientation. *Gay* and
Gay Power were more culturally oriented and supported the liberal reformist politics of GAA when
that organization was set up. Articles in *Come Out* railed against gay bar culture, because these spaces
exploited patrons' marginalization and fears of exposure. *Gay* and *Gay Power* treated the bars as valid
sites of gay cultural activity and explicitly distanced themselves from the GLF position.

18. Shelley, for instance, didn't make the transition to mainstream celebrity, and although
Johnston continues to publish prolifically her writings consist mainly of personal autobiography or art
criticism and commentary. Only a reprinting of some of her *Village Voice* columns in *Admission
Accomplished* (1998) might indicate to younger readers the part she played in articulating the principles, as well as an analysis, of lesbian liberation.

19. The Rubyfruit Jungle Productions press release I located in the New York Public Library's
International Gay Information Center Archives appears to have been designed to mobilize members
of the gay rights movement to pressure recalcitrant film producers. The release explains that they were
not interested in making a low-budget independent film based on the novel "because *we want this
film to have the visibility that can be provided by a major studio*. We are not interested in making a film
that plays to the already sympathetic. The widest possible distribution is a perfect tool to help break
down the barriers of bigotry and reactionism" (emphasis added).

CHAPTER FIVE: IN RETROSPECT

1. Another play, *Jehanne d'Arc*, was produced in Paris, and flopped, like the earlier *Botticelli* piece. Both were conceived as vehicles for de Acosta's lover at the time, Eva Le Gallienne. Her play-writing career garnered her one success: a London production of *Prejudice*, which starred a young John Gielgud, featured Ralph Richardson in a secondary role, and was well received by critics. It ran for an entire season in London's West End in 1928 but was never staged in the U.S.

2. De Acosta was also mentioned in several 1923 articles about the Lucy Stone League, an organization that advocated women not changing their last names when they married (de Acosta Papers).

3. A profile of Rita de Acosta Lydig opens Annette Tapert and Diana Edkins's *The Power of Style: The Women Who Defined the Art of Living Well*, where she is described as "one of the most dazzling personalities in New York" in the first two decades of the twentieth century (Tapert and Edkins 1994, 17). Cecil Beaton also included a profile of Rita in his *The Glass of Fashion* (1954), which was a similar tribute to women known as fashion trendsetters. In 1940, the Museum of Costume Art in New York held an exhibition of Rita's extravagant clothing, which Mercedes had donated, and in 1975 Diana Vreeland paid tribute to Rita by commissioning a mannequin in her likeness to display items from her wardrobe in a show at the Metropolitan Museum of Art entitled "American Women of Style."

4. The play was a London production of *Othello*, about which West wrote: "[T]he actor playing the Moor, although highly accomplished, was physically unsuited to the part. He looked just like Mercedes d'Acosta [*sic*], which is a very good way to look, but not when one is acting 'Othello'" (West 1932).

5. Indeed, in 1961 the National Concerts and Artists Corporation listed a lecture by de Acosta on the topic of "Friends and Celebrities" among their offerings (de Acosta Papers).

6. De Wolfe died in 1950, but in 1997 the *New York Times* ran a feature on her in the weekly "Home" section (Owen 1997). She was also included in a *New York Times Magazine* piece about legendary interior decorators (Etherington-Smith 2000).

7. This anecdote, it turns out, is untrue. According to Alfred Allan Lewis's collective biography of Marbury, de Wolfe, and several of their close friends, the *World* never paid for nor published Wilde's poem. And although Hearst's New York *Journal* did pay Marbury one hundred dollars for the right to print it, this paper also never managed to do so (A. Lewis 2000, 182–185).

8. Marbury also disliked snobs and had strong opinions on many subjects, including modernist art, which she detested, with the exception of the Ballets Russes.

9. De Wolfe's marriage to Charles Mendl did not prevent Marbury from bequeathing most of her estate to her former lover when she died, a gift that made headlines in the New York press (Marbury clippings).

10. Smith's assesment of this episode in de Wolfe's autobiography is a tribute to her ability to respect de Wolfe's actual sexual preference, insofar as her own idea of the de Wolfe–Marbury relationship suffers from a pronounced heterosexual bias, as in the following passage: "Bessie and Elsie in fact assumed the roles of husband and wife according to the most sentimental of late-Victorian models. Bessie's instincts were domestic; she was a paterfamilias looking for a family, and, in Elsie, that was what she found. . . . Photographs of the two women in their first years together are a revealing mimic of the typical family portraits of the day" (Smith 1982, 50–51). The idea that pairings like de Wolfe and Marbury's can be explained as imitations of heterosexual marriage has been thoroughly debunked by Judith Butler (1991).

11. De Acosta notes that the model for Iris March was believed to be Nancy Cunard, "whom I greatly admired" (1960, 128), and who, not surprisingly, was a lesbian. It's just as likely, though, that Arlen's character was based on Marion Barbara (Joe) Carstairs, lesbian Standard Oil heiress and speed boat racer. She and de Acosta knew one another but had a falling out after de Acosta attempted to seduce one of Carstairs's girlfriends (Summerscale 1997, 135), which may be why the infamous speed demon is never mentioned in *Here Lies the Heart*.

12. Paris reports that Garbo's business manager Harry Edington is said to have encouraged her standoffish behavior as a way to incite interest in the star. He also repeats MGM publicity chief Howard Dietz's assertion that, whatever the reason for Garbo's refusal to speak to the press, her silence proved to be "the best publicity notion of the century" (Paris 1995, 179). For an example of the closet-case hypothesis, see Madsen (1995, xiv). Madsen bases his theory on a remark by director Edmund Goulding, although the quote from Goulding states only that Garbo was afraid of reporters snooping in her bedroom; he did not say anything about what they might have found. See also, Michael Bronski's 1990 obituary of Garbo in *Gay Community News*, "She Did Really 'Want to Be Alone'" (quoted in Mayne 1993, 163).

13. A few came close. An article about a stakeout at Garbo's residence produced this tidbit: "Around eight o'clock of that particular morning, a fresh young blonde of some eighteen summers was seen to skip out the front door of Mercedes' house and into the garage, out of which she drove a small closed car into the circular driveway, stopping directly opposite the front entrance. When she jumped out to go inside she left the motor running and the car door open.

"It was all of fifteen minutes before the blonde reappeared with Garbo—blue trousered legs showing beneath a tightly buttoned trench coat and blue beret tilted jauntily over straight blonde hair—following close behind. Both girls hurried into the car" (Palmborg 1932).

14. Hopper's columns were also syndicated, and published in such major dailies as the New York *Daily News* and the *Chicago Tribune*, among others.

15. It is not surprising to learn that neither Parsons nor Hopper was forthright about her own personal history. For details about the elaborate fictions each woman invented for herself, see Eells (1972).

16. Hopper's biographer finds her affinity with gay men difficult to fathom, which is reflected in a disparaging statement he quotes, uttered by David ("Spec") McClure, Hopper's assistant: "She had a strange attraction to fags. They were good dancers. A lot of them were witty, talented people. They didn't paw her. The only problem she had when she got home was to keep them from coming in and drinking all her liquor" (Eells 1972, 207).

17. Still, when her husband finally asked her for a divorce after almost fifteen years of noncohabitation, de Acosta says that the request came as a "great shock. . . . It had never occurred to me that Abram and I would ever be divorced" (de Acosta 1960, 261).

18. On de Wolfe's decision to marry, see Smith (1982, 223–224). According to Smith, Mendl made little secret of his liaisons with young, pretty women, often actresses, and said of his wife, "For all I know . . . the old girl is still a virgin" (304).

19. The presumed heterosexuality of Cornell and McClintic is unquestioned in two relatively recent biographies (Mosel and Macy 1978; Pederson 1994). Castle corrects this misimpression and reproduces a photo of Cornell and Nancy Hamilton basking nude in the sun alongside Coward, McClintic, and Coward's lover. In the caption, Castle matter-of-factly identifies Hamilton as Cornell's lover (Castle 1996, 37).

20. Sheehy documents New York theater critic George Jean Nathan's routine disparagement of Le Gallienne's performances, amidst otherwise positive notices, and notes Nathan's especially nasty item on her in his 1940 *Encyclopaedia of the Theatre*, which was embellished with homophobic jibes (Sheehy 1996, 258). Le Gallienne's lesbianism was also mocked in a 1928 *Vanity Fair* cartoon, reproduced in Schanke (1992, n.p.).

21. Lambert mentions a notice Nazimova received while touring in 1908: "There is not a town of any consequence in the United States today,' a columnist wrote in the *Washington Post*, 'where the coming of this young actress would not create interest among theatregoers, for her fame has spread over the land" (Lambert 1997, 146).

22. Nazimova once told a reporter, "My friends call me Mimi and sometimes Peter" and wore a "blue serge suit of mannish cut" to the interview (Lambert 1997, 210).

23. A Nazimova fan, Anita Owen, wrote a song titled "Alla" around 1920, which became a best-

selling phonograph record and piano roll. The refrain was: "Alla my heart is lonely/I want you only/Your eyes are e'er before me,/Alla I'll pray to Allah/To keep you safe for me" (quoted in Lambert 1997, 228).

24. Many of the lesbians in Flanner's "Letter from Paris" reports also appear in the photographic portraits taken during the late 1920s by Flanner's fellow expatriate Berenice Abbott, whose work featured such lesbians as Djuna Barnes, Margaret Anderson, Jane Heap, Sylvia Beach, Adrienne Monnier, Flanner, and her lover Solita Solano, in the same company as James Joyce, Max Ernst, and Peggy Guggenheim. Abbott's pictures—many of them with women in masculine garb and, my favorite, Flanner in top hat with two masks around it—underscore the point that lesbian invisibility as currently construed was not a problem in the 1920s, although the masks could be interpreted as a reference to lesbian themes like living a double life. A selection of these portraits are published in Abbott (1970).

25. The *WWD* article is not a review but an item about the use of de Acosta's book in a window display at Saks Fifth Avenue, with a mannequin holding the book and wearing a monocle. The writer mistakenly identifies this prop as a "Mercedes trademark," although the monocle *was* a mainstay of early twentieth-century, upper-class lesbian style and could be read as a sly reference to the store's and *WWD*'s awareness of the lesbian dimension of de Acosta's life story.

26. Interestingly, this was the expression used to discuss the frequent trips to Hawaii made by Janet Gaynor, the girl-next-door star, without her husband, just as famous MGM costume designer Adrian, who Hollywood insiders knew well was gay, and applied to him as well when he managed to conceal his whereabouts from reporters. See, York (1932).

27. Before the book was published, though, de Acosta removed a statement crediting Garbo with "*unfailing* honesty" in her dealings with the press, since de Acosta must have realized that this was an insupportable assertion (de Acosta Papers, emphasis added).

28. On Valentino's marriages, see Anger 1975 (108–113). However, the story about Nazimova's introductions is not entirely accurate, insofar as she did not introduce Acker to Valentino, although Acker *was* Nazimova's estranged lover when she married him. On the other hand, Rambova was introduced to Valentino when she was designing the sets and costumes for Nazimova's *Camille*; on both relationships, see Lambert (1997, 210–240).

29. I first became aware of the connection between Garbo and the flurry of outings in the early 1990s when reading Judith Mayne's commentary on this issue (1993, 160–164), which cites three Garbo obituaries in the gay press as harbingers of more widespread acknowledgment of the screen idol's sexual involvement with women. Mayne's point about Garbo's symbolic status in lesbian and gay culture led to my understanding of 1990 as the pivotal year in the consolidation of visibility politics and emergence of lesbian celebrity.

30. The candidates for de Acosta's third important lover who Madsen proposes in the text— Gertrude Stein or Eleanor Roosevelt—betray his preference for sensational speculation, since there is no evidence that de Acosta was more than a distant acquaintance of Stein (which, obviously, Toklas knew very well) or that she and Roosevelt ever met. Curiously, Souhami offers a similar quote, citing a letter from Toklas to Anita Loos as the source, but her version sets the number of lovers at two and names the obvious lovers—Garbo and Dietrich (Souhami 1994, ix).

31. The source Madsen cites for this witticism is Vickers's (1994, 12). Vickers, in turn, acknowledges his correspondence with John Richardson.

32. The text to which I refer concerns Nazimova's career, and reads in part: "She studied music at the St. Petersburg Consevatory. . . . She played leads at the Moscow Art Theater under Konstantin Stanislavsky and emigrated to America in 1906. . . . In 1921, she became Nancy Reagan's godmother when newly divorced Edith Davis toured with her. Nazimova's nephew, Val Lewton (Vladimir Ivan Leventon) . . . became David O. Selznick's story editor and in the 1940s a director of horror movies." (Madsen 1995, 97–98) The errors are these: She did not play leading roles in the Moscow Art Theater, only minor parts. She never studied violin at the St. Petersburg Conservatory, although her

teacher in Yalta did. She came to the U.S. in 1905 and was indeed Nancy Reagan's godmother, although the father was not anyone named Davis but a Kenneth Robbins, to whom Edith Luckett was still married when she toured with Nazimova. Val Lewton produced, and did not direct, horror movies like *The Cat People* and *I Walked with a Zombie*. Lambert's carefully researched *Nazimova* (1997) and materials in the Nazimova clippings files in the Billy Rose Collection at the New York Public Library are the sources for these corrections.

33. My quarrel with Madsen is not that he says that Cornell was a lesbian; she was.

34. Only in the case of Patsy Kelly, who had no reservations about saying, "I'm a big dyke. So what? Big deal!"(Hadleigh 1994, 62)—and that on the condition that these words not appear in print until her career had definitely come to a halt—does Hadleigh not resort to secondhand information to justify who he includes in his book and much of what he says in the text concerning his subjects' sexuality.

35. Other lines also describe Mercedes in terms that situate her unambiguously as an object of desire: "She had a small white body, like a marble park, in which her eyes lived as brown nightingales./Her hair was ligneous, black, and like a combed bush: her ears reddened like the berries./Her appetites were few, and they in her head, living there in grandeur like political prisoners who had changed, not broken, laws./Her shoes were those of ladies who used to be heeded." And the outline of two petals spelling out "Janet" and "Mercedes" adorn the top of the flower. The only other Flanner memorabilia among de Acosta's papers is a series of snapshots of the two and Flanner's lover Natalia Danesi Murray that appear to have been taken on a New York City terrace or rooftop in the 1940s; everyone is smiling (de Acosta Papers).

36. The friend in question is Sybille Bedford (Vickers 1994, 159–160). While reading in William Murray's memoir, which chronicles Flanner's intimate involvement with his mother, that "a well-known seducer with a reputation for scandalmongering" (Murray 2000, 168), spread rumors about Flanner's sexual infidelities during the late 1940s, I was provoked to make another attempt to pin down the accuracy of Vickers's statement. In response to a letter I wrote to Murray, enquiring whether de Acosta was this seducer, he replied, "It's my strong impression . . . that it was she" but went on to say that he isn't absolutely certain because the name of the guilty party was never uttered in his presence (Murray 2002).

37. Although filled with absurd touches, such as having the Nazimova character appear at home wearing a costume and headdress modeled on an outfit she wore in *Salome*, as well as outrageously hyperbolic performances, Russell's film remains remarkably faithful to reputable historical accounts of Valentino's rise and fall as a movie idol.

38. De Acosta died in 1968, and it's tempting to speculate what she would have had to say about the women's and gay liberation movements then taking shape. In a sense, she did stake out a position: her lifelong belief was that art always transcended politics, and she was an artist.

39. Apparently, de Acosta met Warhol through his lover Charles Lisanby, who was a scenic designer and former assistant of Cecil Beaton, also a member of a group of fashionable gay men with whom Warhol was involved socially in the 1950s and early sixties. According to Bob Colacello, Warhol's amanuensis for several decades and the first editor of Warhol's celebrity gossip sheet *Interview*, "Andy considered daCosta [*sic*] the height of elegance because not only were her shoes made in Europe, but her shoe *trees* were made by a violin maker" (Colacello 1990, 23). This is not quite accurate: the shoe trees belonged to Rita Lydig. De Acosta describes them in *Here Lies the Heart* as evidence of her sister's exquisite taste. In his somewhat bitter memoir of his life with Warhol, Colacello then repeats a famous anecdote about a picnic attended by Warhol, de Acosta, and Garbo, where Andy gave a drawing of a butterfly to Greta, which she discarded and he recovered; he inscribed the drawing "butterfly crumpled by Greta Garbo" (ibid.). Warhol's Garbo fetish was also enacted when he commissioned a photograph of himself assuming the same pose Garbo took in a famous portrait by Edward Steichen. Insofar as Warhol is routinely invoked whenever the expansion and influence of celebrity in contemporary culture is considered, it is noteworthy that one of his own celebrity prototypes was the lesbian Garbo.

CHAPTER SIX: POPULAR MECHANICS

1. The book appeared on the the the *New York Times* best-seller list for ten weeks.

2. Other favorite items included in the official Navratilova narrative ca. 1985 were her defection in 1975 and her inability to win the U.S. Open.

3. For a detailed account of the uproar, see Festle (1996).

4. In her autobiography, Brown claims, erroneously, "I inhabited a peculiar territory as the only public lesbian in a nation of 200 million people. . . . It wasn't that other public figures weren't thought to be bisexual or lesbian, for instance Marlene Dietrich, but I said it, no sidestepping or crawfishing" (Brown 1997, 328). This kind of self-aggrandizement isn't particularly unusual for Brown. She also takes credit for single-handedly starting the lesbian liberation movement: "I was going to pull together gay women. This would be a neat trick since, as far as I knew, it had never been done in the context of mass organizing in all of Western history. . . . No one had directly appealed to gay women" (234). She mentions earlier efforts by the Daughters of Bilitis but asserts that they don't count because the group "might as well have come from the Paleolithic Age" (ibid.)

5. For instance, Axthelm (1982) mentions Navratilova's denials about a sexual relationship with Lieberman. Salter (1981) quotes Lieberman's mocking dismissal of reporters' curiosity about Navratilova's sex life and insists that their relationship is chaste.

6. Conventionally, the Grand Slam consists of winning Wimbledon and the Australian, French, and U.S. Opens in one calendar year. Navratilova won the four matches consecutively, but in 1983 and 1984.

7. *New York Times* op-ed columnist Maureen Dowd (2000) cites the example of Anna Kournikova, who was "the highest earning player in women's tennis" when the article appeared, despite her failure to win a major tournament.

8. Navratilova's total income during the years she has played tennis professionally is not public information; therefore, any actual amounts are unavailable.

9. This text appears in a caption for a photo of an elegantly attired and heavily made-up Navratilova during an appearance on the *Tonight* show.

10. Cahn quotes an item from the *Baltimore Sun*, which informed its readers that a 1925 women's track meet, "was a girly show if there ever was one" (Cahn 1994, 78).

11. For commentary on recent appearances of women tennis stars as models in various stylish magazines, see Finn (1998).

12. Not that Navratilova did not dabble in these more conventional post-retirement activities. She performed a brief stint as a columnist on health and fitness for a magazine for women, *Condé Nast Sport*, in 1998, and, as I discuss in this chapter, she has worked as a television commentator at Grand Slam tournaments during the years after her retirement from playing singles as a professional.

13. The line is: "I've been in the twilight of my career longer than most people have careers" (Navratilova and Nickles 1994, 8).

14. For a transcript of much of the interview, see Faulkner (1993, 151–156). For an example of the interpretation of the interview as Navratilova's first public coming out announcement, see Zwerman (1995, 149).

15. Cf. a subsequent *Advocate* cover, with an utterly placid Martina gazing at the camera (*Advocate* 696 [12 December 1995]).

16. In his column on advertising in the *New York Times*, which reproduced the muscular Martina photo, Stuart Elliott (1995) quotes a curious remark by one of the chief executive of Do Tell, the company that created the card and lined up its sponsors, who explains the choice of Navratilova as the spokesperson: "She came out when many of us were in the closet and few were willing to join her and say, 'I'm gay, too.'" Could this be an indirect response to those who reproached the tennis star for her coyness?

17. This is the thesis of the sole book on the topic of contemporary lesbian celebrity that is not a biography to date: Allen (1997).

18. Cathy Griggers (1994) considers the problem but offers no decisive suggestions.

19. As the subtitle of the book in which these lines appear indicates, *Multiple Personality and the Sciences of Memory*, Hacking applies these concepts to people with multiple personalities, although elsewhere he considers the historical production of homosexual people in similar terms. On this topic, see Hacking (1986).

20. In addition to Foucault, one of the best analysts of the factors and forms involved in present-day personhood is Nikolas Rose (1998; 1999).

CHAPTER SEVEN: AFTERWORD

1. McLellan's fantastic account of the Garbo–Dietrich liaison is far too elaborate to be summarized here. Her suppositions, stated as irrefutable fact, are also difficult to accept, since these are premised upon a set of frame enlargements from G. W. Pabst's 1925 film *Die freudlose Gasse* (*Joyless Street*), which she claims prove, beyond doubt, that the two women were intimate. After peering at the photos for a long time, I found that the resemblance between the actress she insists *must* be Dietrich and other photos of the star is not convincing. My disbelief was reinforced by the author's promiscuous use of information in other instances. Like several of her predecessors in the biographical subgenre of lesbian revelation, she confidently asserts that various famous women were lovers, based solely on evidence that they knew each other. McLellan reaches the height of this kind of implausible interpretation with her blithe description of a imaginary affair between Nazimova and Emma Goldman, without mentioning Goldman's close and most likely sexual relationship with Nazimova's mentor and companion, Pavel Orlenev.

BIBLIOGRAPHY

Abbott, Berenice. 1970. *Berenice Abbott/Photographs*. Washington: Smithsonian Institution Press.

Abbott, Sidney, and Barbara Love. [1972] 1985. *Sappho Was a Right-On Woman: A Liberated View of Lesbianism*. New York: Stein and Day.

Alinder, Gary. [1970] 1992. "Gay Liberation Meets the Shrinks." In *Out of the Closets: Voices of Gay Liberation*, rev. ed., ed. Karla Jay and Allen Young, 141–145. New York: New York University Press.

Allen, Louise. 1997. *The Lesbian Idol: Martina, kd, and the Consumption of Lesbian Masculinity*. London: Cassell.

Als, Hilton and Darryl Turner. 1995. "Double Exposure," *Out*, November, 101.

Alwood, Edward. 1996. *Straight News: Gays, Lesbians, and the News Media*. New York: Columbia University Press.

Andur, Neil. 1981. "Homosexuality Sets Off Tremors," *New York Times*, 12 May, sec. B.

Anger, Kenneth. 1975. *Hollywood Babylon*. San Francisco: Straight Arrow Books.

———. 1984. *Hollywood Babylon II*. New York: Penguin.

Angier, Natalie. 1993. "Bias Against Gay People: Hatred of a Special Kind," *New York Times*, 26 December, sec. E.

Appadurai, Arjun. 1986. "Introduction: Commodities and the Politics of Value." In *The Social Life of Things: Commodities in Cultural Perspective*, ed. Arjun Appadurai, 3–63. Cambridge, England: Cambridge University Press.

Axthelm, Pete. 1984. "The Curse of Unlovable Champs," *Newsweek* 104:13 (24 September), 62.

Axthelm, Pete, with Pamela Anderson and Stephanie Russell. 1982. "Martina: A Style All Her Own," *Newsweek* 100:10 (6 September), 44–48.

Bach, Steven. 1992. *Marlene Dietrich: Life and Legend*. New York: William Morrow.

Badgett, M. V. Lee. 2000. "The Myth of Gay and Lesbian Affluence." *Gay and Lesbian Review* 7:2 (30 April).

Baker, Michael. 1985. *Our Three Selves: The Life of Radclyffe Hall*. New York: William Morrow.

Barnes, Djuna. 1930. "Alla Nazimova," *Theatre Guild Magazine* 7:9, 32–34.

Barringer, Felicity. 1993a. "Sex Survey of American Man Finds 1% Are Gay," *New York Times*, 15 April, sec. A.

———. 1993b. "Measuring Sexuality Through Polls Can Be Shaky," *New York Times*, 25 April, sec. A.

Barthes, Roland. 1993. "La vedette: enquêtes d'audience?" In *Oeuvres complètes: Vol. 1, 1942–1965*, 1111–1155. Paris: Editions du Seuil.

Battcock, Gregory. 1970. "The Last Estate," *Gay* 1:11 (6 July).

Beaton, Cecil. 1954. *The Glass of Fashion*. Garden City, NY: Doubleday.

Bennetts, Leslie. 1993. "k.d. lang Cuts It Close," *Vanity Fair* 56:8 (August), 94–99.

Bersani, Leo. 1995. *Homos*. Cambridge: Harvard University Press.

B. G., 1960. "Letters," *Ladder* 4:11 (August), 25–26.

Bird, S. Elizabeth. 1992. *For Enquiring Minds: A Cultural Study of Supermarket Tabloids*. Knoxville: University of Tennessee Press.

Blue, Adrianne. 1994. *Martina Unauthorized*. London: Victor Gollancz.

Blumer, Herbert. 1933. *Movies and Conduct*. New York: Macmillan.

Bodeen, De Witt. 1972. "Nazimova: Her Film Career Was a Pale Reflection of Her Genius as an Actress." *Films in Review* (December): 577–604.

Bono, Chastity, interviewed by Judy Wieder. 1995. "Virtuous Reality," *Advocate* 679 (18 April), 43–52.

———, interviewed by Gabriel Rotello. 1998. "The Sudden Adulthood of Chastity Bono," *Advocate* 770 (13 October), 32–48.

Boorstin, Daniel J. 1961. *The Image: A Guide to Pseudo-Events in America*. New York: Random House.

Boswell, Thomas. 1981. "A Delightful Exception to the Rule," *Washington Post*, 30 June, sec. D.

Braudy, Leo. 1986. *The Frenzy of Renown: Fame and Its History*. New York: Oxford University Press.

Brooks, Peter. 1984. *The Melodramatic Imagination: Balzac, Henry James, Melodrama, and the Mode of Excess*. New Haven: Yale University Press.

Brown, Rita Mae. 1971. *The Hand That Cradles the Rock*. New York: New York University Press.

———. 1972. "Leadership vs Stardom," *Furies* 2 (February), 20–22.

———. [1972] 1992. "Take a Lesbian to Lunch." In *Out of the Closets: Voices of Gay Liberation*, rev. ed., ed. Karla Jay and Allen Young, 185–195. New York: New York University Press.

———. [1973] 1977. *Rubyfruit Jungle*. New York: Bantam Books.

———. 1976. *Plain Brown Rapper*. Oakland: Diana Press.

———. 1983. *Sudden Death*. New York: Bantam Books.

———. 1997. *Rita Will: Memoir of a Literary Rabble-Rouser*. New York: Bantam Books.

Brownmiller, Susan. 1970. "'Sisterhood Is Powerful': A Member of the Women's Liberation Movement Explains Its Aims," *New York Times Magazine*, 15 March, 26–27.

Bruce, Carter. 1932. "Garbo Steps Out—Dietrich Goes into Seclusion," *Modern Screen* 3:3 (February), 70.

Bryan, C. D. B. 1986. "*Architectural Digest* Visits: Martina Navratilova," *Architectural Digest* 43:9 (September), 118–123.

Buffington, Betsy. n.d. "Greta Garbo's Pal Has Much to Tell," review of *Here Lies the Heart*, by Mercedes de Acosta. De Acosta Papers.

Bull, Chris. 1991. "The Magic of Martina," *Advocate* 593 (31 December), 40.

Burchell, Graham, Colin Gordon, and Peter Miller, ed. 1991. *The Foucault Effect: Studies in Governmentality*. Chicago: University of Chicago Press.

Busby, Marquis. 1933. "Hot News," *Movie Mirror* 3:4 (February), 8.

Butler, Judith. 1990. *Gender Trouble: Feminism and the Subversion of Identity*. New York: Routledge.

———. 1991. "Imitation and Gender Insubordination." In *Inside/Out: Lesbian Theories, Gay Theories*, ed. Diana Fuss, 13–31. New York: Routledge.

Cahn, Susan K. 1994. *Coming on Strong: Gender and Sexuality in Twentieth-Century Women's Sport*. Cambridge, MA: Harvard University Press.

Callahan, Tom. 1983. "Martina's Turn at the Top," *Time* 122:2 (11 July), 40.

Cammermeyer, Margarethe, with Chris Fisher. 1994. *Serving in Silence*. New York: Penguin.

Case, Sue-Ellen. 1993. "Toward a Butch-Femme Aesthetic." In *The Lesbian and Gay Studies Reader*, ed. Henry Abelove, Michèle Aina Barale, and David M. Halperin, 294–306. New York: Routledge.

Castle, Terry. 1993. *The Apparitional Lesbian: Female Homosexuality and Modern Culture*. New York: Columbia University Press.

———. 1996. *Noël Coward and Radclyffe Hall: Kindred Spirits*. New York: Columbia University Press.

Cayleff, Susan E. 1995. *Babe: The Life and Legend of Babe Didrikson Zaharias*. Urbana: University of Illinois Press.

Chauncey, George, Jr. 1982–83. "From Sexual Inversion to Homosexuality: Medicine and the Changing Conceptualization of Female Deviance." *Salmagundi* 58/59 (Fall/Winter): 114–146.

———. 1994. *Gay New York: Gender, Urban Culture, and the Making of a Gay Male World, 1890–1940*. New York: HarperCollins.

Chicago Gay Liberation. 1970. *Chicago Gay Liberation Newsletter* 7 (August).

———. [1970] 1992. "Working Paper for the Revolutionary People's Constitutional Convention." In *Out of the Closets: Voices of Gay Liberation*, rev. ed., ed. Karla Jay and Allen Young, 346–352. New York: New York University Press.

Clark, Danae. 1993. "Commodity Lesbianism." In *The Lesbian and Gay Studies Reader*, eds. Henry Abelove, Michèle Aina Barale, and David M. Halperin, 186–201. New York: Routledge.

Class Workshop. 1970. "What Can We Do about the Media?" Quoted in Echols (1989, 208).

Colacello, Bob. 1990. *Holy Terror: Andy Warhol Close Up*. New York: HarperCollins.

Come Out 1:3. 1970 (April/May).

Connell, R. W. 1979. "The Concept of Role and What to Do with It." *Australia and New Zealand Journal of Sociology* 15:3 (November): 7–17.

Cooper, David. 1967. *Psychiatry and Anti-Psychiatry*. London: Tavistock.

———. 1968. *To Free a Generation: The Dialectics of Liberation*. New York: Collier Books.

Cory, Donald Webster [Edward Sagarin]. 1963. "The Loneliness of Radclyffe Hall," *Ladder* 7:10 (July), 4–9.

Coulson, Margaret. 1972. "Role: A Redundant Concept in Sociology? Some Educational Considerations." In *Role*, ed. J. A. Jackson, 107–128. Cambridge, England: Cambridge University Press.

Crimp, Douglas. 1994. "Right On, Girlfriend!" In *Fear of a Queer Planet: Queer Politics and Social Theory*, ed. Michael Warner, 300–320. Minneapolis: University of Minnesota Press.

Crowther, Bosley. 1967. "Alla Nazimova's 1922 Film 'Salome' at the Museum [of Modern Art]," *New York Times*, 15 February.

Cruikshank, Margaret. 1992. *The Gay and Lesbian Liberation Movement*. New York: Routledge.

———, ed. 1985. *The Lesbian Path*. San Francisco: Grey Fox Press.

Damon, Gene. 1962. "Biography of 'The Well,'" *Ladder* 6:7 (April), 10.

Darrach, Brad. 1983. "Portrait: Martina Navratilova," *Life* 6 (February), 19–21.

Davidson, Arnold. 1987. "Sex and the Emergence of Sexuality." *Critical Inquiry* 14 (Autumn): 16–48.

Davis, Tracy C. 1991. *Actresses as Working Women: Their Social Identity in Victorian Culture*. London: Routledge.

de Acosta, Mercedes. Papers. Rosenbach Museum and Library, Philadelphia.

de Acosta, Mercedes. 1919. *Moods*. New York: Moffat and Yard.

———. 1920. *Wind Chaff*. New York: Moffat and Yard.

———. 1921. *Archways of Life*. New York: Moffat and Yard.

———. 1922. *Streets and Shadows*. New York: Moffat and Yard.

———. 1928. *Until the Day Breaks*. New York: Longmans, Green and Company.

———. 1960. *Here Lies the Heart*. New York: Reynal and Company.

Debord, Guy. 1990. *The Society of the Spectacle*, trans. Donald Nicholson-Smith. New York: Swerve Editions.

de Certeau, Michel. 1984. *The Practice of Everyday Life*, trans. Steven Rendall. Berkeley: University of California Press.

deCordova, Richard. 1990. *Picture Personalities: The Emergence of the Star System in America*. Urbana: University of Illinois Press.

———. 1991. " The Emergence of the Star System in America." In *Stardom: Industry of Desire*, ed. Christine Gledhill, 17–29. London: Routledge.

Decter, Midge. 1970. "Liberated Woman," review of *Sexual Politics*, by Kate Millett, *Commentary* 50 (October), 33–44.

Deford, Frank. 1984. "Talk about Strokes of Genius," *Sports Illustrated* 61:3 (16 July), 14–16.

de Lauretis, Teresa. 1984. *Alice Doesn't: Feminism, Semiotics, Cinema*. Bloomington: Indiana University Press.

———. 1987. *Technologies of Gender: Essays on Theory, Film, and Fiction*. Bloomington: Indiana University Press.

———. 1988. "Sexual Indifference and Lesbian Representation." *Theatre Journal* 40:2 (May): 155–177.

———. 1991. "Film and the Visible." In *How Do I Look? Queer Film and Video*, ed. Bad Object Choices, 223–264. Seattle: Bay Press.

———. 1994. *The Practice of Love: Lesbian Sexuality and Perverse Desire*. Bloomington: Indiana University Press.

D'Emilio, John. 1992. Preface to *Out of the Closets: Voices of Gay Liberation*, rev. ed., ed. Karla Jay and Allen Young, xi–xxviii. New York: New York University Press.

D'Emilio, John, and Estelle B. Freedman. 1988. *Intimate Matters: A History of Sexuality in America*. New York: Harper and Row.

de Wolfe, Elsie. 1935. *After All*. New York: Harper and Brothers.

Dittmar, Linda. 1998. "The Straight Goods: Lesbian Chic and Identity Capital on a Not-So-Queer Planet." In *The Passionate Camera: Photography and Bodies of Desire*, ed. Deborah Bright, 319–339. London: Routledge.

Doane, Mary Ann. 1981. "Woman's Stake: Filming the Female Body." *October* 17 (Summer): 23–36.

———. 1987. *The Desire to Desire: The Woman's Film of the 1940s*. Bloomington: Indiana University Press.

Donoghue, Emma. 1993. *Passions Between Women: British Lesbian Culture, 1668–1801*. New York: HarperCollins.

Dowd, Maureen. 1996. "The No Frontier," *New York Times*, 3 October, sec. A.

———. 2000. "Nymphet at the Net," *New York Times*, 4 June, sec. WK.

Duberman, Martin. 1992. *Cures: A Gay Man's Odyssey*. New York: Plume.

Dyer, Richard. 1979. *Stars*. London: British Film Institute.

———. 1986. *Heavenly Bodies: Film Stars and Society*. New York: St. Martin's.

———. 1991. "*A Star Is Born* and the Construction of Authenticity." In *Stardom: Industry of Desire*, ed. Christine Gledhill, 132–140. London: Routledge.

———. 1997. *White*. London: Routledge.

Dyson, Michael Eric. 1993. *Reflecting Black: African-American Cultural Criticism*. Minneapolis: University of Minnesota Press.

Echols, Alice. 1989. *Daring to Be Bad: Radical Feminism in America, 1967–1975*. Minneapolis: University of Minnesota Press.

Eckert, Charles. 1990. "The Carole Lombard in Macy's Window." In *Fabrications: Costume and the Female Body*, ed. Jane Gaines and Charlotte Herzog, 100–121. New York: Routledge.

Eells, George. 1972. *Hedda and Louella*. New York: G. P. Putnam's Sons.

Elliott, Stuart. 1995. "Advertising," *New York Times*, 6 October, sec. D.

Ellis, Havelock. [1901] 1936. *Studies in the Psychology of Sex: Sexual Inversion*, vol. 1. pt. 4. New York: Random House.

Elsaesser, Thomas. 1987. "Tales of Sound and Fury: Observations on the Family Melodrama." In *Home Is Where the Heart Is: Studies in Melodrama and the Women's Film*, ed. Christine Gledhill, 43–69. London: British Film Institute.

Etherington-Smith, Meredith. 2000. "They Did Windows," *New York Times Magazine*, 14 April, 24–32.

Faderman, Lillian. 1991. *Odd Girls and Twilight Lovers: A History of Lesbian Life in the Twentieth Century*. New York: Penguin.

Faulkner, Sandra, with Judy Nelson. 1993. *Love Match: Nelson vs. Navratilova*. New York: Birch Lane Press.

Featherstone, Mike. 1992. "The Heroic Life and Everyday Life." In *Cultural Theory and Cultural Change*, ed. Mike Featherstone, 159–182. London: Sage.

Feinstein, John. 1992. *Hard Courts: Real Life on the Professional Tennis Tours*. New York: Random House.

Festle, Mary Jo. 1996. *Playing Nice: Politics and Apologies in Women's Sports*. New York: Columbia University Press.

Field, Rose. 1960. "Memoirs of a Lady Who Knew Them All," review of *Here Lies the Heart*, by Mercedes de Acosta, *New York Herald Tribune*, 27 March.

"Film Gossip of the Month." 1931. *Modern Screen* 2:6 (November), 15.

Finn, Robin. 1998. "Game, Set, Glamour," *New York Times*, 23 November, sec. B.

Flanner, Janet. 1971. *Paris Was Yesterday, 1925–1939*. New York: Viking.

Fletcher, Adele Whitely. 1932. "Marlene Dietrich's Amazing Secret," *Modern Screen* 3:2 (January).

Foucault, Michel. 1977. *Discipline and Punish: The Birth of the Prison*, trans. Alan Sheridan. New York: Vintage Books.

———. 1978. *The History of Sexuality, Volume I: An Introduction*, trans. Robert Hurley. New York: Random House.

———. 1994. *Ethics: Subjectivity and Truth*, ed. Paul Rabinow. New York: New Press.

Freud, Sigmund. 1963. "Fetishism." In *Sexuality and the Psychology of Love*, 214–219. New York: Macmillan.

Gaba, Lester. 1960. "Lester Gaba Looks at Display," *Women's Wear Daily*, 12 April, 13.

Gabler, Neal. 1994. *Winchell: Gossip, Power and the Culture of Celebrity*. New York: Vintage Books.

Gamson, Joshua. 1994. *Claims to Fame: Celebrity in Contemporary America*. Berkeley: University of California Press.

Gavin, Steve. 1972. "Thoughts on the Movement," *Come Out* 2:8 (Winter), 20.

Gay and Lesbian Alliance Against Defamation. 1997a. *GLAAD Dispatch* 4:7 (October).

———. 1997b. Membership recruitment letter.

Germano, Barbara. 1993. "Letters," *Advocate* 642 (16 November), 12.

Gever, Martha. 1989. "Visibility/Invisibility: Contradictions in Lesbian Representations." *White Walls* 23 (Fall): 52–70.

———. 1990. "The Names We Give Ourselves." In *Out There: Marginalization and Contemporary Cultures*, ed. Russell Ferguson, Martha Gever, Trinh T. Minh-ha, and Cornel West, 191–202. Cambridge, MA, and New York: MIT Press and New Museum.

———. 1991. "Invisibility Made Visible," review of Lookout Lesbian and Gay Video Festival and Experimental Lesbian and Gay Film Festival (New York City), *Art in America* 79:4 (April), 57–63.

———. 1994. "What Becomes a Legend Most?" review of *Forbidden Love: The Unashamed Stories of Lesbian Lives*, dir. Aerlyn Weissman and Lynne Fernie, and *Last Call at Maud's*, dir. Paris Poirier. *GLQ: A Journal of Lesbian and Gay Studies* 1:2: 209–219.

Gingrich, Candace, with Chris Bull. 1996. *The Accidental Activist: A Personal and Political Memoir*. New York: Scribners.

Gitlin, Todd. 1980. *The Whole World Is Watching: Mass Media and the Making and Unmaking of the New Left*. Berkeley: University of California Press.

———. 1993. "Glib, Tawdry, Savvy, and Standardized: Television and American Culture." *Dissent* 40:3 (Fall): 351–355.

Gledhill, Christine. 1987. "The Melodramatic Field: An Investigation." In *Home Is Where the Heart Is: Studies in Melodrama and the Women's Film*, ed. Christine Gledhill, 1–39. London: British Film Institute.

———. 1991. "Signs of Melodrama." In *Stardom: Industry of Desire*, ed. Christine Gledhill, 207–229. London: Routledge.

Gluckman, Amy, and Betsy Reed. 1993. "The Gay Marketing Moment: Leaving Diversity in the Dust," *Dollars and Sense* 190 (November/December), 16–19, 34–35.

Goff, Michael. 1996. "Lifestyles of the Rich and Famous," *Out*, December/January, 16.

Goldsby, Jackie. 1993. "Queen for 307 Days: Looking B[l]ack at Vanessa Williams and the Sex Wars." In *Sisters, Sexperts, and Queers: Beyond Lesbian Nation*, ed. Arlene Stein, 165–188. New York: Plume.

Griggers, Cathy. 1994. "Lesbian Bodies in the Age of (Post) Mechanical Reproduction." In *The Lesbian Postmodern*, ed. Laura Doan, 118–133. New York: Columbia University Press.

Gronowicz, Antoni. 1990. *Garbo: Her Story*. New York: Simon and Schuster.

Gross, Larry. 1989. "Out of the Mainstream: Sexual Minorities and the Mass Media." In *Remote Control: Television, Audiences, and Cultural Power*, ed. Ellen Seiter et al., 130–149. London: Routledge.

———. 1993. *Contested Closets: The Politics and Ethics of Outing*. Minneapolis: University of Minnesota Press.

Hacking, Ian. 1986. "Making Up People." In *Reconstructing Individualism: Autonomy, Individuality, and the Self in Western Thought*, ed. Thomas C. Heller, Morton Sosna, and David E. Wellbery, 222–236. Stanford: Stanford University Press.

———. 1995. *Rewriting the Soul: Multiple Personality and the Sciences of Memory*. Princeton: Princeton University Press.

Hadju, David. 2002. "Queer as Folk," *New York Times Magazine*, 18 August, 38–41.

Hadleigh, Boze. 1994. *Hollywood Lesbians*. New York: Barricade Books.

Hall, Radclyffe. 1928. *The Well of Loneliness*. New York: Doubleday.

Hall, Stuart. 1981. "Notes on Deconstructing 'the Popular.'" In *People's History and Socialist Theory*, ed. Raphael Samuel, 227–240. London: Routledge and Kegan Paul.

Hambourg, Maria Morris, Françoise Heilbrun, and Philippe Néagu, ed. 1995. *Nadar*. New York: Metropolitan Museum of Art.

Hansen, Miriam. 1991. *Babel and Babylon: Spectatorship in American Silent Film*. Cambridge, MA: Harvard University Press.

Haraway, Donna. 1991. *Cyborgs, Simians, and Women: The Reinvention of Nature*. New York: Routledge.

Harris, Helaine. 1972. "Queen Christina: Lesbian Ruler of Sweden," *Furies* 1:1 (January), 10–11.

Harris, Thomas B. 1957. "The Building of Popular Images: Grace Kelly and Marilyn Monroe." *Studies in Public Communication* 1: 45–48.

Hauser, P. M. 1935. *Movies, Delinquency, and Crime*. New York: Macmillan.

"HI!" 1971. *Gay Power* 1:11, 15.

Hollander, Anne. 1994. *Sex and Suits: The Evolution of Modern Dress*. New York: Knopf.

Holmes, Oliver Wendell. [1863] 1980. "Doings of the Sunbeam." In *Photography: Essays and Images*, ed. Beaumont Newhall, 63–77. New York: Museum of Modern Art. Originally published in *Atlantic Monthly* 12 (July).

"Homosexuality in America." 1969. *Time* 94:18 (31 October), 56–67.

"Homosexuals in Revolt: The Year that One Liberation Movement Turned Militant." 1971. *Life* 71:26 (31 December), 62–72.

Howe, Irving. 1970. Review of *Sexual Politics*, by Kate Millett, *Harper's* 241 (December), 110.

Huyssen, Andreas. 1986. *After the Great Divide: Modernism, Mass Culture, Postmodernism*. Bloomington: Indiana University Press.

"Inside Stuff." 1933. *Modern Screen* 5:3 (February).

Irigaray, Luce. 1985. *Speculum of the Other Woman*, trans. Gillian C. Gill. Ithaca: Cornell University Press.

"Is Homosexuality Normal or Not?" 1971. *Life* 7:26 (31 December), 72.

Ivins, William M., Jr. 1981. "Prints and Visual Communications." In *Photography in Print: Writings from 1816 to the Present*, ed. Vicki Goldberg, 387–393. New York: Touchstone.

Jamison, Laura. 1998. "A Feisty Female Rapper Breaks a Hip-Hop Taboo," *New York Times*, 18 January, sec. AR.

Jay, Karla. 1999. *Tales of the Lavender Menace: A Memoir of Liberation*. New York: Basic Books.

Jay, Karla, and Allen Young, ed. 1992. *Out of the Closets: Voices of Gay Liberation*, rev. ed. New York: New York University Press.

——, ed. 1994. *Lavender Culture*, rev. ed. New York: New York University Press.

Johnston, Jill. 1971a. "The Media Macho," *Village Voice*, 15 April, 25–26.

——. 1971b. "Germaine and Guillaume in Baltimore," *Village Voice*, 22 April, 31–32.

——. 1973. *Lesbian Nation: The Feminist Solution.* New York: Simon and Schuster.

——. 1974. *Gullibles Travels.* New York: Links Books.

——. 1998. *Admission Accomplished: The Lesbian Nation Years (1970–75).* London: Serpent's Tail.

Joreen [Jo Freeman]. [1972] 1973. "The Tyranny of Structurelessness." In *Radical Feminism*, eds. Anne Koedt, Ellen Levine, and Anita Rapone, 285–299. New York: Quadrangle Books. Originally published in *Ain't I a Woman?* 2:9 (16 June), 2–4.

——. 1976. "Trashing: The Dark Side of Sisterhood," *Ms.* 4:10 (April), 49–51, 92–98.

Kaiso, Stephen. 1970. "The Well of Possibility," *Gay* 1:5 (2 February), 8.

Kakutani, Michiko. 1996. "The United States of Andy," *New York Times Magazine*, 17 November, 34.

Kalyn, Wayne. 1983. "Building the Brave New Martina," *World Tennis* 30:11 (April), 56–61, 104.

Kaplan, E. Ann. 1983. *Women and Film: Both Sides of the Camera.* New York: Methuen.

Kaplan, Janice. 1985. "Star Secrets: How Martina Does It!" *Vogue* 175:4 (April), 344.

Kasindorf, Jeanne Russell. 1993. "Lesbian Chic: The Bold, Brave New World of Gay Women," *New York* 26:19 (10 May), 30–37.

Katz, Jonathan Ned. 1976. *Gay American History: Lesbians and Gay Men in the U.S.A.* New York: Harper Colophon.

Keller, Ulrich. 1995. "Sorting Out Nadar: An Examination of Nadar's Photographic Legacy." In *Nadar*, ed. Maria Morris Hambourg, Françoise Heilbrun, and Philippe Néagu. New York: Metropolitan Museum of Art.

Kirkpatrick, Curry. 1972. "The Ball in Two Different Courts," *Sports Illustrated*, 25 December. Quoted in Festle (1996, 150).

——. 1994. "The Passion of a Champion," *Newsweek* 126:20 (14 November), 58.

Kirshenbaum, Jerry. 1981. "Facing Up to Billie Jean's Revelations," *Sports Illustrated* 54:20 (11 May), 13–14.

Klemesrud, Judy. 1971. "The Disciples of Sappho, Updated," *New York Times Magazine*, 28 March, 38–52.

Knickerbocker, Cholly. 1935. "Cholly Knickerboker Says," *New York American*, 1 March.

Koffler, Kevin. 1996. "Hooray for Hollywood," *Out*, March, 16.

Kuczynski, Alex. 2002. "She's Out of the Closet. Now What?," *New York Times*, 3 March, Style sec., 1, 5.

Ladder. 1969–1970. 14:3&4 (December–January).

Laing, R. D. 1967. *The Politics of Experience.* New York: Ballantine.

Lambert, Gavin. 1997. *Nazimova: A Biography.* New York: Knopf.

Lawrenson, Helen. 1971. "Feminine Mistake," review of *Sexual Politics*, by Kate Millett, *Esquire* 75 (January), 82–85.

Le Bon, Gustave. [1895] 1981. *The Crowd.* New York: Penguin.

Lee, Alfred McClung. 1937. *The Daily Newspaper in America: The Evolution of a Social Instrument.* New York: Macmillan.

Le Gallienne, Eva. 1934. *At 33.* New York: Longmans, Green and Company.

——. 1953. *With a Quiet Heart.* New York: Viking.

Leitsch, Dick. 1969. "Facts Your History Teacher 'Forgot' to Mention," *Gay* 3 (31 December), 14.

"Lesbians Zap Bandy." 1971. *Gay* 51 (24 May), n.p.

Lewis, Alfred Allan. 2000. *Ladies and Not-So-Gentle Women: Elisabeth Marbury, Anne Morgan, Elsie de Wolfe, Anne Vanderbilt, and Their Times.* New York: Viking.

Lewis, Lloyd, and Henry J. Smith. 1936. *Oscar Wilde Discovers America.* New York: Benjamin Blum.

Lieberman-Cline, Nancy, with N. Jennings. 1992. *Lady Magic.* Champaign, IL: Sagamore.

Lorge, Barry. 1981a. "Clear Skies for Navratilova," *Washington Post*, 8 January, sec. F.

———. 1981b. "The Aftermath: Verbal Vultures Descend on Women's Tour; King Affair Puts Women's Sports on Trial," *Washington Post*, 7 May, sec. D.

Lowenthal, Leo. [1944] 1968. "The Triumph of Mass Idols." In *Literature, Popular Culture, and Society*, 109–140. Palo Alto: Pacific Books. Originally published as "Biographies in Popular Magazines." In *Radio Research, 1942–43*, ed. Paul F. Lazarsfeld and Frank Stanton. New York: Duell, Sloan and Pearce.

Luhan, Mabel Dodge. [1933–1937] 1971. *Intimate Memories*. New York: Kraus Reprint Company.

MacIntosh, Mary. 1968. "The Homosexual Role." *Social Problems* 16 (Fall): 182–192.

Madsen, Axel. 1995. *The Sewing Circle—Hollywood's Greatest Secret: Female Stars Who Loved Other Women*. New York: Carol Publishing Group.

Malcolm, Janet. 1970. "Help!" review of *Sexual Politics*, by Kate Millett, *New Republic* 163 (10 October), 15–17.

Mandel, Ernest. 1984. *Delightful Murder: A Social History of the Crime Story*. Minneapolis: University of Minnesota Press.

Mansfield, Stephanie. 1981. "Rita Mae Brown, Martina Navratilova, and the End of the Affair," *Washington Post*, 13 August, Style sec.

Marbury, Elisabeth. 1923. *My Crystal Ball*. New York: Boni and Liveright.

———. Clippings file. Billy Rose Collection, New York Public Library.

Marotta, Toby. 1981. *The Politics of Homosexuality*. Boston: Houghton Mifflin.

Martello, Leo Louis. 1969. "A Positive Image for Homosexuality," *Come Out* 1:1 (14 November), 16.

Martin, Biddy. 1994. "Sexualities Without Genders and Other Queer Utopias." *Diacritics* 24:2–3 (Summer/Fall): 104–121.

———. 1996. *Femininity Played Straight: The Significance of Being Lesbian*. New York: Routledge.

Martin, W. K. 1995. *Marlene Dietrich*. New York: Chelsea House Publishers.

Marx, Karl. 1977. *Capital*, vol. 1. New York: Vintage Books.

Maxwell, Elsa. 1943. "Elsa Maxwell's Party Line," *New York Post*, 20 April.

Mayne, Judith. 1991. "Lesbian Looks: Dorothy Arzner and Female Authorship." In *How Do I Look? Queer Film and Video*, ed. Bad Object Choices, 103–135. Seattle: Bay Press.

———. 1993. *Cinema and Spectatorship*. London: Routledge.

McCandless, Barbara. 1991. "The Portrait Studio and the Celebrity." In *Photography in Nineteenth-Century America*, ed. Martha A. Sandweiss, 49–75. New York: Abrams.

McCauley, Elizabeth Anne. 1985. *A. A. E. Disdéri and the Carte de Visite Portrait Photograph*. New Haven: Yale University Press.

McLaughlin, Richard. 1960. "Adventures of an Esthete," review of *Here Lies the Heart*, by Mercedes de Acosta, *New Leader*, 13 June, 29.

McLellan, Diana. 2000. *The Girls: Sappho Goes to Hollywood*. New York: St. Martin's Press.

Mendelsohn, Daniel, 1996. "We're Here! We're Queer! Let's Get Coffee!" *New York* 29:38 (30 September), 24–31.

Merck, Mandy. 1993. *Perversions: Deviant Readings*. New York: Routledge.

"The Militant Homosexual." 1971. *Newsweek* 78:8 (23 August), 45–48.

Millett, Kate. 1970. *Sexual Politics*. Garden City, NY: Doubleday.

———. 1974. *Flying*. New York: Knopf.

Modern Screen. 1931. Portrait of Greta Garbo, 2:3 (August), 28.

Modleski, Tania. 1991. "Femininity as Mas(s)querade." In *Feminism Without Women: Culture and Criticism in a "Postfeminist" Age*, 23–34. New York: Routledge.

Morin, Edgar. 1960. *The Stars*, trans. Richard Howard. New York: Grove Press.

Morris, Michael. 1991. *Madam Valentino: The Many Lives of Natacha Rambova*. New York: Abbeville Press.

Mosedale, John. 1981. *The Men Who Invented Broadway: Damon Runyon, Walter Winchell and Their World*. New York: Richard Marek.

Mosel, Tad, and Gertrude Macy. 1978. *Leading Lady: The World and Theatre of Katharine Cornell.* Boston: Little, Brown.

Mott, Frank Luther. 1962. *American Journalism: A History, 1690–1960.* New York: Macmillan.

Mukerji, Chandra. 1983. *From Graven Images: Patterns of Modern Materialism.* New York: Columbia University Press.

Mulvey, Laura. 1989. *Visual and Other Pleasures.* Bloomington: Indiana University Press.

Murray, William. 2000. *Janet, My Mother and Me: A Memoir of Growing Up with Janet Flanner and Natalia Danesi Murray.* New York: Simon and Schuster

Navratilova, Martina, with George Vecsey. 1985. *Martina.* New York: Ballantine Books.

Navratilova, Martina, interviewed by Michele Kort. 1993. "Martina Navratilova," *Advocate* 639 (5 October), 46–53.

———, interviewed by Suzanne Westenhoefer. 1995. "I, Martina," *Advocate* 696 (12 December), 46–64.

———, interviewed by Cathay Che. 2000. "Martina Navratilova," *Advocate*, 30 April, 47–48.

Navratilova, Martina, and Liz Nickles. 1994. *The Total Zone.* New York: Ballantine Books.

———. 1996. *Breaking Point.* New York: Random House.

———. 1997. *Killer Instinct.* New York: Random House.

Nazimova, Alla. Clippings files. Billy Rose Collection, New York Public Library.

Neale, Steve. 1983. "Masculinity as Spectacle: Reflections on Men and Mainstream Cinema." *Screen* 24:6 (November-December): 2–16.

Nelson, Cary. 1997. "Superstars." *Academe* 83:1 (January–February): 38–43.

Newsweek. 1960. Photoessay on *Here Lies the Heart*, by Mercedes de Acosta, 7 March, 102.

Newton, Esther. 1989. "The Mythic Mannish Lesbian: Radclyffe Hall and the New Woman." In *Hidden from History: Reclaiming the Gay and Lesbian Past*, ed. Martin Duberman, Martha Vicinus, and George Chauncey Jr., 281–293. New York: Penguin.

Ogren, Peter. 1971. "Woman Objects to 'Gay' as Sexist, Tears Up Paper at Rutgers: A Personal View," *Gay* 52 (7 June), 6, 9.

Owen, Mitchell, 1997. "Can't Great Rooms Outlive Movie Sets?" *New York Times*, 20 March, sec. C.

Owles, Jim, interviewed by Jim Francis Hunter. 1970. "Where the Action Is," *Gay* 1:31 (7 September), 15.

Palmborg, Rita Page. 1932. "What's Really Happening to Garbo?" *Modern Screen* 4:6 (November), 28.

Parenti, Michael. 1992. *Make-Believe Media: The Politics of Entertainment.* New York: St. Martin's Press.

Paris, Barry. 1995. *Garbo: A Biography.* New York: Knopf.

Parsons, Louella. 1945. "Alla Nazimova," *Los Angeles Examiner*, 14 July.

Parsons, Talcott, and Robert F. Bales. 1955. *Family, Socialization, and the Interaction Process.* Glencoe, IL: Free Press.

Parsons, Talcott and James Olds. 1955. "The Mechanisms of Personality Functioning with Special Reference to Socialization." In Talcott Parsons Bales.

Patton, Cindy. 1994. Preface to *Lavender Culture*, ed. Karla Jay and Allen Young, ix–xxviii. New York: New York University Press.

Pederson, Lucille M. 1994. *Katharine Cornell: A Bio-Bibliography.* Westwood, CN: Greenwood Press.

Penelope, Julia, and Susan J. Wolfe, ed. 1989. *The Original Coming Out Stories*, second ed. Freedom, CA: Crossing Press.

Phelan, Peggy. 1993. *Unmarked: The Politics of Performance.* New York: Routledge.

Pileggi, Sarah. 1981. "Martina's Garden Party," *Sports Illustrated* 54:15 (6 April), 63–64.

———. 1982. "Merrily She Rolls Along," *Sports Illustrated* 56:21 (24 May), 102–116.

Pogrebin, Robin. 1998. "Magazines Bowing to Demands for Star Treatment," *New York Times*, 18 May, sec. A.

Radicalesbians. [1970] 1973. "The Woman Identified Woman." In *Radical Feminism*, ed. Anne Koedt, Ellen Levine, and Anita Rapone, 240–245. New York: Quadrangle Books.

Rich, Adrienne. 1980. "Compulsory Heterosexuality and Lesbian Existence." *Signs* 5:4 (Summer): 631–660.

Rich, Frank. 1998. "Ring Out the Old Celebs," *New York Times*, 3 January, sec. A.

Rivère, Joan. [1929] 1986. "Womanliness as a Masquerade." In *Formations of Fantasy*, ed. Victor Burgin, James Donald, and Cora Kaplan, 35–44. London: Methuen. Originally published in *International Journal of Psychoanalysis* 10.

Riva, Maria. 1993. *Marlene Dietrich, by Her Daughter*. New York: Knopf.

Roof, Judith. 1991. *A Lure of Knowledge: Lesbian Sexuality and Theory*. New York: Columbia University Press.

Rose, Jacqueline. 1986. *Sexuality in the Field of Vision*. London: Verso.

Rose, Nikolas. 1998. *Inventing Our Selves: Psychology, Power, and Personhood*. Cambridge, England: Cambridge University Press.

———. 1999. *Powers of Freedom: Reframing Political Thought*. Cambridge, England: Cambridge University Press.

Rubyfruit Jungle Productions. n.d. (ca. 1977). Press release. Rita Mae Brown folder, International Gay Information Center Archives, New York Public Library.

Sahlins, Marshall. 1976. "La Pensée Bourgeois: Western Society as Culture." In *Culture and Practical Reason*, 166–205. Chicago: University of Chicago Press.

Salholz, Eloise. 1993. "The Power and the Pride," *Newsweek* 121:25 (21 June), 54–60.

Salter, Stephanie. 1981. "Citizen Navratilova: Is She Home at Last?" *World Tennis* 29:7 (December), 30–35.

Schanke, Robert A. 1992. *Shattered Applause: The Lives of Eva Le Gallienne*. Carbondale: Southern Illinois University Press.

Scharf, Aaron. 1975. *Pioneers of Photography: An Album of Pictures and Words*. New York: Abrams.

Schickel, Richard. 1973. *His Picture in the Papers: A Speculation on Celebrity in America, Based on the Life of Douglas Fairbanks, Sr*. New York: Charterhouse.

———. 1985. *Intimate Strangers: The Culture of Celebrities*. Garden City, NY: Doubleday.

Schudson, Michael. 1978. *Discovering the News: A Social History of American Newspapers*. New York: Basic Books.

Scott, Janny. 1997. "'Academostars Find Sky's the Limit as Schools Woo Talented Professors," *New York Times*, 20 December.

Scott, Joan W. 1990. "Deconstructing Equality-Versus-Difference: Or the Use of Poststructuralist Theory for Feminism." In *Conflicts in Feminism*, ed. Marianne Hirsch and Evelyn Fox Keller, 134–148. New York: Routledge.

———. 1993. "The Evidence of Experience." In *The Lesbian and Gay Studies Reader*, ed. Henry Abelove, Michéle Aina Barale, and David M. Halperin, 397–415. New York: Routledge.

Sedgwick, Eve Kosofsky. 1991. *Epistemology of the Closet*. Berkeley: University of California Press.

Sheehy, Helen. 1996. *Eva Le Gallienne*. New York: Knopf.

Shelley, Martha. 1970. "Come Out," *Rat*, 24 February, quoted in *Detroit Gay Liberator* 1:8 (January 1971), 15.

———. 1970–71. "Subversion in the Women's Movement," *Come Out* 1:7 (December-January), n.p.

———. [1970] 1992. "Gay Is Good." In *Out of the Closets: Voices from Gay Liberation*, rev. ed., ed. Karla Jay and Allen Young, 31–34. New York: New York University Press.

Shumway, David R. 1997. "The Star System in Literary Studies." *Publications of the Modern Language Association* 112:1 (January): 85–99.

Slater, Don. 1993. "Going Shopping: Markets, Crowds and Consumption." In *Cultural Reproduction*, ed. Christopher Jenks, 188–209. London: Routledge.

———. 1995. "Photography and Modern Vision." In *Visual Culture*, ed. Chris Jenks, 218–237. London: Routledge.

———. 1997. *Consumer Culture and Modernity*. London: Polity Press.

S. M. A. 1960. "Aberrant Hedonist Writes All," review of *Here Lies the Heart*, by Mercedes de Acosta, *Houston Chronicle*, 3 April.

Smith, Jane S. 1982. *Elsie de Wolfe: A Life in High Style*. New York: Atheneum.

Sobel, Bernard. 1953. *Broadway Heartbeat: Memoirs of a Press Agent*. New York: Hermitage House.

Souhami, Diana. 1994. *Greta and Cecil*. New York: HarperCollins.

Spivak, Gayatri Chakravorty. 1988. "Can the Subaltern Speak?" In *Marxism and Interpretations of Culture*, ed. Cary Nelson and Lawrence Grossberg, 271–313. Urbana: University of Illinois Press.

Spoto, Donald. 1992. *Blue Angel: The Life of Marlene Dietrich*. New York: Doubleday.

Stacey, Jackie. 1994. *Star Gazing: Hollywood Cinema and Female Spectatorship*. London: Routledge.

Staiger, Janet. 1991. "Seeing Stars." In *Stardom: Industry of Desire*, ed. Christine Gledhill, 3–16. London: Routledge.

"Star Tracks." 1996. *People* 45:18 (6 May), 13.

Stein, Arlene. 1989. "All Dressed Up but No Place to Go? Style Wars and the New Lesbianism." *Out/Look* 1:4 (Winter): 34–42.

Strand, Mark. 1985. "Martina! . . . the Woman, the Champion," *Vogue* 175:4 (April), 342–347.

Summerscale, Kate. 1997. *The Queen of Whale Cay: The Eccentric Story of Joe' Carstairs, Fastest Woman on Water*. London: Fourth Estate.

Symons, Julian. 1972. *Bloody Murder: From the Detective Story to the Crime Novel, A History*. Harmondsworth: Penguin.

Taft, Robert. 1938. *Photography and the American Scene: A Social History, 1839–1889*. New York: Macmillan.

Tapert, Annette, and Diana Edkins. 1994. *The Power of Style: The Women Who Defined the Art of Living Well*. New York: Crown Publishers.

Tauber, Michelle. 2002. "Oh by the Way," *People*, 18 March, 80–86.

Taylor, Leslie A. 2001. "'I Made Up My Mind to Get It': The American Trial of *The Well of Loneliness*, New York City, 1928–1929." *Journal of Sexuality* 10:2 (April): 250–286.

Terry, Jennifer. 1990. "Lesbians Under the Medical Gaze: Scientists Search for Remarkable Sexual Differences." *Journal of Sex Research* 27:3 (August): 317–340.

Third World Gay Revolution. [1971] 1992. "What We Want, What We Believe." In *Out of the Closets: Voices of Gay Liberation*, rev. ed., ed. Karla Jay and Allen Young, 363–367. New York: New York University Press.

Todd, Arthur. 1960. "'The Place Cards Read Like an All-Star Cast at a Benefit,'" review of *Here Lies the Heart*, by Mercedes de Acosta, *New York Times Book Review*, 29 March, 6.

Troubridge, Una. 1961. *The Life and Death of Radclyffe Hall*. London: Hammond and Hammond.

Tyler, Carole-Anne. 1990. "The Feminine Look." In *Theory Between the Disciplines: Authority/Vision/Politics*, ed. Martin Kreiswirth and Mark A. Cheetham, 191–212. Ann Arbor: University of Michigan Press.

———. 1991. "Boys Will Be Girls: The Politics of Gay Drag." In *Inside/Out: Lesbian Theories, Gay Theories*, ed. Diana Fuss, 32–70. New York: Routledge.

Urry, John. 1970. "Role Analysis and the Sociological Enterprise." *Sociological Review* 18:3 (November): 351–363.

Vicinus, Martha. 1993. "'They Wonder to Which Sex I Belong': The Historical Roots of Lesbian Identity." In *The Lesbian and Gay Studies Reader*, ed. Henry Abelove, Michèle Aina Barale, and David M. Halperin, 432–452. New York: Routledge.

Vickers, Hugo. 1994. *Loving Garbo: The Story of Greta Garbo, Cecil Beaton, and Mercedes de Acosta*. New York: Random House.

Walker, Lisa M. 1993. "How to Recognize a Lesbian: The Cultural Politics of Looking Like What You Are." *Signs* 18:4 (Summer): 866–890.

Warshawsky, Allan, and Ellen Bedoz. 1970. "G.L.F. and the Movement," *Come Out* 1:2 (January 10), 4.

Watney, Simon. 1989. "The Warhol Effect." In *The Work of Andy Warhol*, ed. Gary Garrells, 115–123. Seattle: Bay Press.

Weeks, Jeffrey. 1977. *Coming Out: Homosexual Politics in Britain from the Nineteenth Century to the Present*. London: Quartet Books.

———. 1985. *Sexuality and Its Discontents: Meanings, Myths, and Modern Sexualities*. London: Routledge, Kegan Paul.

———. 1991. *Against Nature: Essays on History, Sexuality, and Identity*. London: Rivers Oram Press.

Welling, William. 1978. *Photography in America: The Formative Years, 1839–1900*. Albuquerque: University of New Mexico Press.

Wershba, Joseph. 1960. "Daily Closeup," *New York Post*, 18 April.

West, Rebecca. 1932. "I Said to Me," *Los Angeles Herald Examiner*, 31 May.

W. G. R. 1960. "Writer 'Drops Names' Through Autobiography," review of *Here Lies the Heart*, by Mercedes de Acosta, *Indianapolis Star*, 6 March.

"Who's Come a Long Way, Baby?" 1970. *Time* 96:9 (31 August), 16–23.

"Who's Married to Who." 1917. *Photoplay* 11:6 (May), 67–68.

Wilson, Elizabeth. 1985. *Adorned in Dreams: Fashion and Modernity*. Berkeley: University of California Press.

Witchel, Alex. 1997. "Growing Up in Public: From Babe in Arms to Gay Advocate," *New York Times*, 9 July, sec. C.

"Women's Lib: A Second Look." 1970. *Time* 96:24 (14 December), 50.

Wrenn, Marie-Claude. 1970. "Women Arise: The Furious Young Philosopher Who Got It Down on Paper," *Life* 69:10 (4 September), 16–23.

Wrong, Dennis. 1957. "The Oversocialized Conception of Man in Modern Sociology." In *Sociological Theory: A Book of Readings*, ed. Lewis A. Coser and Bernard Rosenberg, 122–132. New York: Macmillan.

York, Cal. 1921. "Plays and Players," *Photoplay* 21:1 (December), 80.

———. 1932. "Gossip—East and West," *Photoplay* 23:5 (April).

Zimmerman, Bonnie. 1990. *The Safe Sea of Women: Lesbian Fiction, 1969–1989*. Boston: Beacon Press.

Zwerman, Gilda. 1995. *Martina Navratilova*. New York: Chelsea House Publishers.

INDEX

Page numbers in italics indicate a photograph of the person or entity named, or an image by that person.